FOR MARX

(For Brad)

FOR MARX

Louis Althusser

Translated by Ben Brewster

VERSO

London • New York

VERSO

London – New York

Originally published as *Pour Marx* by
François Maspero, Paris 1965
© François Maspero 1965
First published in English 1969
Translation © Ben Brewster 1969
This edition published by Verso 2005

3 5 7 9 10 8 6 4 2

Verso
UK: 6 Meard Street, London W1F 0EG
USA: 180 Varick Street, New York NY 10014–4606
www.versobooks.com

Verso is the imprint of New Left Books

ISBN 1-84467-662-0

British Library Cataloguing in Publication Data
A catalogue record for this book is available from the British Library

Library of Congress Cataloging-in-Publication Data
A catalog record for this book is available from the Library of Congress

Typeset in Fournier by Hewer Text UK Ltd, Edinburgh
Printed in Sweden by ScandBook AB

These pages are dedicated
to the memory of Jacques Martin,
the friend
who, in the most terrible ordeal,
alone
discovered the road to
Marx's philosophy
– and guided me onto it.

L.A.

Contents

To My English Readers

I should like briefly to present this translation of *Pour Marx* to an English audience and, on the same occasion, to make use of the time that has elapsed since it was written to take some 'bearings' on the philosophical content and the ideological significance of this small book.

Pour Marx appeared in France in 1965. But only its Introduction ('Today') dates from that year. All the other chapters were published earlier, between 1960 and 1964, in the form of articles in French Communist Party journals.[1] They were collected together exactly as originally written, without any corrections or alterations.

To understand these essays and to pass judgement on them, it is essential to realize that they were conceived, written and published by a Communist philosopher in a particular ideological and theoretical conjuncture.[2] So these texts must be taken for what they are. They are *philosophical* essays, the first stages of a long-term investigation, preliminary results which obviously demand correction; this investigation concerns the specific nature of the principles of the science and philosophy founded by Marx. However, these philosophical essays do not derive from a merely erudite or speculative investigation. They are, *simultaneously*, interventions in a definite conjuncture.

---

1 With the exception of the article on Bertolazzi and Brecht, which was published in the Catholic review *Esprit*.

2 For explanation of terms used see Glossary, page 215.

I

As the Introduction shows, this conjuncture is, first, the theoretical and ideological conjuncture in France, more particularly the present conjuncture in the French Communist Party and in French philosophy. But as well as this peculiarly French conjuncture, it is also the present ideological and theoretical conjuncture in the international Communist movement.

Of course, the essays you are about to read do not bear on the *political* elements of this conjuncture (the policies of the Communist Parties, the split in the international Communist movement). They deal with the ideological and theoretical problems present in the conjuncture and produced by it. In certain respects these problems are new ones; in others they refer us back to debates which have long characterized the history of the workers' movement.

A consideration of the *recent* elements of this conjuncture reveals that, since Stalin's death, the International Communist movement has lived in a conjuncture dominated by two great events: the critique of the 'cult of personality' by the Twentieth Congress, and the rupture that has occurred between the Chinese Communist Party and the Soviet Communist Party.

The denunciation of the 'cult of personality', the abrupt conditions and the forms in which it took place, have had profound repercussions, not only in the political domain, but in the ideological domain as well. In what follows I shall deal only with the ideological reactions of Communist intellectuals.

The critique of Stalinist 'dogmatism' was generally 'lived' by Communist intellectuals as a 'liberation'. This 'liberation' gave birth to a profound ideological reaction, 'liberal' and 'ethical' in tendency, which spontaneously rediscovered the old philosophical themes of 'freedom', 'man', the 'human person' and 'alienation'. This ideological tendency looked for theoretical justification to Marx's Early Works, which do indeed contain all the arguments of a philosophy of man, his alienation and liberation. These conditions have paradoxically turned the tables in Marxist philosophy. Since the 1930s Marx's Early Works have been a war-horse for petty bourgeois intellectuals in their struggle against Marxism; but little by little, and then massively, they have been set to work in the interests of a new 'interpretation' of Marxism which is today being openly developed by many Communist intellectuals, 'liberated' from Stalinist dogmatism by the Twentieth Congress. The themes of 'Marxist Humanism' and the 'humanist' interpretation of Marx's work have progressively and irresistibly imposed themselves on recent Marxist philosophy, even inside Soviet and Western Communist Parties.

If this ideological reaction, characteristic above all of Communist intellectuals, has, despite some resistance, been capable of such a development, it is because it has benefited from the direct or indirect support of certain *political* slogans laid down by the Communist Parties of the U.S.S.R. and the West. On one side, for example, the Twenty-second Congress of the C.P.S.U. declared that with the disappearance of the class struggle, the dictatorship of the proletariat had been 'superseded' in the U.S.S.R., that the Soviet State is no longer a class State but the 'State of the Whole People'; and that the U.S.S.R. has embarked on the 'construction of communism', guided by the 'humanist' slogan, 'Everything for Man'. On the other, for example, Western Communist Parties have pursued policies of unity with socialists, democrats and Catholics, guided by certain slogans of related resonance, in which the accent is put on the 'peaceful transition to socialism', on 'Marxist' or 'socialist humanism', on 'dialogue', etc.

The 'humanist' interpretations of Marxist theory which have developed under these definite circumstances represent a *new* phenomenon as compared with the period just past (the period between 1930 and 1956). However, they have many historical *precedents* in the history of the workers' movement. Marx, Engels and Lenin, to refer only to them, ceaselessly struggled against ideological interpretations of an idealist, humanist type that threatened Marxist theory. Here it will suffice to recall Marx's rupture with Feuerbach's humanism, Engels's struggle against Dühring, Lenin's long battle with the Russian populists, and so on. This whole past, this whole heritage, is obviously part of the present theoretical and ideological conjuncture of the international Communist movement.

To return to the recent aspects of this conjuncture, I shall add the following remark.

In the text entitled 'Marxism and Humanism', dating from 1963, I have already interpreted the present inflation of the themes of Marxist or socialist 'Humanism' as an *ideological* phenomenon. In no sense was I condemning ideology as a social reality: as Marx says, it is in ideology that men 'become conscious' of their class conflict and 'fight it out'; in its religious, ethical, legal and political forms, etc., ideology is an objective social reality; the ideological struggle is an organic part of the class struggle. On the other hand, I criticized the *theoretical* effects of ideology, which are always a threat or a hindrance to scientific knowledge. And I pointed out that the inflation of the themes of 'Marxist humanism' and their encroachment on Marxist theory should be interpreted as a possible historical symptom of a double inability and a double danger. An inability to think the specificity of Marxist theory, and, correlatively, a revisionist danger of confusing it with pre-Marxist ideological interpretations. An inability to resolve the real (basically *political* and *economic*) problems posed by the conjuncture since the Twentieth Congress, and a danger of masking these problems with the false 'solution' of some merely *ideological* formulae.

II

It was in this conjuncture that the texts you are about to read were conceived and published. They must be related to this conjuncture to appreciate fully their nature and function: they are *philosophical* essays, with theoretical investigations as their objects, and as their aim an intervention in the present theoretico-ideological conjuncture in reaction to its dangerous tendencies.

Very schematically, I should say that these theoretical texts contain a double 'intervention', or, if you prefer, they 'intervene' on two fronts, to trace, in Lenin's excellent expression, a 'line of demarcation' between Marxist theory on the one hand, and ideological tendencies foreign to Marxism on the other.

The object of *the first intervention* is to 'draw a line of demarcation' between Marxist theory and the forms of philosophical (and political) subjectivism which have compromised it or threaten it: above all, *empiricism* and its variants, classical and modern – pragmatism, voluntarism, historicism, etc. The essential moments of this first intervention are: a recognition of the importance of Marxist *theory* in the revolutionary class struggle, a distinction of the different practices, a demonstration of the specificity of 'theoretical practice', a first investigation into the revolutionary specificity of Marxist theory (a total distinction between the idealist dialectic and the materialist dialectic), etc.

This first intervention is situated essentially in the terrain of the confrontation between Marx and Hegel.

The object of *the second intervention* is to 'draw a line of demarcation' between the true theoretical bases of the Marxist science of history and Marxist philosophy on the one hand, and, on the other, the pre-Marxist idealist notions on which depend contemporary interpretations of Marxism as a 'philosophy of man' or a 'Humanism'. The essential moments of this second intervention are: the demonstration of an 'epistemological break' in the history of Marx's thought, a basic difference between the ideological 'problematic' of the Early Works and the scientific 'problematic' of *Capital*; first investigations into the specificity of Marx's theoretical discovery, etc.

This second intervention is situated essentially in the terrain of the confrontation between Marx's Early Works and *Capital*.

Behind the detail of the arguments, textual analyses and theoretical discussions, these two interventions reveal a major opposition; the opposition that separates science from ideology, or more precisely, that separates a new science in process of self-constitution from the pre-scientific *theoretical* ideologies that occupy the 'terrain' in which it is establishing itself. This is an important point; what we are dealing with in the opposition science/ideologies concerns the 'break' relationship between a science and the *theoretical* ideology in which the object it gave the knowledge of was 'thought' before the foundation of the science. This 'break' leaves intact the objective social domain occupied by ideologies (religion, ethics, legal and political ideologies, etc.). In this domain of non-theoretical ideologies, too, there are 'ruptures' and 'breaks', but they are *political* (effects of political practice, of great revolutionary events) and not 'epistemological'.

This opposition between science and ideology and the notion of an 'epistemological break' that helps us to think its historical character refer to a thesis that, although always present in the background of these analyses, is never explicitly developed: the thesis that Marx's discovery is a scientific discovery without historical precedent, in its nature and effects.

Indeed, in conformity with the tradition constantly reiterated by the classics of Marxism, we may claim that Marx established a new *science*: the science of the history of 'social formations'. To be more precise, I should say that Marx 'opened up' for scientific knowledge a new 'continent', that of *history* – just as Thales opened up the 'continent' of mathematics for scientific knowledge, and Galileo opened up the 'continent' of physical nature for scientific knowledge.

I should add that, just as the foundation of mathematics by Thales 'induced' the birth of the Platonic philosophy, just as the foundation of physics by Galileo 'induced' the birth of Cartesian philosophy, etc., so the foundation of the science of history by Marx has 'induced' the birth of a new, theoretically and practically revolutionary philosophy, Marxist philosophy or dialectical materialism. The fact that, from the standpoint of its theoretical elaboration, this unprecedented philosophy still lags behind the Marxist science of history (historical materialism) is explained by historico-political reasons and *also* simultaneously by theoretical reasons: great philosophical revolutions are always preceded and 'borne along' by the great scientific revolutions 'active' in them, but long theoretical labour and long historical maturing are required before they can acquire an explicit and adequate form. If the accent is laid on Marxist philosophy in the texts you are about to read, it is to assess both its reality and its right to existence, but also its lateness, and to begin to provide it with a theoretical form of existence a little more adequate to its nature.

III

Naturally, these texts are marked, and sometimes sensibly so, not only by errors and inaccuracies, but also by silences or half-silences. Neither the impossibility of saying everything at once nor the urgency of the conjuncture completely explain all these silences and their effects. In fact, I was not equipped for an adequate treatment of certain questions, some difficult points were obscure to me; as a result, in my texts I did not take into account certain important problems and realities, as I should have. As a 'self-criticism', I should like to signal two particularly important points.

If I did lay stress on the vital necessity of *theory* for revolutionary practice, and therefore denounced all forms of empiricism, I did not discuss the problem of the 'union of theory and practice' which has played such a major role in the Marxist-Leninist tradition. No doubt I did speak of the union of theory and practice within 'theoretical practice', but I did not enter into the question of the union of theory and practice within *political practice*. Let us be precise; I did not examine the general form of historical existence of this union: the 'fusion' of Marxist theory and the *workers' movement*. I did not examine the *concrete forms of existence* of this 'fusion' (organization of the class struggle – trade unions, parties – the means and methods of direction of the class struggle by these organizations, etc.). I did not give precise indications as to the function, place and role of Marxist theory in these concrete forms of existence: where and how Marxist theory intervenes in the development of political practice, where and how political practice intervenes in the development of Marxist theory.

I have learnt from experience that my silence on these questions has not been without its consequences for certain ('theoreticist') 'readings' of my essays.

Similarly, if I did insist on the theoretically revolutionary character of Marx's discovery, and pointed out that Marx had founded a new science and a new philosophy, I left vague the difference distinguishing philosophy from science, a difference which is, however, of great importance. I did not show what it is, as distinct from science, that constitutes *philosophy proper*: the organic relation between every philosophy, as a *theoretical* discipline and even within its *theoretical* forms of existence and exigencies, and *politics*. I did not point out the nature of this relation, which, in Marxist philosophy, has nothing to do with a *pragmatic* relation. So I did not show clearly enough what in this respect distinguishes Marxist philosophy from earlier philosophies.

I have learnt from experience that my half-silence on these questions has not been without its consequences for certain ('positivist') 'readings' of my essays.

I intend to return to these two important questions, which are intimately connected from a theoretical and practical point of view, in later studies.

October 1967

Acknowledgements

'Feuerbach's "Philosophical Manifestoes" ' first appeared in *La Nouvelle Critique*, December 1960.

'On the Young Marx: Theoretical Questions' first appeared in *La Pensée*, March–April 1961.

'Contradiction and Overdetermination' first appeared in *La Pensée*, December 1962. Its appendix is published here for the first time.

'Notes on a Materialist Theatre' first appeared in *Esprit*, December 1962.

'The "1844 Manuscripts" ' first appeared in *La Pensée*, February 1963.

'On the Materialist Dialectic' first appeared in *La Pensée*, August 1963.

'Marxism and Humanism' first appeared in the *Cahiers de l'I.S.E.A.*, June 1964.

'A Complementary Note on "Real Humanism" ' first appeared in *La Nouvelle Critique*, March 1965.

I should like to thank all those editors of magazines who were obliging enough to allow me to collect these pieces together into the present volume.

Introduction: Today

I venture to publish together these jottings, which have appeared in various magazines during the last four years. Some of them are now unobtainable; this is my first, purely practical, excuse. If, hesitant and incomplete as they are, they nevertheless make some sense, this should be brought out by grouping them together; this is my second excuse. Ultimately, I must present them for what they are: the documentation of a particular *history*.

Nearly all these pieces were born of some conjuncture: a comment on a book, an answer to criticisms or objections, an analysis of a theatrical production, etc. They are marked by their date of birth, even in their inconsistencies, which I have decided not to correct. I have struck out a few passages of unduly personal polemic; I have inserted the small number of words, notes or pages that had then to be cut, either to spare the feelings of those with certain prejudices, or to reduce my expositions to a suitable length; I have also corrected a few references.

Each the result of a special occasion, these pieces are none the less products of the same epoch and the same history. In their own way they are witnesses to the unique experience which all the philosophers of my generation who tried to think with Marx had to live: the *investigation* of Marx's *philosophical* thought, indispensable if we were to escape from the theoretical impasse in which history had put us.

History: it had stolen our youth with the Popular Front and the Spanish Civil War, and in the War as such it had imprinted in us the terrible education of deeds. It surprised us just as we entered the world, and turned us students of bourgeois or petty bourgeois origin into men advised of the existence of classes, of their struggles and aims. From the evidence it forced on us we drew the only possible conclusion, and rallied to the political organization of the working class, the Communist Party.

The War was just over. We were brutally cast into the Party's great political and ideological battles: we had to measure up to our choice and take the consequences.

In our political memory this period remains the time of huge strikes and demonstrations, of the Stockholm Appeal and of the Peace Movement – the time when the great hopes aroused by the Resistance faltered and the long and bitter struggle began in which innumerable human hands would push back the shadow of catastrophe into the Cold War horizon. In our philosophical memory it remains the period of intellectuals in arms, hunting out error from all its hiding-places; of the philosophers we were, without writings of our own, but making politics out of all writing, and slicing up the world with a single blade, arts, literatures, philosophies, sciences with the pitiless demarcation of class – the period summed up in caricature by a single phrase, a banner flapping in the void: 'bourgeois science, proletarian science'.

To defend Marxism, imperilled as it was by Lysenko's 'biology', from the fury of bourgeois spite, some leaders had relaunched this old 'Left-wing' formula, once the slogan of Bogdanov and the Proletkult. Once proclaimed it dominated everything. Under its imperative line, what then counted as philosophy could only choose between commentary and silence, between conviction, whether inspired or forced, and dumb embarrassment. Paradoxically, it was none other than Stalin, whose contagious and implacable system of government and thought had induced this delirium, who reduced the madness to a little more reason. Reading between the lines of the few simple pages in which he reproached the zeal of those who were making strenuous efforts to prove language a superstructure, we could see that there were limits to the use of the class criterion, and that we had been made to treat science, a status claimed by every page of Marx, as merely the first-comer among ideologies. We had to retreat, and, in semi-disarray, return to first principles.

I write these lines for my own part and as a Communist, inquiring into our past solely for some light on our present which will then illuminate our future.

Neither bitterness nor nostalgia makes me recall this episode – but the wish to sanction it by a comment that will supersede it. We were at the age of enthusiasm and trust; we lived at a time when the enemy gave no quarter, the language of slander sustaining his aggression. But this did not save us from remaining long confused by this detour into which certain of our leaders, far from holding us back from the slope of theoretical 'Leftism', had actively led us, without the others showing any sign of restraining them or giving us any warning or advice. So we spent the best part of our time in agitation when we would have been better employed in the defence of our right and duty to know, and in study for production as such. For we did not even take this time. We knew nothing of Bogdanov and the Proletkult, or of Lenin's historic struggle against political and theoretical Leftism; we were not even intimately familiar with Marx's mature works, as we were only too eager and happy to rediscover our own burning passions in the ideological flame of his Early Works. But what of our elders? Those whose responsibility it was to show us the way – how was it that they too were living in the same ignorance? This long theoretical tradition, worked out in so many trials and struggles, blazoned by the testimony of so many great texts, how could it have become a dead letter for them?

In this way we came to realize that under the protection of the reigning dogmatism a second, negative, tradition, a French one this time, had prevailed over the first, a second tradition, or rather what, echoing Heine's 'German misery', we might call, our 'French misery': the stubborn, profound absence of any real *theoretical* culture in the history of the French workers' movement. The French Party may have been able to reach its present position by using the general theory of the two sciences in the form of a radical proclamation, it may have been able to make it the test and proof of its indisputable political courage, but this also meant that it was living on meagre theoretical reserves: those it had inherited from the past of the French workers' movement as a whole. In fact, other than the utopians Saint-Simon and Fourier whom Marx loved to invoke, Proudhon who was not a Marxist at all, and Jaurès who was, but only slightly, where were our theoreticians? In Germany there were Marx and Engels and the earlier Kautsky; in Poland, Rosa Luxemburg; in Russia, Plekhanov and Lenin; in Italy, Labriola, who (when we had Sorel!) could correspond with Engels as equal to equal, then Gramsci. Who were our theoreticians? Guesde? Lafargue?

A whole theoretical analysis would be necessary to account for this poverty, so striking when compared with the richness of other traditions. With no pretensions to undertake this analysis, a few reference points can at least be established. Without the efforts of intellectual workers there could be no *theoretical* tradition (in history or philosophy) in the workers' movement of the nineteenth and early twentieth centuries. The founders of historical and dialectical materialism were intellectuals (Marx and Engels), their theory was developed by intellectuals (Kautsky, Plekhanov, Labriola, Rosa Luxemburg, Lenin, Gramsci). Neither at the beginning, nor long afterwards, could it have been otherwise – it cannot be otherwise, neither now nor in the future: what can change and will change is the class origin of intellectual workers, but not their characterization as intellectuals.[1] This is so for those reasons of principle that Lenin, following Kautsky, impressed upon us: on the one hand, the 'spontaneous' ideology of the workers, if left to itself, could only produce utopian socialism, trade-unionism, anarchism and anarcho-syndicalism; on the other hand, Marxist socialism, presupposing as it does the massive theoretical labour of the establishment and development of a science and

---

1   Naturally this term 'intellectuals' denotes a very specific type of militant intellectual, a type unprecedented in many respects. These are real initiates, armed with the most authentic scientific and theoretical culture, forewarned of the crushing reality and manifold mechanisms of all forms of the ruling ideology and constantly on the watch for them, and able in their theoretical practice to borrow – against the stream of all 'accepted truths' – the fertile paths opened up by Marx but bolted and barred by all the reigning prejudices. An undertaking of this nature and this rigour is unthinkable without an unshakeable and lucid confidence in the working class and direct participation in its struggles.

a philosophy without precedent, could only be the work of men with a thorough historical, scientific and philosophical formation, intellectuals of very high quality. That such intellectuals appeared in Germany, Russia, Poland and Italy, either to found Marxist theory or to become masters of it, is not a matter of isolated accidents; the social, political, religious, ideological and moral conditions prevailing in these countries quite simply denied their intellectuals any activity, the ruling classes (the nobility and the bourgeoisie, allied and united in their class interests and supported by the Churches) could in general only offer them servile and derisory employment. Under these conditions, the intellectuals could only seek their freedom and future at the side of the working class, the only revolutionary class. In France, on the contrary, the bourgeoisie had been revolutionary; it had long been able to assimilate intellectuals to its revolution and to keep them as a whole at its side after the seizure and consolidation of power. The French bourgeoisie had successfully carried through a complete, clear revolution; driving the feudal class from the political stage (1789, 1830, 1848), it had set the seal of its own command on the unity of the nation in the process of revolution itself, it had defeated the Church and then adopted it, but only to separate itself at the right moment and cover itself with the slogans of liberty and equality. It had been able to use both its position of strength and its past standing to offer the intellectuals a sufficient space and future, sufficiently honourable functions and a sufficient margin of freedom and illusion to keep them within its authority and under the control of its ideology. With a few important exceptions, who were precisely exceptions, French intellectuals accepted this situation and felt no vital need to seek their salvation at the side of the working class; and when they did rally to the working class, they could not radically cast off the bourgeois ideology in which they were steeped and which survived in their idealism and reformism (Jaurès) or in their positivism. Nor was it accidental that the French Party had to devote a long and courageous struggle to the reduction and destruction of a reflex '*ouvriériste*' distrust of intellectuals, which was in its own way the expression of a long historical experience of continual deception. Thus it was that the forms of bourgeois domination themselves long deprived the French workers' movement of the intellectuals indispensable to the formation of an authentic *theoretical* tradition.

Need I add another national reason? This is the pitiful history of French philosophy in the 130 years following the Revolution of 1789, its spiritualist persistence in reaction, not just conservatism, from Maine de Biran and Cousin to Bergson, its contempt for history and for the people, its deep but narrow-minded ties with religion, its relentless hostility to the only mind worthy of interest that it produced, Auguste Comte, its incredible ignorance and lack of culture. In the last thirty years things have taken another turn. But the burden of a long century of official philosophical stupidity has also played a part in crushing theory in the workers' movement itself.

The French Party was born into this theoretical vacuum, and it grew despite this vacuum, filling in as best it could the existing lacunas, nourishing itself from our sole authentic national tradition, the *political* tradition for which Marx had the most profound respect. Despite itself it has been marked by this primacy of *politics* and a certain failure to appreciate the role of theory, particularly *philosophical* theory as opposed to political and economic theory. If it was able to rally itself some famous intellectuals, these were above all great writers, novelists, poets and painters, great natural scientists and also a few first-rate historians and psychologists – and they came primarily for political reasons; but it very rarely attracted men of sufficient *philosophical* formation to realize that Marxism should not be simply a political doctrine, a 'method' of analysis and action, but also, over and above the rest, the *theoretical domain of a fundamental investigation*, indispensable not only to the development of the science of society and of the various 'human sciences', but also to that of the natural sciences and philosophy. It was the fate of the French Party to be born and to grow up in these conditions: without the heritage and assistance of a national *theoretical* tradition, and as an inevitable consequence, without a theoretical school which could produce masters.

This was the reality we had to learn to spell out, and that all by ourselves. By ourselves because there were no really great philosophical *maîtres* in Marxist philosophy amongst us to guide our steps. Politzer, who might have become one if he had not sacrificed the great philosophical achievements he had in him to urgent economic tasks, left us only the genius of the errors in his *Critique des Fondements de la Psychologie*. He was dead, assassinated by the Nazis. We had no *maîtres*. There was no lack of willing spirits, nor of highly cultivated minds, scholars, literary figures and many more. But I mean masters of Marxist philosophy, emerging from our own history, accessible and close to us. This last condition is not a superfluous detail. For we have inherited from our national past not only a theoretical vacuum, but also a monstrous philosophical and cultural provincialism (our form of chauvinism), we do not read foreign languages, and more or less ignore anything that happens to be thought beyond a line of mountains, the course of a river or the width of a sea. Is it an accident that in France the study and commentary of Marx's work has long been the work of a few courageous and tenacious Germanists? If the only name fit for display beyond our frontiers is that of a quiet lone hero, who, unknown to French learning, spent many years in a minutely detailed study of the left neo-Hegelian movement and the Young Marx: Auguste Cornu?

These reflections throw some light on our predicament, but they do not abolish it. We are indebted to Stalin for the first shock, even within the evil for which he bears the prime responsibility. His death set off the second – his death and the Twentieth Congress. But meanwhile life had done its work among us as well.

Neither a political organization nor a real theoretical culture can be created overnight or by a simple *fiat*. So many of the young philosophers who had come of age in the War or just after it were worn out by exhausting political tasks but had taken no time off from them for scientific work! It is also characteristic of our social history that the intellectuals of petty bourgeois origin who came to the Party at that time felt that they had to pay in pure activity, if not in political activism, the imaginary Debt they thought they had contracted *by not being proletarians*. In his own way, Sartre provides us with an honest witness to this baptism of history: we were of his race as well; it is no doubt a gain of recent years that our younger comrades seem free of this Debt, which perhaps they pay in some other way. *Philosophically* speaking, our generation sacrificed itself and was sacrificed to political and ideological conflict alone, implying that it was sacrificed in its intellectual and scientific work. A number of scientists, occasionally even historians, and even a few rare literary figures came through unscathed or at least only slightly bruised. There was no way out for a philosopher. If he spoke and wrote the philosophy the Party wanted he was restricted to commentary and slight idiosyncrasies in his own way of using the Famous Quotations. We had no audience among our peers. Our enemies flung in our faces the charge that we were merely politicians; our most enlightened colleagues argued that we ought to study our authors before judging them, justify our principles objectively before proclaiming and applying them. To force their best opponents to pay them some attention, some Marxist philosophers were reduced, and by a natural movement which did not conceal a conscious tactic, to *disguising themselves* – disguising Marx as Husserl, Marx as Hegel, Marx as the ethical and humanist Young Marx – at the risk of some day taking the masks for the reality. This is no exaggeration, simply the facts. We are still living the consequences today. We were politically and philosophically convinced that we had reached the only firm ground in the world, but as we could not demonstrate its existence or firmness philosophically, no one else could see any firm ground beneath our feet – only conviction. I am not discussing the spread of Marxism, which luckily can radiate from other spheres than the philosophical: I am discussing the paradoxically precarious existence of Marxist philosophy as such. We thought we knew the principles of all possible philosophy, and of the impossibility of all philosophical ideology, but we failed to offer an objective and public proof of the apodicity of our convictions.

Once aware of the vacuity of the dogmatic approach we were left with only one way of accepting the impossible situation we had been reduced to in our efforts towards a real grasp of our philosophy: to treat philosophy itself as *impossible*. So we were led into that great, subtle temptation, the '*end of philosophy*', encouraged by some enigmatically clear texts in Marx's Early Works (1840–45) and of his epistemological break (1845). Those of us who were the most militant and the most generous tended towards an interpretation of the 'end of philosophy' as its 'realization' and celebrated the death of philosophy in action, in its political realization and proletarian consummation, unreservedly endorsing the famous Thesis on Feuerbach which, in theoretically ambiguous words, counterposes the transformation of the world to its interpretation. It was, *and always will be*, only a short step from here to theoretical pragmatism. Others, of more scientific bent, proclaimed the 'end of philosophy' in the manner of certain positivistic formulations in *The German Ideology*, in which it is no longer the proletariat or revolutionary action which take in charge the realization and thereby the death of philosophy, but science pure and simple: does not Marx call on us to stop philosophizing, that is, stop developing ideological reveries so that we can move on to the study of reality itself? Politically speaking, the former of these two readings was that of the majority of those philosophical militants who gave themselves completely to politics, making philosophy the religion of their action; the latter on the contrary was that of those critics who hoped that a scientific approach would fill out the empty proclamations of dogmatic philosophy. But if both groups made their peace with politics, both paid for it with a bad philosophical conscience: a practico-religious or positivist death of philosophy is not really a *philosophical* death of philosophy.

So we contorted ourselves to give philosophy a death worthy of it: a philosophical death. Here again we sought support from more texts of Marx and from a third reading of the others. We proceeded on the assumption that the end of philosophy could not but be *critical*, as the subtitle of *Capital* proclaims that book to be of Political Economy: it is essential to go to the things themselves, to finish with philosophical ideologies and to turn to the study of the real world – *but*, and this we hoped would secure us from positivism, in turning against ideology, we saw that it constantly threatened 'the understanding of positive things', besieged science and obscured real characteristics. So we entrusted philosophy with the continual critical reduction of the thread of ideological illusion, and in doing so we made philosophy the conscience of science pure and simple, reduced it completely to the letter and body of science, but merely turned against its negative surroundings as its vigilant conscience, the consciousness of those surroundings that could reduce them to nothing. Thus philosophy was certainly *at an end*, but it survived none the less as an *evanescent* critical consciousness for just long enough to project the positive essence of science on to the threatening ideology, and to destroy the enemy's ideological phantasms, before returning to its place amongst its allies. The critical death of philosophy, identified with its *evanescent* philosophical existence, gave us at last the status and deserts of a really philosophical death, consummated in the ambiguous act of *criticism*. Now philosophy had no fate other than the consummation of its critical death in the *recognition* of the real, and in the return to the real, real *history*, the progenitor of men, of their acts and their thoughts. Philosophy meant retracing on our own account the Young Marx's critical Odyssey, breaking through the layer of illusion that was hiding the real world from us, and arriving at last in our native land: the land of history, to find there at last the rest afforded by reality and science in concord under the perpetual vigilance of *criticism*. According to this reading, there could no longer be any question of a history of philosophy; how could there be a history of dissipated phantasms, of shadows traversed? The only history possible is that of reality, which may dimly arouse in the sleeper incoherent dreams, but these dreams, whose only continuity is derived from their anchorage in these depths, can never make up a continent of history in their own right. Marx said so himself in *The German Ideology*: 'Philosophy has no history.' When you come to read the essay 'On the Young Marx' you will be able to judge if it is not still partly trapped in the mythical hope for a philosophy which will achieve its philosophical end in the living death of a critical consciousness.

*

I have recalled these investigations and these choices because in their own way they carry the traces of our history. And also because the end of Stalinist dogmatism has not completely dissipated them as mere circumstantial reflexes; *they are still our problems*. Those who impute all our disappointments, all our mistakes and all our disarray *in whatever domain*, to Stalin, along with his crimes and errors, are likely to be disconcerted by having to admit that the end of Stalinist dogmatism has not restored Marxist philosophy to us in its integrity.

After all, it is never possible to liberate, even from dogmatism, more than already *exists*. The end of dogmatism produced a real freedom of investigation, and also in some a feverish haste to make philosophy an ideological commentary on their feeling of liberation and their taste for freedom. Fevers sink as surely as stones. What the end of dogmatism has restored to us is the right to assess exactly what we have, to give both our wealth and our poverty their true names, to think and pose our problems in the open, and to undertake in rigour a true investigation. It makes it possible for us to emerge partly from our theoretical provincialism, to recognize and acquaint ourselves with those who did exist and do exist outside us, and as we see this outside, we can begin to see ourselves from the outside and discover the place we occupy in the knowledge and ignorance of Marxism, and thereby begin to know ourselves. The end of dogmatism puts us face to face with this reality: that Marxist philosophy, founded by Marx in the very act of founding his theory of history, has still largely to be constituted, since, as Lenin said, only the corner-stones have been laid down; that the theoretical difficulties we debated in the dogmatist night were not completely artificial – rather they were largely the result of a meagrely elaborated Marxist philosophy; or better, that in the rigid caricatural forms we suffered or maintained, including the theoretical monstrosity of the two sciences, something of an unsettled problem was really present in grotesque and blind forms – the writings of theoretical Leftism (the young Lukács and Korsch) which have recently been re-published are a sufficient witness to this; and finally, that our lot and our duty today is quite simply to pose and confront these problems in the light of day, if Marxist philosophy is to acquire some real existence or achieve a little theoretical consistency.

II

I should like to give some guidance to the road traversed by the notes you are about to read.

The piece on the Young Marx is still trapped in the myth of an evanescent critical philosophy. Nevertheless, it does contain *the* essential *question*, irresistibly drawn from us even by our trials, failures and impotence: *What is Marxist philosophy? Has it any theo-retical right to existence? And if it does exist in principle, how can its specificity be defined?* This essential question was raised practically by another, apparently historical but really theoretical, question: the question of reading and interpreting Marx's Early Works. It was no accident that it seemed indispensable to submit these famous texts to a serious critical examination, these texts which had been inscribed on every banner, in every field, these openly philosophical texts in which we had hoped to read Marx's personal philosophy more or less spon-taneously. The question of Marxist philosophy and of its specificity with respect to Marx's Early Works necessarily implied the question of Marx's relation to the philosophies he had espoused or traversed, those of Hegel and Feuerbach, and therefore the question of where he differed with them.

It was the study of the works of Marx's youth that first led me to a reading of Feuerbach, and to the publication of the most impor-tant of his theoretical writings in the period from 1839 to 1845 (cf. my remarks on pp. 3–8). The same reasoning quite naturally led me to begin studying the nature of the relation of Hegel's philosophy to Marx's in the detail of their respective concepts. The question of the specific difference of Marxist philosophy thus assumed the form of the question as to whether or no there was an *epistemological break* in Marx's intellectual development indicating the emergence of a new conception of philosophy – and the related question of the precise *location* of this break. Within the field defined by this question the study of Marx's Early Works acquired a decisive theoretical impor-tance (does this break exist?) as well as a historical importance (where is it located?).

Of course, the quotation in which Marx himself attests to and locates this break ('we resolved . . . to settle accounts with our erst-while philosophical conscience') in 1845 at the level of *The German Ideology* can only be treated as a declaration to be examined, and falsified or confirmed, not as a proof of the existence of the break and a definition of its location. The examination of the status of this declaration called for a theory and a method – the *Marxist theoreti-cal concepts* in which the reality of theoretical formations in general (philosophical ideologies and science) can be considered must be applied to Marx himself. Without a theory of the history of theoretical formations it would be impossible to grasp and indicate the specific difference that distinguishes two different theoretical formations. I thought it possible to borrow for this purpose the concept of a *'problematic'* from Jacques Martin to designate the particular unity of a theoretical formation and hence the location to be assigned to this specific difference, and the concept of an *'epistemological break'* from Gaston Bachelard to designate the mutation in the theoretical problematic contemporary with the foundation of a scientific discipline. That one of these concepts had to be constructed and the other borrowed does not imply at all that either is arbitrary or foreign to Marx; on the contrary, it can be shown that both are present and active in Marx's scientific thought, even if this presence is most often in the practical state.[2] These two concepts provided me with the indispensable theoretical minimum authorizing a pertinent analysis of the process of the theoretical transformation of the Young Marx, and leading to some precise conclusions.

Let me summarize here in extremely abbreviated form some of the results of a study which took several years and to which the pieces I am presenting here bear only partial witness.

(1) There is an unequivocal *'epistemological break'* in Marx's work which does in fact occur at the point where Marx himself locates it, in the book, unpublished in his lifetime, which is a critique of his erstwhile philosophical (ideological) conscience: *The German Ideology*. The *Theses on Feuerbach*, which are only a few sentences long, mark out the earlier limit of this break, the point at which the new theoretical consciousness is already beginning to show through in the erstwhile consciousness and the erstwhile language, that is, as *necessarily ambiguous and unbalanced concepts*.

---

2   On this dual theme of the *problematic* and of the *epistemological break* (the break indicating the mutation of a pre-scientific problematic into a scientific problematic), see the pages of extraordinary theoretical profundity in Engels's Preface to the Second Volume of *Capital* (English translation, Moscow 1961, pp. 14–18). I shall give a brief commentary on them in *Lire le Capital*, Vol. II.

(2) This 'epistemological break' concerns conjointly *two distinct theoretical disciplines*. By founding the theory of history (historical materialism), Marx simultaneously broke with his erstwhile ideological philosophy and established a new philosophy (dialectical materialism). I am deliberately using the traditionally accepted terminology (historical materialism, dialectical materialism) to designate this double foundation in a single break. And I should point out two important problems implied by this exceptional circumstance. Of course, if the birth of a new philosophy is simultaneous with the foundation of a new science, and this science is the science of history, a crucial theoretical problem arises: by what necessity of principle should the foundation of the scientific theory of history *ipso facto* imply a theoretical revolution in philosophy? This same circumstance also entails a considerable practical consequence: as the new philosophy was only implicit in the new science it might be tempted *to confuse itself with it*. *The German Ideology* sanctions this confusion as it reduces philosophy, as we have noted, to a faint shadow of science, if not to the empty generality of positivism. This practical consequence is one of the keys to the remarkable history of Marxist philosophy, from its origins to the present day.

I shall examine these two problems later.

(3) This 'epistemological break' divides Marx's thought into two long essential periods: the 'ideological' period before, and the scientific period after, the break in 1845. The second period can itself be divided into two moments, the moment of Marx's theoretical transition and that of his theoretical maturity. To simplify the philosophical and historical labours in front of us, I should like to propose the following provisional terminology which registers the above periodization.

(*a*) I propose to designate the works of the earlier period, that is, everything Marx wrote from his Doctoral Dissertation to the *1844 Manuscripts* and *The Holy Family* by the already accepted formula: *Marx's Early Works*.

(*b*) I propose to designate the writings of the break in 1845, that is, the *Theses on Feuerbach* and *The German Ideology* which first introduce Marx's new problematic, though usually still in a partially negative and sharply polemical and critical form, by a new formula: *the Works of the Break*.

(*c*) I propose to designate the works of the period 1845–57 by a new formula: *the Transitional Works*. While it is possible to assign the crucial date of the works of 1845 (the *Theses on Feuerbach* and *The German Ideology*) to the break separating the scientific from the ideological, it must be remembered that this mutation could not produce immediately, in *positive* and *consummated* form, the new theoretical problematic which it inaugurated, in the theory of history as well as in that of philosophy. In fact, *The German Ideology* is a commentary, usually a negative and critical one, on the different forms of the ideological problematic Marx had rejected. Long years of *positive* study and elaboration were necessary before Marx could produce, fashion and establish a conceptual terminology and systematics that were adequate to his revolutionary theoretical project. That is why I propose to designate the works written between 1845 and the first drafts of *Capital* (around 1845–57), that is, the *Manifesto*, the *Poverty of Philosophy*, *Value, Price and Profit*, etc., as the *Works of Marx's Theoretical Transition*.

(*d*) Finally, I propose to designate all the works after 1857 as *Marx's Mature Works*.

This gives us the following classification:

> 1840–45: the Early Works.
>
> 1845: the Works of the Break.
>
> 1845–57: the Transitional Works.
>
> 1857–83: the Mature Works.

(4) The period of Marx's Early Works (1840–5), that is, the period of his ideological works, can itself be subdivided into two moments:

(*a*) the liberal-rationalist moment of his articles in *Die Rheinische Zeitung* (up to 1842).

(*b*) the communalist-rationalist moment of the years 1842–5.

As my essay on 'Marxism and Humanism' briefly suggests, the presupposition of the works of the first moment is a problematic of Kantian-Fichtean type. Those of the second moment, on the contrary, rest on Feuerbach's anthropological problematic. The Hegelian problematic inspires one absolutely *unique* text, which is a rigorous attempt to 'invert' Hegelian idealism, in the *strict* sense, into Feuerbach's pseudo-materialism: this text is the *1844 Manuscripts*.

Paradoxically, therefore, if we exclude the Doctoral Dissertation, which is still the work of a student, the Young Marx *was never strictly speaking a Hegelian*, except in the *last* text of his ideologico-philosophical period; rather, he was first a Kantian-Fichtean, then a Feuerbachian. So the thesis that the Young Marx was a Hegelian, though widely believed today, is in general a myth. On the contrary, it seems that Marx's one and only resort to Hegel in his youth, on the eve of his rupture with his 'erstwhile philosophical conscience', produced the prodigious 'abreaction' indispensable to the liquidation of his 'disordered' consciousness. Until then he had always kept his distance from Hegel, and to grasp the movement whereby he passed from his *Hegelian university studies* to a Kantian-Fichtean problematic and thence to a Feuerbachian problematic, we must realize that, far from being close to Hegel, Marx moved *further and further away from him*. With Fichte and Kant he had worked his way back to the end of the eighteenth century, and then, with Feuerbach, he regressed to the heart of the theoretical past of that century, for in his own way Feuerbach may be said to represent the 'ideal' eighteenth-century philosopher, the synthesis of sensualist materialism and ethico-historical idealism, the real union of Diderot and Rousseau. It would be difficult not to speculate that Marx's sudden and total last return to Hegel in that genial synthesis of Feuerbach and Hegel, the *1844 Manuscripts*, might not have been an explosive experiment uniting the substances of the two extremes of the theoretical field which he had until then frequented, that this extraordinarily rigorous and conscientious experiment, the most extreme test of the 'inversion' of Hegel ever attempted might not have been the way Marx lived practically and achieved his own transformation, in a text which *he never published*. Some idea of the logic of this prodigious mutation is given by the extraordinary theoretical tension of the *1844 Manuscripts*, for we know in advance the paradox that the text of the last hours of the night is, theoretically speaking, the text the furthest removed from the day that is about to dawn.

(5) The *Works of the Break* raise delicate problems of interpretation, precisely as a function of their place in the theoretical formation of Marx's thought. Those brief sparks, the *Theses on Feuerbach*, light

up every philosopher who comes near them, but as is well known, a spark dazzles rather than illuminates: nothing is more difficult to locate in the darkness of the night than the point of light which breaks it. One day we will have to show that these eleven deceptively transparent theses are really riddles. As for *The German Ideology*, it offers us precisely a thought in a state of rupture with its past, playing a pitiless game of deadly criticism with all its erstwhile theoretical presuppositions: primarily with Feuerbach and Hegel and all the forms of a philosophy of consciousness and an anthropological philosophy. But this new thought, so firm and precise in its interrogation of ideological error, cannot define itself without difficulties and ambiguities. It is impossible to break with a theoretical past at one blow: in every case, words and concepts are needed to break with words and concepts, and often the old words are charged with the conduct of the rupture throughout the period of the search for new ones. *The German Ideology* presents the spectacle of a re-enlisted conceptual reserve standing in for new concepts still in training ... and as we usually judge these old concepts by their bearing, taking them at their *word*, it is easy to stray into a positivist conception (the end of all philosophy) or an individualist-humanist conception (the subjects of history are 'real, concrete men'). Or again, it is possible to be taken in by the ambiguous role of the *division of labour*, which, in this book, plays the principal part taken by alienation in the writings of his youth, and commands the whole theory of *ideology* and the whole theory of science. This all arises from its proximity to the break, and that is why *The German Ideology* alone demands a major critical effort to distinguish the suppletory theoretical *function* of particular concepts from the concepts themselves. I shall return to this.

(6) Locating the break in 1845 is not without important theoretical consequences as regards not only the relation between Marx and Feuerbach, but also the relation between Marx and Hegel. Indeed, Marx did not first develop a systematic critique of Hegel after 1845; he had been doing so since the beginning of the second moment of his Youthful period, in the *Critique of Hegel's Philosophy of Right* (1843 Manuscript), the *Introduction to a Critique of Hegel's Philosophy of Right* (1843), the *1844 Manuscripts* and *The Holy Family*. But the

theoretical principles on which this critique of Hegel was based are *merely* a reprise, a commentary or a development and extension of the admirable critique of Hegel repeatedly formulated by Feuerbach. It is a critique of Hegelian philosophy as *speculative* and *abstract*, a critique appealing to the concrete-materialist against the abstract-speculative, i.e. a critique which remains a prisoner of the idealist problematic it hoped to free itself from, and therefore a critique which belongs by right to the theoretical problematic with which Marx broke in 1845.

In the search for Marxist philosophy and in its definition, it is clear that the Marxist critique of Hegel should not be confused with the Feuerbachian critique of Hegel, even if Marx started it in his name. The decision as to whether or no the critique in Marx's writings of 1843 is Marxist (in fact it is Feuerbachian through and through) makes a major difference to our idea of the nature of Marx's later philosophy. I stress this as a crucial point for contemporary interpretations of Marxist philosophy, by which I mean serious, systematic interpretations, based on real philosophical, epistemological and historical knowledge, and on rigorous reading methods – not mere opinions (books can be written on this basis too). For example, there are the writings of Colletti and Della Volpe in Italy, which I regard as of the greatest importance, because in our time they are the only scholars who have made an irreconcilable theoretical distinction between Marx and Hegel and a definition of the specificity of Marxist philosophy the conscious centre of their investigations. Their work certainly presupposes the existence of a break between Marx and Hegel, and between Marx and Feuerbach, but they locate it in 1843, at the level of the *Introduction to the Critique of Hegel's Philosophy of Right*! Such a simple displacement of the break profoundly affects all the theoretical conclusions drawn from it, and not only their conception of Marxist philosophy, but also, as a later work will show, their reading and interpretation of *Capital*.

*

I have permitted myself these remarks so as to clarify the meaning of the pages devoted to Feuerbach and the Young Marx, and so as to reveal the unity of the problem dominating these Notes, since the

essays on contradiction and on the dialectic equally concern a definition of the irreducible specificity of Marxist theory.

That this definition cannot be *read* directly in Marx's writings,
that a complete prior critique is indispensable to an identification of
the location of the real concepts of Marx's maturity; that the identification of these concepts is the same thing as the identification of
their location; that all this critical effort, the absolute precondition
of any interpretation, in itself presupposes activating a minimum of
provisional Marxist theoretical concepts bearing on the nature of
theoretical formations and their history; that the precondition of a
reading of Marx is a Marxist theory of the differential nature of theoretical formations and their history, that is, a theory of epistemological
history, which is Marxist philosophy itself; that this operation in itself
constitutes an indispensable circle in which the application of Marxist
theory to Marx himself appears to be the absolute precondition of an
understanding of Marx and at the same time as the precondition even
of the constitution and development of Marxist philosophy, so much
is clear. But the circle implied by this operation is, like all circles of this
kind, simply the dialectical circle of the question asked of an object as
to its nature, on the basis of a theoretical problematic which in putting
its object to the test puts itself to the test of its object. That Marxism
can and must itself be the object of the epistemological question, that
this epistemological question can only be asked as a function of the
Marxist theoretical problematic, that is necessity itself for a theory
which defines itself dialectically, not merely as a science of history
(historical materialism) but also and simultaneously as a philosophy,
a philosophy that is capable of accounting for the nature of theoretical
formations and their history, and therefore *capable of accounting for
itself*, by taking itself as its own object. Marxism is the only philosophy that theoretically faces up to this test.

All this critical effort is indispensable, not only to a reading of
Marx which is not just an immediate reading, deceived either by
the false transparency of his youthful ideological conceptions, or
by the perhaps still more dangerous false transparency of the apparently familiar concepts of the works of the break. This work which

is essential to a *reading* of Marx is, in the strict sense, simultaneously the work of theoretical elaboration of Marxist philosophy. A theory which enables us to see clearly in Marx, to distinguish science from ideology, to deal with the difference between them within the historical relation between them and to deal with the discontinuity of the epistemological break within the continuity of a historical process; a theory which makes it possible to distinguish a word from a concept, to distinguish the existence or non-existence of a concept behind a word, to discern the existence of a concept by a word's function in the theoretical discourse, to define the nature of a concept by its function in the problematic, and thus by the location it occupies in the system of the 'theory'; this theory which alone makes possible an authentic reading of Marx's writings, a reading which is both epistemological and historical, this theory is in fact simply Marxist philosophy itself.

We set out in search of it. And here it begins to emerge, along with its own first, most elementary demand: the demand for a simple definition of the preconditions of this search.

March 1965

Part One

Feuerbach's 'Philosophical Manifestoes'

La Nouvelle Critique has asked me to situate the writings by Feuerbach published a few months ago in the *Collection Epiméthée* (PUF). I am glad to be able to do so by giving brief answers to a number of questions.

Under the title *Philosophical Manifestoes*, I have gathered together the most important texts and articles published by Feuerbach between 1839 and 1845: *A Contribution to the Critique of Hegel's Philosophy* (1839), the Introduction to *The Essence of Christianity* (1841), the *Provisional Theses for the Reform of Philosophy* (1842), the *Principles of the Philosophy of the Future* (1843), the preface to the second edition of *The Essence of Christianity* (1843) and an article replying to Stirner's attacks (1845). This selection does not include all of Feuerbach's output between 1839 and 1845, but it does represent the essentials of his thought during these historic years.

Why the title Philosophical Manifestoes?

The expression is not Feuerbach's own. I hazard it for two reasons, one subjective, the other objective.

Anyone who reads the texts on the Reform of Philosophy and the Preface to the Principles will realize that they are true proclamations, a passionate annunciation of the theoretical revelation which is to deliver man from his chains. Feuerbach calls out to Humanity. He tears the veils from universal History, destroys myths and lies, uncovers the *truth* of man and restores it to him. The fullness of time has come. Humanity is pregnant with the imminent revolution which will give it possession of its own being. Let men at last become conscious of this, and they will be in reality what they are in truth: free, equal and fraternal beings.

Such exhortations are certainly manifestoes as far as their author is concerned.

So were they for their readers. Particularly for the young radical intellectuals of the 1840s, arguing one another through the contradictions of the 'German misery' and neo-Hegelian philosophy. Why the 1840s? Because they were the *testing years* of this philosophy. In 1840, the Young Hegelians, who believed there was a goal to history – the realm of reason and liberty – looked to the heir to the throne for the realization of their hopes – the end of the autocratic and feudal Prussian order, the abolition of censorship, the reduction to reason of the Church, in short, the installation of a regime of political, intellectual and religious liberty. But hardly had he reached the throne than this so-called 'liberal' heir, now Frederick William IV, returned to despotism. This confirmation and reaffirmation of tyranny was a terrible blow to the theory which was the basis and sum of all their hopes. In principle, history should be reason and liberty; in fact, it was merely unreason and slavery. The facts had provided a lesson to be learnt: this very contradiction. *But how could it be grasped?* At this point *The Essence of Christianity* appeared, and then the pamphlets on the *Reform of Philosophy*. These texts may not have liberated humanity, but they did release the Young Hegelians from their theoretical impasse. Precisely at the moment of their greatest disarray, Feuerbach gave them an *exact* answer to the dramatic question they were asking each other about man and history! The echo of this relief and enthusiasm can be seen forty years later in Engels. Feuerbach was precisely the '*New Philosophy*' that made *tabula rasa* of Hegel and all speculative philosophy, that put the world which philosophy had made to walk *on its head* back *on to its feet* again, that denounced every alienation and every illusion but also *gave reasons for them*, and made the *unreason* of history thinkable and criticizable in the name of reason itself, that at last reconciled *idea* and *fact*, and made the necessity of a world's contradiction and the necessity of its liberation comprehensible. This is why the neo-Hegelians, as the old Engels had to admit, 'all became at once Feuerbachians'. This is why they received his books as Manifestoes announcing the Paths of the Future.

I should add that these Manifestoes are *philosophical*. For, quite obviously, everything was still taking place in philosophy. But philosophical events had become historical events *as well*.

What is particularly interesting about these writings?

First of all, they are of *historical* interest. I did not choose these works of the 1840s simply because they were the most famous and the most lasting (indeed they have lasted until today, when certain existentialists and theologians look to them for the origins of a modern tendency), but also and primarily because they belong to a historical *moment* and had a historical role (among a restricted circle, of course, but one with a great future). Feuerbach was both *witness* to and *actor* in the crisis in the theoretical development of the Young Hegelian movement. It is essential to read Feuerbach to understand the writings of the Young Hegelians between 1840 and 1845. In particular, this reveals the extent to which Marx's early works are impregnated with Feuerbach's thought. Not only is Marx's terminology from 1842 and 1845 Feuerbachian (alienation, species being, total being, 'inversion' of subject and predicate, etc.) but, what is probably more important, so is the basic *philosophical problematic*. Articles like *On the Jewish Question* or the *Critique of Hegel's Philosophy of Right* cannot be understood outside the context of the Feuerbachian problematic. Naturally, Marx's themes go beyond Feuerbach's immediate preoccupations, but the theoretical schemata and problematic are *the same*. To use his own expression, Marx did not really 'settle accounts' with this problematic until 1845. *The German Ideology* is the first work indicating a conscious and definitive rupture with Feuerbach's philosophy and his influence.

A comparative study of Feuerbach's writings and Marx's early works makes possible a *historical reading* of Marx's writings, and a better understanding of his development.

Does this historical understanding have any theoretical significance?

Certainly. Once Feuerbach's writings in the years from 1839 to 1845 have been read it is impossible to make any mistakes as to the *derivation* of the majority of the concepts traditionally used to justify '*ethical*' interpretations of Marx. Such famous expressions as 'philosophy's world-to-be', 'the inversion of subject and predicate', 'for man the root is man himself', 'the political State is the species-life of man', the 'suppression and realization of philosophy', 'philosophy is the head of human emancipation and the proletariat is its heart', etc., etc., are expressions *directly* borrowed from Feuerbach, or directly inspired by him. All the expressions of

Marx's idealist 'humanism' are Feuerbachian. Admittedly, Marx did
not merely quote or repeat Feuerbach, who, as these Manifestoes show,
was always thinking about politics but hardly ever talked about it. His
whole concern was with the criticism of religion, of theology, and with
that secular disguise for theology known as speculative philosophy. The
Young Marx, on the contrary, was haunted first by politics and then by
that for which politics is merely the 'heaven': the concrete life of alienated
men. But in *On the Jewish Question, Hegel's Philosophy of the State*, etc.,
and even usually in *The Holy Family*, he is no more than an *avant-garde*
Feuerbachian applying *an ethical problematic to the understanding of human
history*. In other words, we can say that at this time Marx was merely
applying the theory of alienation, that is, Feuerbach's theory of 'human
nature', to politics and the concrete activity of man, before extending it
(in large part) to political economy in the *Manuscripts*. It is important
that the real origin of these Feuerbachian concepts should be recognized,
not so as to assess everything according to a standard of attribution (this
is Marx's, that Feuerbach's, etc.), but so as to avoid attributing to Marx
the *invention* of concepts and a problematic he had only *borrowed*. It is
even more important that it be recognized that these borrowed concepts
were not borrowed one by one, in isolation, but *en bloc, as a set*: this set
being precisely Feuerbach's problematic. This is the essential point. For
borrowing a concept in isolation may only be of accidental and secondary significance. Borrowing a concept in isolation (from its context) does
not bind the borrower *vis-à-vis* the context from which he extracted it
(for example, the borrowings from Smith, Ricardo and Hegel in *Capital*).
But borrowing a systematically interrelated set of concepts, borrowing a
real *problematic*, cannot be accidental, it *binds* the borrower. I believe that
a comparison of the Manifestoes and of Marx's early works shows quite
clearly that for two or three years Marx literally *espoused* Feuerbach's
problematic, that he profoundly *identified himself* with it, and that to
understand the meaning of most of his statements during this period, even
where these bear on the material of later studies (for example, politics,
social life, the proletariat, revolution, etc.) and might therefore seem fully
Marxist, it is essential *to situate oneself at the very heart of this identification*,
and to explore all its theoretical consequences and inferences.

I feel that this requirement is a crucial one, for if it is true that Marx espoused a whole problematic, then his rupture with Feuerbach, his famous 'settling of accounts with our erstwhile philosophical conscience', implied the adoption of a *new problematic* which even if it did integrate a certain number of the old concepts, did so into a whole which confers on them a radically new significance. I am pleased to be able to express this in an image from Greek history which Marx himself used: after serious set-backs in the War against the Persians, Themistocles advised the Athenians to leave the land and base the future of their city *on another element* – the sea. Marx's theoretical revolution was precisely to base his theory on *a new element* after liberating it from its *old element*: the element of Hegelian and Feuerbachian philosophy.

But this new problematic can be looked at in two ways:

Firstly, in Marx's mature writings – *The German Ideology*, *The Poverty of Philosophy*, *Capital*, etc. But these works do not contain any systematic exposition of Marx's theoretical position comparable to the exposition of Hegel's philosophy in *The Phenomenology of Mind*, the *Encyclopaedia*, and the *Larger Logic*, or the exposition of Feuerbach's philosophy in the *Principles of the Philosophy of the Future*. Marx's writings are either polemics (*The German Ideology*, *The Poverty of Philosophy*) or positive studies (*Capital*). Marx's theoretical position, what can be called, ambiguously, his 'philosophy', is certainly active in these works, but it is buried in them, and confused with his own critical or heuristic concerns, and rarely, if ever, explicitly discussed for its own sake in a systematic and extensive form. Naturally, this situation does not simplify the interpreter's task.

At this point a knowledge of Feuerbach's problematic and of why Marx broke with Feuerbach can come to our aid. For through Feuerbach we have an indirect access to Marx's new problematic. We can find out *what was the problematic that Marx broke with*, and we can discover the theoretical horizons 'opened up' by this rupture. If it is true that we can learn as much about a man by what he rejects as by what he adheres to, then *a thinker as exacting as Marx should be illuminated by his break with Feuerbach as much as by his own later statements*. As this rupture with Feuerbach occurred at the decisive point in the constitution of Marx's definitive theoretical position, a knowledge of Feuerbach thereby becomes an irreplaceable means of access to Marx's philosophical position, rich in theoretical implications.

In the same way, I feel that it makes possible a better understanding of the relation between Marx and Hegel. If there was this rupture between Marx and Feuerbach, the critique of Hegel to be found in most of the former's early works must, at least as far as its *ultimate* philosophical presuppositions are concerned, be regarded as inadequate, or even incorrect, to the extent that it was a critique *from a Feuerbachian viewpoint*, that is, a viewpoint that Marx later rejected. Now, usually for reasons of convenience, there is a constant and innocent tendency to believe that, even though Marx later modified his viewpoint, the critique of Hegel to be found in the early works is none the less justifiable and can therefore be 'retained'. But to do so is to neglect the basic fact that Marx set himself apart from Feuerbach when he realized that *the Feuerbachian critique of Hegel was a critique 'from within Hegelian philosophy itself'*, that Feuerbach was still a 'philosopher', who had, indeed, 'inverted' the body of the Hegelian edifice, but had retained its ultimate structure and bases, that is, its theoretical presuppositions. In Marx's eyes, Feuerbach had stopped within Hegelian territory, he was as much a prisoner of it as its critic since he had merely turned Hegel's own principles against Hegel himself. He had not changed '*elements*'. The truly Marxist critique of Hegel depends precisely on this change of elements, that is, on the abandonment of the philosophical problematic whose recalcitrant prisoner Feuerbach remained.

To summarize the theoretical interest of this privileged confrontation between Marx and Feuerbach's thought in a manner which is not without its bearing on contemporary polemic, I should say that what is at stake in this double rupture, first with Hegel, then with Feuerbach, is the very meaning of the word *philosophy*. What can Marxist '*philosophy*' be in contrast to the classical models of philosophy? Or, what can be the theoretical position which has broken with the traditional philosophical problematic whose last theoretician was Hegel and from which Feuerbach tried desperately but in vain to free himself? The answer to this question can largely be drawn negatively from Feuerbach himself, from this last witness of Marx's early 'philosophical conscience', the last mirror in which Marx contemplated himself before rejecting the borrowed image to put on his own true features.

October 1960

Part Two

On the Young Marx

THEORETICAL QUESTIONS

To Auguste Cornu, who devoted his life to a young man called Marx.

'German criticism has, right up to its latest efforts, never quitted the realm of philosophy. Far from examining its general philosophical premises, the whole body of its inquiries has actually sprung from the soil of a definite philosophical system, that of Hegel. Not only in their answers but also in their questions there was a mystification.'

Karl Marx, *The German Ideology*

The periodical *Recherches Internationales* offers us eleven studies by Marxists from abroad 'on the Young Marx'. One article by Togliatti, already old (1954), five from the Soviet Union (three of which are by young scholars, twenty-seven to twenty-eight years old), four from the German Democratic Republic, and one from Poland. Exegesis of the Young Marx might have been thought the privilege and the cross of Western Marxists. This work and its Presentation show them that they are no longer alone in the perils and rewards of this task.[1]

Reading this interesting but uneven[2] collection has given me the opportunity to examine a number of problems, clear up certain confusions and put forward some clarifications on my own account.

Convenience of exposition is my excuse for entering on the question of Marx's Early Works in three basic aspects: political, theoretical and philosophical.

The Political Problem

First of all, any discussion of Marx's Early Works is a *political* discussion. Need we be reminded that Marx's Early Works, whose history and significance were well enough described by Mehring, were exhumed by Social-Democrats and exploited by them to the detriment

---

1   The interest shown in the study of Marx's Early Works by young Soviet scholars is particularly noteworthy. It is an important sign of the present direction of cultural development in the U.S.S.R. (cf. the 'Presentation', p. 4, n. 7).

2   Incontestably dominated by the remarkable essay by Hoeppner: '*À propos de quelques conceptions erronées du passage de Hegel à Marx*' (pp. 175–90).

of Marxism-Leninism? The heroic ancestors of this operation were named Landshut and Mayer (1931). The Preface to their edition may be read in Molitor's translation in the Costes edition of Marx (*Œuvres philosophiques de Marx*, t. IV, pp. XIII–LI). The position is quite clearly put. *Capital* is an *ethical* theory, the silent philosophy of which is openly spoken in Marx's Early Works.[3] Thus, reduced to two propositions, is the thesis which has had such extraordinary success. And not only in France and in Italy, but also, as these articles from abroad show, in contemporary Germany and Poland. Philosophers, ideologues, theologians have all launched into a gigantic enterprise of criticism and *conversion*: let Marx be restored to his source, and let him admit at last that in him, the mature man is merely the young man in disguise. Or if he stubbornly insists on his age, let him admit the sins of his maturity, let him recognize that he sacrificed philosophy to economics, ethics to science, man to history. Let him consent to this or refuse it, his truth, everything that will survive him, everything which helps the men that we are to live and think, is contained in these few Early Works.

---

3   See Molitor, trans., *Œuvres philosophiques de Marx*, Ed. Costes, Vol. IV, 'Introduction' by Landshut and Mayer: 'It is clear that the basis for the tendency which presided over the analysis made in *Capital* is . . . the tacit hypothesis that can alone restore an intrinsic justification to the whole tendency of Marx's most important work . . . these hypotheses were precisely the formal theme of Marx's work before 1847. For the author of *Capital* they by no means represent youthful errors from which he progressively liberated himself as his knowledge matured, and which were cast aside as waste in the process of his personal purification. Rather, in the works from 1840 to 1847 Marx opened up the whole horizon of historical conditions and made safe the general humane foundation without which any explanation of economic relations would remain merely the work of a good economist. Anyone who fails to grasp this hidden thread which is the subject-matter of his early works and which runs through his works as a whole will be unable to understand Marx . . . the principles of his economic analysis are directly derived from "the true reality of man" ' (pp. XV–XVII). 'A slight alteration in the first sentence of the *Communist Manifesto* would give us: "The history of all hitherto existing society is the history of the self-alienation of man . . ." ' (p. XLII), etc. Pajitnov's article '*Les Manuscrits de 1844*' (*Recherches*, pp. 80–96) is a valuable review of the main authors of this 'Young-Marxist' revisionist current.

So these good critics leave us with but a single choice: we must admit that *Capital* (and 'mature Marxism' in general) is *either an expression of the Young Marx's philosophy, or its betrayal*. In either case, the established interpretation must be totally revised and we must return to the Young Marx, the Marx through whom spoke the Truth.

This is the *location* of the discussion: the Young Marx. Really *at stake* in it: Marxism. The *terms of the discussion*: whether the Young Marx was already and wholly Marx.

The discussion once joined, it seems that Marxists have a choice between two parrying dispositions within the ideal order of the tactical combinatory.[4]

Very schematically, if they want to rescue Marx from the perils of his youth with which his opponents threaten them, they can *either agree that the Young Marx is not Marx; or that the Young Marx is Marx*. These extreme theses may be *nuanced*; but their inspiration extends even to their nuances.

Of course, this inventory of possibilities may well seem derisory. Where disputed history is concerned, there is no place for tactics, the verdict must be sought solely in a scientific examination of the facts and documents. However, past experience, and even a reading of the present collection, proves that on occasion it may be difficult to abstract from relatively enlightened tactical considerations or defensive reactions where facing up to a *political attack* is concerned. Jahn sees this quite clearly:[5] it was not Marxists who opened the debate on Marx's Early Works. And no doubt because they had not grasped the true value of Mehring's classic work or of the scholarly and scrupulous research of Auguste Cornu, young Marxists were caught out, ill-prepared for a struggle they had not foreseen. They reacted as best they could. There is some of this surprise left in the present defence, in its reflex movement, its confusion, its awkwardness. I should also

---

4   Obviously, they could calmly adopt their opponents' theses (without realizing it) and rethink Marx through his youth – and this paradox has been tried, in France itself. But ultimately history always dissipates misunderstandings.
5   W. Jahn, '*Le contenu économique de l'aliénation*' (*Recherches*, p. 158).

add: *in its bad conscience*. For this attack surprised Marxists on their own ground: that of Marx. If it had been a question of a simple concept they might have felt themselves to have less of a special responsibility, but the problem raised was one that directly concerned Marx's history and Marx himself. So they fell victim to a *second reaction* which came to reinforce the first reflex defence: the fear of failing in their duty, of letting the charge entrusted to them come to harm, before themselves and before history. In plain words: if it is not studied, criticized and dominated, this reaction could lead Marxist philosophy into a '*cata-strophic' parrying movement*, a global response which in fact *suppresses* the problem in its attempt to deal with it.

To discomfit those who set up against Marx his own youth, the *opposite position* is resolutely taken up: Marx is reconciled with his youth – *Capital* is no longer read as *On the Jewish Question*, *On the Jewish Question* is read as *Capital*; the shadow of the Young Marx is no longer projected onto Marx, but that of Marx onto the young Marx; and a pseudo-theory of the history of philosophy in the '*future anterior*' is erected to justify this counter-position, without realizing that this pseudo-theory is quite simply Hegelian.[6] A devout fear of

---

6   Cf. Schaff: '*Le vrai visage du jeune Marx*' (*Recherches*, p. 193) and also the following extract from the Presentation (pp. 7–8): 'Marx's work as a whole cannot be seriously understood, nor Marxism itself as thought and as action, on the basis of the conception of his early works he happened to have when he was working them out. Only the opposite approach is valuable, that is, the approach which understands the significance and appreciates the value of these first fruits (?) and enters those creative laboratories of Marxist thought represented by writings such as the Kreuznach notebooks and the *1844 Manuscripts*, via Marxism as we have inherited it from Marx and also – it must be plainly stated – as it has been enriched by a century in the heat of historical practice. In default of this there is nothing to prevent an evalua-tion of Marx by criteria taken from Hegelianism if not from Thomism. *The history of philosophy is written in the future anterior: ultimately, a refusal to admit this is a denial of this history and the erection of oneself as its founder in the manner of Hegel.*' I have emphasized the last sentence deliberately. But the reader will have done so himself, astonished to see attributed to Marxism precisely the Hegelian conception of the history of philosophy and, as the summit of this confusion!, find himself accused of Hegelianism if he rejects it. . . . We shall soon see that there are other motives at issue

a blow to Marx's *integrity* inspires as its reflex a resolute acceptance of *the whole of Marx*: Marx is declared to be a whole, '*the young Marx is part of Marxism*'[7] – as if we risked losing the *whole of Marx* if we were to submit his youth to the radical critique of history, not *the history he was going to live*, but *the history he did live*, not an immediate history, but the reflected history for which, in his maturity, he gave us, not the '*truth*' in the Hegelian sense, but the principles of its scientific understanding.

Even where parrying is concerned, there can be no good policy without good theory.

The Theoretical Problem

This brings us to the *second problem* posed by a study of Marx's Early Works: the *theoretical* problem. I must insist on it, as it seems to me that it has not always been resolved, or even correctly posed in the majority of studies inspired by this subject.

Indeed, only too often the form of the *reading* of Marx's early writings adopted depends more on free association of ideas or on a simple comparison of terms than on a historical critique.[8] This is not

in such a conception. At any rate, this quotation clearly demonstrates the movement I have been pointing out: Marx is threatened in everything by his youth, so he is recuperated as a *moment of the whole*, and a philosophy of the history of philosophy is constructed to this end, a philosophy which is quite simply – Hegelian. Hoeppner calmly brings this into perspective in his article '*A propos du passage de Hegel à Marx*' (*Recherches*, p. 180): 'History must not be studied from the front backwards, searching for the heights of Marxist knowledge its ideal germs in the past. The evolution of philosophical thought must be traced on the basis of the real evolution of society.' This is Marx's own position, extensively developed in *The German Ideology*, for example.

7   'Presentation', p. 7. The reasoning is unambiguous.
8   Cf. Hoeppner (*op. cit.*, p. 178): '*It is not a question of knowing what Marxist content a Marxist investigator might today be able to read into such passages, but rather of knowing what social content they had for Hegel himself.*' Hoeppner's excellent position on Hegel, opposing Kuczynski who looks in Hegel for 'Marxist' themes, *is also unreservedly valid for Marx himself* when his early works are being read from the standpoint of his mature works.

to dispute that such a reading can give theoretical results, but these results are merely *the precondition* of a real understanding of the texts. For example, Marx's Dissertation may be read by comparing its terms with those of Hegel's thought;[9] the *Critique of Hegel's Philosophy of Right* by comparing its principles with those of Feuerbach or those of Marx's maturity;[10] the *1844 Manuscripts* by comparing their principles with those of *Capital*.[11] Even then, the comparison may be either superficial or profound. It may give rise to misunderstandings[12] which are errors for all that. On the other hand, it can open up interesting perspectives.[13] But such comparison is not always its own justification.

Indeed, to stick to spontaneous or even enlightened association of theoretical *elements* is to run the risk of remaining the prisoner of an implicit conception only too close to the current academic conception of the comparison, opposition and approximation of elements that culminates in a theory of *sources* – or, what comes to the same thing, in a theory of anticipation. A sophisticated reading of Hegel 'thinks of Hegel' when it reads the *1841 Dissertation* or even the *1844 Manuscripts*. A sophisticated reading of Marx 'thinks of Marx' when it reads the *Critique of the Philosophy of Right*.[14]

---

9   Togliatti, '*De Hegel au marxisme*' (*Recherches*, pp. 38–40).

10   N. Lapine, '*Critique de la philosophie de Hegel*' (*Recherches*, pp. 52–71).

11   W. Jahn, '*Le contenu économique du concept d'aliénation du travail dans les œuvres de jeunesse de Marx*' (*Recherches*, pp. 157–74).

12   For example, the two quotations invoked by Togliatti to prove that Marx superseded Hegel are precisely a plagiarism of writings of Feuerbach! Hoeppner, hawk-eyed, has spotted this: 'The two quotations from the *Manuscripts* (of 1844) used by Togliatti to show that Marx had by then liberated himself from Feuerbach merely reproduce in essentials the ideas of Feuerbach expressed in the *Provisional Theses* and the *Principles of the Philosophy of the Future*' (*op. cit.*, p. 184, n. 11). It would be possible to dispute the proof-value of the quotations invoked by Pajitnov on pp. 88 and 109 of his article '*Les Manuscrits de 1844*' in the same way. The moral of these mistakes is that one should closely read one's authors. It is not superfluous where Feuerbach is concerned. Marx and Engels discuss him so much, and so well, that it is easy to believe that one knows him intimately.

13   For example, Jahn: a suggestive comparison between the theory of alienation in the *1844 Manuscripts* and the theory of value in *Capital*.

14   See footnote 5.

Perhaps it is not realized often enough that whether this conception is a theory of sources or a theory of anticipation, it is, in its naïve immediacy, based on *three theoretical presuppositions* which are always tacitly active in it. The *first presupposition is analytic*: it holds that any theoretical system and any constituted thought is *reducible to its elements*: a precondition that enables one to think any element of this system *on its own*, and to compare it with *another* similar element from *another* system.[15] The *second presupposition* is *teleological*: it institutes a secret tribunal of history which *judges* the ideas submitted to it, or rather, which permits the dissolution of (different) systems into their elements, institutes these elements as elements in order to proceed to their measurement according to its own norms as if to *their truth*.[16] Finally, these two presuppositions depend on a *third*, which regards the history of ideas as its own element, maintains that nothing happens there which is not a product of the history of ideas itself and that the world of ideology is *its own principle of intelligibility*.

I believe it is necessary to dig down to these foundations if we are to understand the possibility and meaning of this method's most striking feature: its *eclecticism*. Where this surface eclecticism is not hiding completely meaningless forms a search beneath it will always reveal this *theoretical teleology* and this *auto-intelligibility of ideology* as such. When reading some of the articles in this collection, one cannot help feeling that even in their efforts to free themselves from this conception, they still remain contaminated by its implicit logic. Indeed it seems as if writing the history of Marx's early theoretical development entailed the reduction of his thought into its '*elements*', grouped in general under two rubrics: the materialist elements and the idealist elements; as if a comparison of these elements, a confrontation of the weight of each, could determine the *meaning* of the text under examination. Thus, in the articles from the *Rheinische Zeitung* the external form of a thought which is *still* Hegelian can be shown to conceal the

---

15   This formalism is excellently criticized by Hoeppner with respect to Kuczynski (*op. cit.*, pp. 177–8).

16   In the theory of sources it is the origin that measures the development. In the theory of anticipation it is the goal that decides the meaning of the moments of the process.

presence of *materialist elements* such as the political nature of censor-ship, the social (class) nature of the laws on the theft of wood, etc.; in the 1843 Manuscript (*Critique of Hegel's Philosophy of Right*), the exposition and formulation, though still *inspired* by Feuerbach or *still* Hegelian, conceal the presence of *materialist elements* such as the reality of social classes, of private property and its relation to the State, and even of dialectical materialism itself, etc. It is clear that this discrimination between *elements* detached from the internal context of the thought expressed and conceived in isolation, is only possible on condition that the reading of these texts is *slanted*, that is, *teleologi-cal*. One of the most clear-headed of the authors in this collection, N. Lapine, expressly recognizes this: '*This kind of characterization . . . is, in fact, very eclectic, as it does not answer the question as to how these different elements are combined together in Marx's world outlook.*'[17] He sees clearly that this decomposition of a text into what is *already mate-rialist* and what is *still idealist* does not preserve *its unity*, and that this decomposition is induced precisely by reading the early texts through the content of the mature texts. Fully developed Marxism, the Goal are the members of the tribunal which pronounces and executes this judgement, separating the body of an earlier text into its *elements*, thereby destroying its unity. '*If we start with the conception Marx then had of his philosophical position, the 1843 Manuscript emerges as a perfectly consistent and complete work*', whereas '*from the viewpoint of developed Marxism the 1843 Manuscript does not emerge as an organi-cally complete whole, in which the methodological value of each element has been rigorously demonstrated. An obvious lack of maturity means that an exaggerated attention is paid to certain problems, whereas others of basic importance are no more than outlined. . . .*'[18] We could not ask for a more honest recognition that the decomposition into elements and the *constitution of these elements* is induced by their insertion into a finalist perspective. I might further add that a sort of '*delegation of reference*' often occurs, which fully developed Marxism confers on an interme-diate author, for example, on *Feuerbach*. As Feuerbach is reckoned to

---

17   Lapine, '*Critique de la Philosophie de Hegel*' (*Recherches*, p. 68).
18   Lapine, *op. cit.*, p. 69.

be a 'materialist' (though, strictly speaking, Feuerbach's 'materialism' depends essentially on taking Feuerbach's own *declarations of materialism* at their face value) he can serve as a *second centre of reference*, and in his turn make possible the acceptance of certain elements in Marx's Early Works as materialist by-products, by virtue of his own pronouncement and his own 'sincerity'. Thus the subject-predicate inversion, the Feuerbachian critique of speculative philosophy, his critique of religion, the human essence objectified in its productions, etc., are all declared to be 'materialist'. . . . . This 'by-production' of elements via Feuerbach combined with the production of elements via the mature Marx occasionally gives rise to strange redundancies and misunderstandings; for example, when it is a matter of deciding just what does distinguish the materialist elements authenticated by Feuerbach from the materialist elements authenticated by Marx himself.[19] Ultimately, as this procedure enables us to find *materialist elements* in all Marx's early texts, including even the letter to his father in which he refuses to separate the ideal from the real, it is very difficult to decide *when* Marx can be regarded as materialist, or rather, when he could not have been! For *Jahn*, for example, although they '*still*' contain '*a whole series of abstract elements*' the *1844 Manuscripts* mark '*the birth of scientific socialism*'.[20] For *Pajitnov*, these manuscripts '*form the crucial pivot around which Marx reoriented the social sciences. The theoretical premises of Marxism had been laid down*.'[21] For *Lapine*, '*unlike the articles in the* Rheinische Zeitung *in which certain elements of materialism only appear spontaneously, the 1843 Manuscript witnesses to Marx's conscious passage to materialism*', and in fact '*Marx's critique of Hegel starts from materialist positions*' (it is true that this '*conscious passage*' is called '*implicit*' and '*unconscious*' in the same article).[22] As for Schaff, he writes squarely, '*We know (from later statements of Engels) that Marx became a materialist in 1841*.'[23]

---

19 Cf., e.g. Bakouradzé, '*La formation des idées philosophiques de K. Marx*' (*Recherches*, pp. 29–32).

20 Jahn, *op. cit.*, pp. 160 and 169.

21 Pajitnov, *op. cit.*, p. 117.

22 Lapine, *op. cit.*, pp. 58, 67 and 69.

23 Schaff, *op. cit.*, p. 202.

I am not trying to make an easy argument out of these contradictions (which might at little cost be set aside as signs of an 'open' investigation). But it is legitimate to ask whether this uncertainty about the moment when Marx *passed on* to materialism, etc., is not related to the spontaneous and implicit use of an analytico-teleological theory. We cannot but notice that this theory seems to have no valid criterion whereby it could pronounce upon the body of thought it has decomposed into its elements, that is, whose effective unity it has destroyed. And this lack arises precisely because this very decomposition deprives it of such a criterion: in fact, if an idealist element is an idealist element and a materialist element is a materialist element, who can really decide what meaning they constitute once they are assembled together in *the effective living unity of a text*? Ultimately, the paradoxical result of this decomposition is that even the question of *the global meaning of a text* such as *On the Jewish Question* or the 1843 Manuscript *vanishes, it is not asked* because the means whereby it might have been asked have been rejected. But this is a question of the highest importance that neither real life nor a living critique can ever avoid! Suppose by chance that a reader of our own time came to take seriously the philosophy of *On the Jewish Question* or of the *1844 Manuscripts*, and espoused it (it has happened! I was about to say, it has happened to us all! and how many of those to whom it has happened have *failed* to become Marxists!). Just what, I wonder, could we then say about his thought, considered as what it is, that is, as a whole. Would we regard it as idealist or materialist? Marxist or non-Marxist?[24] Or should we regard its meaning as *in abeyance*, waiting on a stage it has not yet reached? But this is the way Marx's early texts are only too often treated, as if they belonged

---

24   I ask this question with regard to some third party. But we all know that it is asked of all Marxists who make use of Marx's Early Writings. If their use of them lacks discernment, if they take essays like *On the Jewish Question* or the 1843 Manuscript and *1844 Manuscripts* for Marxist writings, if this inspiration gives rise to conclusions for theory and for ideological action, *they have in fact answered the question*, what they do answers for them: the Young Marx can be taken as Marx, the Young Marx was a Marxist. They give openly the answer that the critique I am discussing gives under its breath (by avoiding any answer at all). In both cases, the same principles are at work, and at stake.

to a reserved domain, sheltered from the '*basic question*' solely because they *must* develop into Marxism. . . . As if their meaning had been held in abeyance until the end, as if it was necessary to wait on the final synthesis before their elements could be at last resorbed *into a whole*, as if, before this final synthesis, the question of the whole could not be raised, just because all totalities earlier than the final synthesis have been destroyed? But this brings us to the height of the paradox from behind which this analytico-teleological method breaks out: this method which is constantly *judging* cannot *make the slightest judgement of any totality unlike itself.* Could there be a franker admission that it merely *judges itself, recognizes itself behind the objects it considers*, that it *never moves outside itself*, that the development it hopes to think it cannot definitively think other than as *a development of itself within itself*? And to anyone whose response to the ultimate logic that I have drawn from this method is to say '*that is precisely what makes it dialectical*' – my answer is '*Dialectical, yes, but Hegelian!*'

In fact, once it is a matter of thinking precisely the *development* of a thought which has been reduced to its elements in this way, once Lapine's naïve but honest question has been asked: '*how are these different elements combined together in Marx's final world outlook?*', once it is a matter of conceiving the relations between these elements whose destiny we know, the arguments we can see emerging are those of the Hegelian dialectic, in superficial or profound forms. An example of the superficial form is a recourse to the contradiction between form and content, or more precisely, between content and its *conceptual expression*. The 'materialist content' comes into contradiction with its 'idealist form', and the idealist form itself tends to be reduced to a mere matter of *terminology* (it had to dissolve in the end; it was nothing but *words*). Marx was *already* a materialist, but he was *still* using Feuerbachian concepts, he was borrowing Feuerbachian *terminology* although he was no longer and had never been a pure Feuerbachian: between the *1844 Manuscripts* and the Mature Works Marx discovered his definitive terminology;[25] it is merely a question of *language*. The

---

25   Jahn, *op. cit.*, p. 173, 'In *The German Ideology* . . . historical materialism found its *adequate terminology*.' But as Jahn's own essay shows, it is a matter of something quite different from terminology.

whole development occurred in the words. I know this is to schema-
tize, but it makes it easier to see the hidden meaning of the procedure.
It can on occasion be considerably elaborated, for example, in *Lapine's*
theory which, not content with opposing form (terminology) and
content, opposes *consciousness* and *tendency*. Lapine does not reduce
the differences between Marx's thought at different times to a mere
difference of terminology. He admits that *the language had a meaning*: this meaning was that of Marx's consciousness (of himself) at a
particular moment in his development. Thus, in the 1843 Manuscript
(*Critique of Hegel's Philosophy of Right*) Marx's self-consciousness
was Feuerbachian. Marx spoke the language of Feuerbach because *he
believed himself* to be a Feuerbachian. But this language-conscious-
ness was objectively in contradiction with his '*materialist tendency*'. It
is this contradiction which constitutes the motor of his development.
This conception may well be Marxist in appearance (cf. the 'delay of
consciousness'), but only in appearance, for if it is possible within it
to define the *consciousness* of a text (its global meaning, its language-
meaning), it is hard to see how concretely to define its '*tendency*'. Or,
rather, it is perfectly clear how it has been defined once we realize
that, for Lapine, the distinction between materialist tendency and
consciousness (of self) coincides exactly with '*the difference between
the appearance of the objective content of the 1843 Manuscript from the
viewpoint of developed Marxism and what Marx himself regarded as the
content at the time*'.[26] Rigorously understood, this sentence suggests
that the '*tendency*' is nothing but a retrospective abstraction of the
result, which was precisely what had to be explained, that is, it is the
Hegelian *in-itself* conceived on the basis of its end as its real origin.
The contradiction between consciousness and tendency can thus be
reduced to the contradiction between the in-itself and the for-itself.
Lapine immediately goes on to say that this tendency is 'implicit' and
'unconscious'. We are given *an abstraction from the problem itself as
if it were the solution*. Naturally, I am not denying that in Lapine's
essay there are not indications of a way to a *different* conception (now
I shall be accused of lapsing into the theory of elements! The very

---

26 Lapine, *op.cit.*, p. 69.

concept of 'tendency' must be renounced if it is to be really possible to think these elements), but it must be admitted that his systematic is Hegelian.

It is not possible to commit oneself to a Marxist study of Marx's Early Works (and of the problems they pose) without rejecting the spontaneous or reflected temptations of an analytico-teleological method which is always more or less haunted by *Hegelian principles*. It is essential to break with the presuppositions of this method, and to apply the Marxist principles of a theory of ideological development to our object.

These principles are quite different from those hitherto considered. They imply:

(1) Every ideology must be regarded as a real whole, internally unified by its own problematic, so that it is impossible to extract one element without altering its meaning.

(2) The meaning of this whole, of a particular ideology (in this case an individual's thought), depends not on its relation to a *truth* other than itself but on its relation to the existing *ideological field* and on the *social problems and social structure* which sustain the ideology and are reflected in it; the sense of the *development* of a particular ideology depends not on the relation of this development to its origins or its end, considered as *its truth*, but to the relation found within this development between the mutations of the particular ideology and the mutations in the ideological field and the social problems and relations that sustain it.

(3) Therefore, the developmental motor principle of a particular ideology cannot be found within ideology itself but outside it, in what *underlies* (*l'en-deça de*) the particular ideology: its author as a concrete individual and the actual history reflected in this individual development according to the complex ties between the individual and this history.

I should add that these principles, unlike the previous ones, are not *in the strict sense ideological principles, but scientific ones*: in other words, they are not *the truth* of the process to be studied (as are all the principles of a history in the 'future anterior'). They are not *the truth of*, they are the *truth for*, they are *true* as a precondition to legitimately posing a problem, and thus through this problem, to the production of a true solution. So these principles too presuppose 'fully developed Marxism', but not as the *truth* of its own genesis, rather, as *the theory which makes possible an understanding* of its own genesis as of any other historical process. Anyway, this is the absolute precondition if Marxism is to explain *other things than itself*: not only its own genesis as something different from itself, but also all the other transformations produced in history *including* those marked by the practical consequences of the intervention of Marxism in history. If it is not the *truth of* in the Hegelian and Feuerbachian sense, but a discipline of scientific investigation, Marxism need be no more embarrassed by its own genesis than by the historical movement it has marked by its intervention: where Marx came from, as well as what comes from Marx must, if they are to be understood, *both* suffer the application of Marxist *principles* of investigation.[27]

If the problem of Marx's Early Works is really to be posed, the first condition to fulfil is to admit that *even philosophers* are young men for a time. They must be born somewhere, some time, and begin to think and write. The scholar who insisted that his early works should never be published, or even written (for there is bound to be at least some doctoral candidate to publish them!) was certainly no Hegelian ... for from the Hegelian viewpoint, Early Works are as inevitable and as impossible as the singular object displayed by Jarry: '*the skull of the child Voltaire*'. They are as inevitable as all beginnings. They are impossible because *it is impossible to choose one's beginnings*. Marx did not choose to be born to the thought German history had concentrated in its university education, nor to think its ideological world. He grew up in this world, in it he learned to live and move, with it he 'settled accounts', from it he liberated himself. I shall return to *the necessity and contingency of this beginning* later. The fact is that there was a *beginning*, and that to work out the history of Marx's particular

---

27 Of course, like any other scientific discipline, Marxism did not *stop* at Marx any more than physics stopped at Galileo, who founded it. Like any other scientific discipline, Marxism developed even in Marx's own lifetime. New discoveries were made possible by Marx's basic discovery. It would be very rash to believe that everything has been said.

thoughts their movement must be grasped at the precise instant when that concrete individual the Young Marx emerged into the *thought world* of his own time, to *think in it* in his turn, and to enter into the exchange and debate with the thoughts of his time which was to be his whole life as an ideologue. At this level of the exchanges and conflicts that are the very substance of the *texts* in which his living thoughts have come down to us, it is as if the authors of these thoughts were themselves *absent*. The concrete individual who expresses himself in his thoughts and his writings is absent, so is the actual history expressed in the existing ideological field. As the author effaces himself in the presence of his published thoughts, reducing himself to their rigour, so concrete history effaces itself in the presence of its ideological themes, reducing itself to their system. This double absence will also have to be put to the test. But for the moment, everything is in play between the rigour of a single thought and the thematic system of an ideological field. Their relation is this *beginning* and *this* beginning has no end. This is the relationship that has to be thought: the relation between the (internal) unity of a single thought (at each moment of its development) and the existing ideological field (at each moment of its development). But if this relationship is to be thought, so, in the same movement, must its terms.

This methodological demand immediately implies *an effective knowledge* of the substance and structure of this basic ideological field, and not just an allusive knowledge. It implies that as neutral a representation of the ideological world as that of a stage, on which characters as famous as they are non-existent make chance encounters, will not do. Marx's fate in the years from 1840 to 1845 was not decided by an ideal debate between characters called Hegel, Feuerbach, Stirner, Hess, etc. Nor was it decided by the same Hegel, Feuerbach, Stirner and Hess as they appeared in Marx's own works at the time. Even less by later evocations of great generality by Engels and Lenin. It was decided by *concrete* ideological characters on whom the ideological context imposed *determinate features* which do not necessarily coincide with their literal historical identities (e.g. Hegel), which are much more extensive than the explicit representations Marx gave them of in these same writings, quoting, invoking and criticizing them (e.g.

Feuerbach), and, of course, the general characteristics outlined by
Engels forty years later. As a concrete illustration of these remarks,
the Hegel who was the opponent of the Young Marx from the time of
his Doctoral Dissertation was not the library Hegel we can meditate on
in the solitude of 1960; it was *the Hegel of the neo-Hegelian movement*,
a Hegel already summoned to provide German intellectuals of the
1840s with the means to think their own history and their own hopes;
a Hegel already made to contradict himself, invoked against himself,
in spite of himself. The idea of *a philosophy transforming itself into a
will*, emerging from the world of reflection to transform the political
world, in which we can see Marx's first rebellion against his master,
is perfectly in accord with the interpretation dominant among the
neo-Hegelians.[28] I do not dispute the claim that in his thesis Marx
already showed that acute sense of concepts, that implacably rigorous grasp and that genius of conception which were the admiration
of his friends. But this idea was not his invention. In the same way, it
would be very rash to reduce Feuerbach's presence in Marx's writings
between 1841 and 1844 to explicit *references* alone. For many passages
directly reproduce or paraphrase Feuerbachian arguments without
his name ever being mentioned. The passage Togliatti extracted from
the *1844 Manuscripts* comes straight from Feuerbach; many others
could be invoked which have been too hastily attributed to Marx.
Why should Marx have referred to Feuerbach when everyone knew
his work, and above all, when *he had appreciated Feuerbach's thought*
and was thinking in his thoughts as if they were his own? But as we
shall see in a moment, we must go further than the unmentioned presence of the thoughts of a living author to the presence of his *potential
thoughts*, to his *problematic*, that is, to the constitutive unity of the
effective thoughts that make up the domain of the existing *ideological
field* with which a particular author must settle accounts in his own

---

28   Cf. Auguste Cornu: *Karl Marx et F. Engels* (PUF Paris), Vol. I, 'Les
années d'enfance et de jeunesse, La Gauche hégélienne', the chapter on '*la
formation de la Gauche hégélienne*', especially pp. 141 ff. Cornu quite correctly
insists on the role of *von Cieskowski* in the elaboration of a *philosophy of action*
of neo-Hegelian inspiration, adopted by all the young liberal intellectuals of
the movement.

thought. It is immediately obvious that if it is impossible to think the unity of an individual's thought while ignoring its ideological field, if this field is itself to be thought it requires the thought of this *unity*.

So what is this unity? Let us return to Feuerbach for an illustration whereby we can answer this question, but this time to pose the problem of the internal unity of Marx's thought when *the two were related*. Most of the commentators in our collection are manifestly troubled by the nature of this relation, and it gives rise to many conflicting interpretations. This embarrassment is not merely the result of a lack of familiarity with Feuerbach's writings (they can be read). It arises because they do not succeed in conceiving what it is that constitutes the basic unity of a text, the internal essence of an ideological thought, that is, its *problematic*. I put this term forward – Marx never directly used it, but it constantly animates the ideological analyses of his maturity (particularly *The German Ideology*)[29] – because it is the concept that gives the best *grasp* on the facts without falling into the Hegelian ambiguities of '*totality*'. Indeed, to say that an ideology constitutes an (organic) totality is only valid *descriptively* – not *theoretically*, for this description converted into a theory exposes us to the danger of thinking nothing but the empty unity of the described whole, not a *determinate unitary structure*. On the contrary, to think the unity of a determinate ideological unity (which presents itself explicitly as a whole, and which is explicitly or implicitly 'lived' as a whole or as an intention of 'totalization') by means of the concept of its *problematic* is to allow the *typical systematic structure* unifying all the elements of the thought to be brought to light, and therefore to discover in this unity a *determinate content* which makes it possible both to conceive

---

29 This is not the place to embark on a study of the concepts at work in the analyses of *The German Ideology*. Instead, one quotation that says everything. On 'German criticism' he says: '*The whole body of its inquiries has actually sprung from the soil of a definite philosophical system, that of Hegel. Not only in their answers, but in their very questions there was a mystification.*' It could not be better said that it is not answers which make philosophy but the *questions* posed by the philosophy, and that it is *in the question* itself, that is, *in the way it reflects that object* (and not in the object itself) that ideological mystification (or on the contrary an authentic relationship with the object) should be sought.

the *meaning* of the 'elements' of the ideology concerned – *and to relate this ideology to the problems left or posed to every thinker by the historical period in which he lives.*[30]

Take a specific example: Marx's 1843 Manuscript (*The Critique of Hegel's Philosophy of Right*). According to the commentators this contains a series of Feuerbachian themes (the subject-predicate inversion, the critique of speculative philosophy, the theory of the species-man, etc.), but also some analyses which are not to be found in Feuerbach (the interrelation of politics, the State and private property, the reality of social classes, etc.). To remain at the level of *elements* would be to fall into the impasse of the analytico-teleological critique we discussed above, and into its pseudo-solution: terminology and meaning, tendency and consciousness, etc. We must go further and ask whether the presence in Marx of analyses and *objects* about which Feuerbach says little or nothing is a sufficient justification for this division into Feuerbachian and non-Feuerbachian (that is, already Marxist) elements. But no answer can be hoped for from *the elements themselves*. For the object discussed does not directly qualify the thought. The many authors who talked of social classes or even of the class struggle before Marx have never to my knowledge been taken for Marxists simply because they dealt with objects

---

30   This conclusion is crucial. What actually distinguishes the concept of the *problematic* from the subjectivist concepts of an idealist interpretation of the development of ideologies is that it brings out within the thought *the objective internal reference system of its particular* themes, the system of *questions* commanding the *answers* given by the ideology. If the meaning of an ideology's answers is to be understood at this internal level it must first be asked *the question of its questions*. But this problematic is *itself an answer*, no longer to its own internal questions – problems – but to *the objective problems posed* for ideology *by its time*. A comparison of the problems posed by the ideologue (his problematic) with the *real problems* posed for the ideologue by his time, makes possible a demonstration of the truly ideological element of the ideology, that is, what characterizes ideology as such, its *deformation*. So it is not *the interiority of the problematic* which constitutes its essence but its relation to real problems: *the problematic of an ideology* cannot be demonstrated without *relating* and *submitting* it to the real problems to which its deformed enunciation gives a false answer. But I must not anticipate the third point in my exposition (see footnote 45).

which were eventually destined to attract Marx's attention. It is not the material reflected on that characterizes and qualifies a reflection, but, at this level the *modality of the reflection*,[31] the actual relation the reflection has with its objects, that is, the *basic problematic* that is the starting-point for the reflection of the objects of the thought. This is not to say that the material reflected may not *under certain conditions* modify the modality of the reflection, but that is another question (to which we shall return), and in any case, this modification in the modality of a reflection, this restructuration of the problematic of an ideology can proceed by many other routes than that of the simple immediate relation of object and reflection! So anyone who still wants to pose the problem of elements in this perspective must recognize that everything depends on a question which must have priority over them: the question of *the nature of the problematic which is the starting-point for actually thinking them*, in a given text. In our example, the question takes the following form: in the *Critique of Hegel's Philosophy of Right*, has Marx's reflection on his new objects, social class, the private property/State relation, etc., swept aside Feuerbach's theoretical presuppositions, has it reduced them to the level of mere phrases? Or are these new objects thought from the starting-point of *the same presuppositions?* This question is possible precisely because the *problematic* of a thought is not limited to the domain of the objects considered by its author, because it is not an abstraction for the thought as a totality, but the concrete determinate structure of a thought and of all the thoughts possible within this thought. Thus Feuerbach's anthropology can become the problematic not only of religion (*The Essence of Christianity*), but also of politics (*On the Jewish Question*, the 1843 Manuscript), or even of history and economics (the *1844 Manuscripts*) without ceasing to be in essentials an *anthropological problematic*, even if the 'letter' of Feuerbach is itself abandoned or superseded.[32] It is, of course, possible to regard it as politically important to have moved from

---

31   Such is the meaning of the 'basic question' distinguishing materialism from all the forms of idealism.

32   Cf. the excellent passage by Hoeppner, *op. cit.*, p. 188. See also p. 184, n. 11.

a religious anthropology to a political anthropology, and finally to an economic anthropology, and I would agree completely that in Germany in 1843 anthropology represented an advanced ideological form. But to make this judgement presupposes that the nature of the ideology under consideration is already familiar, that is, that its *effective problematic* has been defined.

I should add that if it is not so much the immediate content of the objects reflected as the way the problems are posed which constitutes the ultimate ideological essence of an ideology, this problematic is not of itself immediately present to the historian's reflection, for good reason: in general a philosopher *thinks in it rather than thinking of it*, and his 'order of reasons' does not coincide with the 'order of reasons' of his philosophy. An ideology (in the strict Marxist sense of the term – the sense in which Marxism is not itself an ideology) can be regarded as characterized in this particular respect by the fact that *its own problematic is not conscious of itself*. When Marx tells us (and he continually repeats it) not to take an ideology's consciousness of itself for its essence, he also means that before it is unconscious of the real problems it is a response (or non-response) to, an ideology is already unconscious of its 'theoretical presuppositions', that is, the active but unavowed problematic which fixes for it the meaning and movement of *its problems* and thereby of their solutions. So a problematic cannot generally be read like an open book, it must be dragged up from the depths of the ideology in which it is buried but active, and usually despite the ideology itself, its own statements and proclamations. Anyone who is prepared to go this far will, I imagine, feel obliged to stop confusing the *materialist proclamations* of certain 'materialists' (above all Feuerbach) with *materialism itself*. There is much to suggest that this would clarify some problems and dissipate some other, false, problems. Marxism would thereby gain an ever more exact consciousness of its own problematic, that is, of itself, and even in its historical works – which, after all, is its due, and, if I may say so, its duty.

Let me summarize these reflections. Understanding an ideological argument implies, at the level of the ideology itself, simultaneous, conjoint knowledge of the *ideological field* in which a thought emerges and grows; and the exposure of the internal unity of this thought: its *problematic*. Knowledge of the ideological field itself presupposes knowledge of the problematics compounded or opposed in it. This interrelation of the particular problematic of the thought of the individual under consideration with the particular problematics of the thoughts belonging to the ideological field allows of a decision as to its author's specific difference, i.e., *whether a new meaning has emerged*. Of course, this complex process is all haunted by real history. But everything cannot be said at once.

It is now clear that this method, breaking directly with the first theoretical presupposition of eclectic criticism, has already[33] detached itself from the illusions of the second presupposition, the silent tribunal over ideological history whose values and verdicts are decided even before investigation starts. The *truth* of ideological history is neither in its principle (its source) nor in its end (its goal). It is *in the facts* themselves, in that nodal constitution of ideological meanings, themes and objects, against the deceptive backcloth of their problematic, itself evolving against the backcloth of an 'anchylose' and unstable ideological world, itself in the sway of real history. Of course, we now know that the Young Marx *did* become Marx, but we should not want to live faster than he did, we should not want to live in his place, reject for him or discover for him. We shall not be waiting for him at the end of the course to throw round him as round a runner the mantle of repose, for at last it is over, he has arrived. Rousseau remarked that with children and adolescents the whole art of education consists of knowing how to *lose time*. The art of historical criticism also consists of knowing how to lose time so that young authors can grow up. This lost time is simply the time we give them to live. We *scan* the necessity of their lives in our understanding of its nodal points, its reversals and mutations. In this area there is perhaps no greater joy than to be able to witness in an emerging life, once the Gods of Origins and Goals have been dethroned, the birth of necessity.

---

33 *Already*, because the success of this rupture as of the whole of this liberation process, presupposes that *real history* is being taken seriously.

The Historical Problem

But all this seems to leave the third presupposition of the eclectic method in the air; the presupposition that the whole of ideological history occurs within ideology. Let us take up this point.

I am afraid that, with the exception of the articles by Togliatti and Lapine and above all Hoeppner's *very remarkable* piece,[34] the majority of the studies offered here ignore this problem or devote only a few paragraphs to it.

But ultimately, no Marxist can avoid posing what used a few years ago to be called the problem of 'Marx's path', that is, the problem of the relation between the *events* of his thought and the one but double real history which was its true *subject*. We must fill in this double absence and reveal the real authors of these as yet subjectless thoughts: the concrete man and the real history that produced them. For without these real subjects how can we account for the emergence of a thought and its mutations?

I shall not pose the problem of Marx's own personality here, the problem of the origin and structure of that extraordinary theoretical temperament, animated by an insatiable critical passion, an intransigent insistence on reality, and a prodigious feeling for the concrete. A study of the psychological structure of Marx's personality and of its origins and history would certainly cast light on the *style of intervention, conception and investigation* which are so striking in these Early Writings themselves. From it we would obtain, if not the root origin of his undertaking in Sartre's sense (the author's 'basic project'), at least the origins of the profound and far-reaching insistence on a *grasp* on reality, which would give a first sense to the actual continuity of Marx's development, to what Lapine has, in part, tried to think in the term 'tendency'. Without such a study we risk a failure to grasp what precisely it was that saved Marx from the fate of most of his contemporaries, who issued from the same environment and confronted

---

34   *op. cit.*

the same ideological themes as he did, that is, the Young Hegelians. Mehring and Cornu have carried out the substance of this study and it is worth completing so that we may be able to understand how it was that the son of a Rhenish bourgeois became the theoretician and leader of the workers' movement in the Europe of the railway epoch.

But as well as giving us *Marx's psychology* this study would lead us to real history, and the *direct apprehension of it by Marx himself*. I must stop here for a moment to pose the problem of the meaning of Marx's evolution and of its 'motor'.

When eclectic criticism is faced with the question, 'how were Marx's growth to maturity and change possible', it is apt to give an answer which remains *within ideological history itself*. For example, it is said that Marx knew how to distinguish Hegel's *method* from his *content*, and that he proceeded to apply the former to history. Or else, that he set the Hegelian system *back onto its feet* (a statement not without a certain humour if we recall that the Hegelian system was 'a sphere of spheres'). Or, that Marx *extended* Feuerbach's materialism to history, as if a localized materialism was not rather suspect as a materialism; that Marx *applied* the (Hegelian or Feuerbachian) theory of alienation to the world of social relations, as if this 'application' could change the theory's basic meaning. Or finally, and this is the crucial point, that the old materialists were '*inconsistent*' where Marx, on the contrary, was *consistent*. This inconsistency–consistency theory which haunts many a Marxist in ideological history is a little wonder of ideology, constructed for their personal use by the Philosophers of the Enlightenment. Feuerbach inherited and, alas, made good use of it! It deserves a short treatise all to itself, for it is the quintessence of historical idealism: it is indeed obvious that if ideas were self-reproducing, then any historical (or theoretical) aberration could only be a logical error.

Even when they do contain a certain degree of truth,[35] taken literally

---

35 Let us say: of pedagogic truth. As for the famous 'inversion' of Hegel, it is a perfect expression for Feuerbach's project. It was Feuerbach who introduced it and sanctioned it for Hegel's posterity. And it is remarkable that Marx correctly attacked Feuerbach in *The German Ideology* for having *remained a prisoner* of Hegelian philosophy precisely when he was claiming

these formulations remain prisoner to the illusion that the Young
Marx's evolution was fought out and decided *in the sphere of ideas*,
and that it was achieved *by virtue of a reflection* on ideas put forward
by Hegel, Feuerbach, etc. It is as if there was agreement that the
ideas inherited from Hegel by the young German intellectuals of
1840 *contained in themselves*, contrary to appearances, a certain tacit,
veiled, masked, refracted truth which Marx's critical abilities finally
succeeded in tearing from them, and forcing them to admit and recognize, after years of intellectual effort. This is the basic logic implied
by the famous theme of the 'inversion', the 'setting back onto its feet'
of the Hegelian philosophy (dialectic), for if it were really a matter
merely of an inversion, a restoration of what had been upside down, it
is clear that to turn an object right round changes neither its nature
nor its content by virtue merely of a rotation! A man on his head is
the same man when he is finally walking on his feet. And a philosophy inverted in this way cannot be regarded as *anything more* than the
philosophy *reversed* except in theoretical metaphor: in fact, its structure, its problems and the meaning of these problems are still haunted
by the *same problematic*.[36] This is the logic that most often *seems* to
be at work in the Young Marx's writings and which is most apt to be
attributed to him.

Whatever the status of this view, I do not believe that it corresponds to reality. Naturally, no reader of Marx's Early Works could
remain insensible to the gigantic effort of theoretical criticism which
Marx made on all the ideas he came across. Rare are the authors who
have possessed so many virtues (acuity, perseverance, rigour) in the
treatment of ideas. For Marx, the latter were concrete objects which

---

to have 'inverted' it. He attacked him for accepting the presuppositions of
Hegel's questions, for giving different answers, but to the same questions.
In philosophy *only the questions are indiscreet*, as opposed to everyday life,
where it is the answers. Once the questions have been changed it is no longer
possible to talk of an *inversion*. No doubt a comparison of the new *relative
rank* of questions and answers to the old one still allows us to talk of an inversion. But it has then become an analogy since *the questions are no longer the
same* and the domains they constitute *are not comparable*, except, as I have
suggested, for *pedagogic* purposes.
36   Cf. footnote 35.

he interrogated as the physicist does the objects of his experiments, to draw from them a little of the truth, of their truth. See his treatment of the idea of censorship in his article on the Prussian Censorship, or the apparently insignificant difference between green and dead wood in his article on the Theft of Wood, or the ideas of the freedom of the press, of private property, of alienation, etc. The reader cannot resist the transparency of this reflective rigour and logical strength in Marx's early writings. And this transparency quite naturally inclines him to believe that *the logic of Marx's intelligence coincides with the logic of his reflection*, and that he did draw from the ideological world he was working on a *truth it really contained*. And this conviction is further reinforced by Marx's own conviction, the conviction that shines through all his efforts and even through his enthusiasms, in short, by his *consciousness*.

So I will go so far as to say that it is not only essential to avoid the spontaneous illusions of the idealist conception of ideological history, but also, and perhaps even more, it is essential to avoid any concession to the impression made on us by the Young Marx's writings and any *acceptance of his own consciousness of himself*. But to understand this it is necessary to go on to speak of real history, that is, *to question 'Marx's path' itself*.

With this I have returned to the *beginning*. Yes, we all have to be born some day, somewhere, and begin thinking and writing in a *given* world. For a thinker, this world is immediately the world of the living thoughts of his time, the ideological world where he is born into thought. For Marx, this world was the world of the German ideology of the 1830s and 1840s, dominated by the problems of German idealism, and by what has been given the abstract name of the 'decomposition of Hegel'. It was not *any world*, of course, but this general truth is not enough. For the world of the German ideology was then *without any possible comparison the world that was worst crushed beneath its ideology* (in the strict sense), that is, the world farthest from the actual realities of history, *the most mystified, the most alienated world that then existed* in a Europe of ideologies. This was the world into which Marx was born and took up thought. *The contingency of Marx's beginnings was this enormous layer of ideology* beneath which he was born, *this crushing layer* which he succeeded in breaking through. Precisely because he *did* deliver himself, we tend too easily to believe that the freedom he achieved at the cost of such prodigious efforts and decisive encounters was already inscribed in this world, and that the only problem was to *reflect*. We tend too easily to project Marx's later consciousness onto this epoch and, as has been said, to write this history in the 'future anterior', when it is not a matter of projecting a consciousness of self onto another consciousness of self, but of applying to the content of an enslaved consciousness the scientific principles of historical intelligibility (not the content of another consciousness of self) later acquired by a liberated consciousness.

In his later works, Marx showed why this prodigious layer of ideology was characteristic of Germany rather than of France or England: for the *two reasons* of the *historical backwardness of Germany* (in economics and politics) and the state of the *social classes* corresponding to this backwardness. At the beginning of the nineteenth century, Germany emerged from the gigantic upheaval of the French Revolution and the Napoleonic Wars deeply marked by its historical inability either to realize *national unity or bourgeois revolution*. And this 'fatality' was to dominate the history of Germany throughout the nineteenth century and even to be felt distantly much later. This situation, whose origins can be traced back to the period of the Peasants' War, made Germany both object and spectator of the real history which was going on around it. It was this German inability that *constituted* and deeply *marked* the German ideology which was formed during the eighteenth and nineteenth centuries. It was this inability which obliged German intellectuals to '*think what the others had done*' and to think it in precisely the conditions implied by their inability: in the hopeful, nostalgic, idealized forms characteristic of the aspirations of their social circle: the petty bourgeoisie of functionaries, teachers, writers, etc. – and with the immediate *objects* of their own servitude as starting-point: in particular, *religion*. The result of this set of historical conditions and demands was precisely a prodigious development of the '*German idealist philosophy*' *whereby German intellectuals thought their conditions, their hopes and even their* '*activity*'.

It was not the attraction of a witty turn of phrase that led Marx to declare that the French have political minds, the English economic minds, while the Germans have *theoretical* minds. The counterpart to Germany's *historical underdevelopment* was an *ideological and theoretical 'overdevelopment'* incomparable with anything offered by other European nations. But the crucial point is that this theoretical development was an *alienated ideological* development, without concrete relation to the real problems and the real objects which were *reflected in it*. From the viewpoint we have adopted, that is Hegel's tragedy. His philosophy was truly the encyclopedia of the eighteenth century, the sum of all knowledge then acquired, and even of history. But all the objects of its reflection have been 'assimilated' in their reflection, that is, by the particular form of ideological reflection which was the tyrant of all Germany's intelligence. So it is easy to imagine what could be and what had to be the basic precondition for the liberation of a German youth who started to think between 1830 and 1840 in Germany itself. This precondition was the rediscovery of real history, of real objects, beyond the enormous layer of ideology which had hemmed them in and deformed them, not being content with reducing them to their shades. Hence the paradoxical conclusion: to free himself from this ideology, Marx was inevitably obliged to realize that Germany's *ideological overdevelopment* was at the same time in fact an expression of her *historical underdevelopment*, and that therefore it was necessary to retreat *from* this ideological flight forward in order to reach the things themselves, to touch real history and at last come face to face with the beings that haunted the mists of German consciousness.[37] Without this *retreat*, the story of the Young Marx's liberation is incomprehensible; without this *retreat*, Marx's relation to the German ideology, and in particular to Hegel, is incomprehensible;

---

37   This desire to dissipate all ideology and return to 'the things themselves', to 'unveil existence' (*zur Sache selbst . . . Dasein zu enthüllen*) animates the whole of Feuerbach's philosophy. His terms are the moving expression of this. His tragedy was to have carried out his intentions and yet to have remained a prisoner of the very ideology he desperately hoped to deliver himself from, because he thought his liberation from speculative philosophy in the concepts and problematic of this same philosophy. It was essential to 'change elements'.

without this *return to real history* (which was also to a certain extent a retreat) the Young Marx's relation to the labour movement remains a mystery.

I have deliberately stressed this *'retreat'*. The too frequent use of formulae such as the 'supersession' of Hegel, Feuerbach, etc., tends to suggest some *continuous* pattern of development, or at least a development whose discontinuities themselves should be thought (precisely along the lines of a Hegelian dialectic of *'Aufhebung'*) within the same *element of continuity* sustained by the *temporality* of history itself (the story of Marx and his time); whereas the critique of this ideological element implies largely a return to the authentic objects which are (logically and historically) prior to the ideology which has reflected them and hemmed them in.

Let me illustrate this formula of the *retreat* by two examples.

The first concerns those authors whose substance Hegel 'assimilated', among them the English economists and the French philosophers and politicians, and the historical events whose meaning they interpreted: above all, the French Revolution. When, in 1843, Marx sat down and read the English economists, when he took up the study of Machiavelli, Montesquieu, Rousseau, Diderot, etc., when he studied concretely the history of the French Revolution,[38] it was not just a return to Hegel's sources to verify Hegel by his sources: on the contrary, it was to *discover* the reality of the objects Hegel had stolen by imposing on them the meaning of his own ideology. To a very great extent, Marx's return to the theoretical products of the English and French eighteenth century was a real *return to the pre-Hegelian*, to the *objects themselves* in their reality. The 'supersession' of Hegel

---

38 Lapine (*op. cit.*, pp. 60–61) is excellent on this point. But these intellectual 'experiments' of Marx's do not measure up to the concept of 'tendency' (a concept too broad and abstract for them, and one which also reflects the end of the development in progress) in which Lapine wants to think them. On the other hand, I am in profound agreement with Hoeppner (*op. cit.*, pp. 186–7): 'Marx did not reach his solution by resorting to some manipulations of the Hegelian dialectic, but essentially on the basis of very concrete investigations into history, sociology and political economy . . . the Marxist dialectic was in its essentials born of the new lands which Marx cleared and opened up for theory . . . Hegel and Marx did not drink at the same source.'

was not at all an 'Aufhebung' in the Hegelian sense, that is, an exposition of *the truth of* what is contained in Hegel; *it was not a supersession of error towards its truth, on the contrary, it was a supersession of illusion towards its truth, or better, rather than a 'supersession' of illusion towards truth it was a dissipation of illusion and a retreat from the dissipated illusion back towards reality*: the term 'supersession' is thus robbed of all meaning.[39] Marx never disavowed this, his decisive experience of the *direct discovery* of reality via those who had *lived* it directly and *thought it with the least possible deformation*: the English economists (they had economic heads because *there was* an economy in England!) and the French philosophers and politicians (they had political heads because *there was* politics in France!) of the eighteenth century. And, as his critique of French utilitarianism, precisely for its lack of the advantage of direct experience,[40] shows, he was extremely sensitive to the ideological 'distanciation' produced by this absence: the French

---

39   If there is any meaning to the term 'supersede' in its Hegelian sense, it is not established by substituting for it the concept of 'the negation-which-contains-in-itself-the-term-negated', thereby stressing the *rupture* in the conservation, for this rupture in conservation presupposes *a substantial unity in the process*, translated in the Hegelian dialectic by the passage of the in-itself into the for-itself, then to the in-itself-for-itself, etc. But it is precisely the substantial continuity of a process containing its own future *in germ in its own interiority* which is in dispute here. Hegelian supersession pre-supposes that the later form of the process is the 'truth' of the earlier form. But Marx's position and his whole critique of ideology implies on the contrary that science (which apprehends reality) constitutes *in its very meaning* a *rupture* with ideology and that it sets itself up in *another terrain*, that it constitutes itself *on the basis of new questions*, that it raises *other questions* about reality than ideology, or what comes to the same thing, it *defines its object* differently from ideology. Therefore science can by no criteria be regarded as the truth of ideology in the Hegelian sense. If we want a historical predecessor to Marx in this respect we must appeal to Spinoza rather than Hegel. Spinoza established a relation between the first and the second kind of knowledge which, in its immediacy (abstracting from the totality in God), presupposed precisely a radical *discontinuity*. Although the second kind makes possible the understanding of the first, it is not *its truth*.

40   Cf. *The German Ideology*, pp. 447–54: 'The theory which for the English still was simply the registration of a fact becomes for the French a philosophical system.' (p. 452).

utilitarians made a 'philosophical' theory out of the economic relation of utilization and exploitation whose *actual mechanism* was described by the English economists as they saw it in action in English reality. I feel that the problem of the relation between Marx and Hegel will remain insoluble until we take this readjustment (*décalage*) of viewpoint seriously, and realize that this *retreat* established Marx in a domain and a terrain which were no longer Hegel's domain and terrain. What were the meanings of Marx's loans from Hegel, of his Hegelian heritage and in particular of the dialectic, are questions that can only be asked from the vantage point of this '*change of elements*'.[41]

My second example: In their arguments within the Hegel they had constructed to answer to their needs, the Young Hegelians constantly asked the questions *which were in fact posed them by the backwardness of the German history of the day* when they compared it with that of France and England. The Napoleonic defeat had not indeed greatly altered the historical dislocation (*décalage*) between Germany and the great nations of Western Europe. The German intellectuals of the 1830s and 1840s looked to France and England as the lands of freedom and reason, particularly after the July Revolution and the English Reform Act of 1832. Once again, unable to live it, they thought what others had done. But as they thought it in the element of philosophy, the French constitution and the English Reform became for them the

---

41   See Hoeppner, *op. cit.*, pp. 186–7. One further word on the term 'retreat'. Obviously it should not be understood as meaning the exact opposite of 'supersession', except metaphorically. It is not a question of substituting for the understanding of an ideology via its end some kind of understanding of it through its *origins*. All I wanted to illustrate was the fact that even within his ideological consciousness the Young Marx demonstrated an exemplary critical insistence: an insistence on consulting the *originals* (French political philosophers, English economists, revolutionaries, etc.) which Hegel had discussed. But with Marx himself, this 'retreat' ultimately lost the retrospective aspect of a search for the *original* in the form of an *origin*, as soon as he returned to German history itself and destroyed the illusion of its 'backwardness', that is, thought it in its reality without measuring it against an external model as its norm. This *retreat* was therefore really the current *restoration*, *recuperation* and *restitution* of a reality which had been stolen and made unrecognizable by ideology.

reign of Reason, and they therefore awaited the German liberal revolution primarily from Reason.[42] When the failure of 1840 revealed
the impotence of (German) Reason alone, they looked for aid from
outside; and they came up with the incredibly naïve yet moving
theme, the theme which was simply an admission of their backwardness and their illusions, but an admission still within those illusions,
that *the future belonged to the mystical union of France and Germany,
the union of French political sense and German theory.*[43] Thus they were
haunted by realities which they could only perceive through their
own *ideological schema*, their *own problematic*, in the deformations
produced by this medium.[44]

---

42   This was the 'liberal' moment of the Young Hegelian movement. Cf.
Cornu, *op. cit.*, Ch. IV, pp. 132 ff.

43   A theme widely developed by the neo-Hegelians. Cf. Feuerbach:
Provisional Theses for the Reform of Philosophy, paras. 46 and 47 (*Manifestes
philosophiques*, *op. cit.*, pp. 116–17).

44   At the heart of this problematic was the implication of the *deformation*
of real historical problems into *philosophical* problems. The *real problems* of
bourgeois revolution, political liberalism, the freedom of the Press, the end
of censorship, the struggle against the Church, etc., were transformed into a
philosophical problem: the problem of the reign of Reason whose victory was
promised by History despite the *appearances* of reality. This contradiction
between Reason, which is the internal essence and goal of History, and the
reality of present history was the neo-Hegelians' basic *problem*. This *formulation of the problem* (this problematic) naturally *commanded its solutions*: if
Reason is the goal of History and its essence, it is enough to *show its presence*
even in its most contradictory appearances: the whole solution is thus to be
found in the *critical omnipotence* of philosophy which must become *practical* by dissipating the aberrations of History in the name of its truth. For a
denunciation of the unreasons of real History is merely an exposition of its
own reason at work even in its unreasons. Thus the State is indeed truth in
action, the incarnation of the truth of History. It is enough to *convert* it to this
truth. That is why this 'practice' can be definitively reduced to philosophical
critique and theoretical propaganda: it is enough to denounce the unreasons
to make them give way, and enough to *speak* reason for it to carry them
away. So everything depends on philosophy which is *par excellence* the head
and heart (after 1840, it is only the head – the heart is to be French) of the
Revolution. So much for *the solutions required by the way the basic problem was
posed*. But what is infinitely more revealing, and of the problematic itself, is
to discover by comparing it to the problems raised for the neo-Hegelians

And when, in 1843, Marx was disillusioned by his failure to teach the Germans Reason and Freedom and he decided at last to *leave for France*, he still went largely *in search of a myth*, just as a few years ago it was still possible for the majority of the students of colonial subject nations to leave home in search of their Myth in France.[45] But when he got there, he made the fundamental *discovery* that *France and England did not correspond to their myth*, the discovery of the class struggle, of flesh and blood capitalism, and of the organized proletariat. Thus an extraordinary division of labour led to Marx discovering the reality of France while Engels did the same for England. Once again we must use the term *retreat* (not 'supersession'), that is, the retreat from *myth to reality*, when we are dealing with the *actual experience* which tore off the veils of illusion behind which Marx and Engels had been living as a result of their *beginnings*.

But this retreat from ideology towards reality came to coincide with the discovery *of a radically new reality* of which Marx and Engels could find *no echo in the writings of 'German philosophy'*. In France, Marx *discovered* the *organized working class*, in England, Engels discovered *developed capitalism* and *a class struggle obeying its own laws and ignoring philosophy and philosophers.*[46]

This double discovery played a decisive part in the Young Marx's intellectual evolution: the discovery beneath (*en-deça*) the ideology

---

by real History that although *this problematic does provide solutions to real problems, it does not correspond to any of these real problems*; there is nothing at issue between reason and unreason, the unreason is neither an unreason nor an appearance, the State is not liberty in action, etc., that is, the objects which this ideology seems to reflect in its problems are not even represented in their 'immediate' reality. By the end of such a comparison, not only do the solutions given by an ideology to its own problems fall (they are merely the reflection of these problems on themselves), but also the problematic itself – and the full extent of the *ideological deformation* then appears: its mystification of problems and objects. Then we can see what Marx meant when he spoke of the need *to abandon the terrain of Hegelian* philosophy, since 'not only in their answers, but in their questions there was a mystification'.

45   Cf. Marx, Letter to Ruge, September 1843.
46   Cf. Engels: '*Umrisse ʒu einer Kritik der Nationalökonomie*'; Marx later referred to this article as 'genial' – it had a great influence on him. Its importance has generally been underestimated.

which had deformed it of *the reality it referred to* – and the discovery beyond contemporary ideology, *which knew it not*, of *a new reality*. Marx became himself by thinking this double reality in a rigorous theory, by changing elements – and by thinking the unity and reality of this new element. Of course, it should be understood that these discoveries are inseparable from Marx's total personal experience, which was itself inseparable from the German history which he directly lived. For *something was happening in Germany none the less*. Events there were not just feeble echoes of events abroad. The idea that everything happened outside and nothing inside was itself an illusion of despair and impotence: for a history that fails, makes no headway and repeats itself is, as we know only too well, still a history. The whole theoretical and practical experience I have been discussing was in fact bound up with the progressive experimental discovery of German reality itself. The disappointment of 1840 which broke down the whole theoretical system behind the neo-Hegelians' hopes, when Frederick William IV, the pseudo-'liberal', changed into a despot – the failure of the Revolution of Reason attempted by the *Rheinische Zeitung*, persecution, Marx's exile, abandoned by the German bourgeois elements who had supported him at first, taught him *with facts* what was concealed by the famous 'German misery', the 'philistinism' denounced with such moral indignation, and *this moral indignation itself*: a concrete historical situation which was no *misunderstanding*, rigid and brutal class relations, reflex exploitation and fear, stronger in the German bourgeoisie than any proof by Reason. This swept everything aside, and Marx at last discovered the reality of the ideological opacity which had blinded him; he realized that he could no longer project German myths onto foreign realities and had to recognize that these myths were meaningless not only abroad but even in Germany itself which was cradling in them its own bondage to dreams: and that on the contrary, he had to project onto Germany the light of experience acquired abroad to see it in the light of day.

I hope it is now clear that if we are truly to be able to think this dramatic genesis of Marx's thought, it is essential to reject the term '*supersede*' and turn to that of *discoveries*, to renounce the spirit of Hegelian logic implied in the innocent but sly concept of 'supersession'

(*Aufhebung*) which is merely the empty anticipation of its end in the illusion of an immanence of truth, and to adopt instead a *logic of actual experience and real emergence*, one that would put an end to the illusions of *ideological immanence*; in short, to adopt a logic of *the irruption of real history in ideology itself*, and thereby – as is absolutely indispensable to the Marxist perspective, and, moreover, demanded by it – give at last some real meaning to the *personal style* of Marx's experience, to the extraordinary sensitivity to the concrete which gave such force of conviction and revelation to each of his encounters with reality.[47]

I do not propose to give a chronology or a dialectic of the *actual experience* of history which united in that remarkable individual the Young Marx one man's particular psychology and world history so as to produce in him the *discoveries* which are still our nourishment today. The details should be sought in '*Père*' Cornu's works, for, with

---

47   It will be readily understood that to speak of a logic of emergence is not to suggest, with Bergson, a *philosophy of invention*. For this emergence is not the manifestation of I know not what empty essence, freedom or choice; on the contrary, it is merely the effect of its own empirical conditions. I should add that this logic is required by Marx's own conception of *the history of ideologies*. For ultimately, our conclusion as to the real history of Marx's discoveries arising from this development *challenges the very existence of the history of ideology*. Once it is clear that the immanentist thesis of the idealist critique has been refuted, that ideological history is not its own principle of intelligibility, once it has been grasped that ideological history can only be understood through the real history which explains its formations, its deformation and their restructurations, and which emerges in it, then it is essential to ask, what survives of this *ideological history* itself as a *history*, and admit that the answer is nothing. As Marx says, 'Morality, religion, metaphysics, all the rest of ideology and their corresponding forms of consciousness, thus no longer retain the semblance of independence. *They have no history*, no development; but men, developing their material production and their material intercourse, alter, along with their real existence, their thinking and the products of their thinking' (*The German Ideology*, p. 38). To return to our starting-point, I say – and the following two reasons are *one and the same reason* – that 'the history of philosophy' cannot be written 'in the future anterior', not simply because the future anterior is not a category of historical understanding – but also because strictly speaking the history of philosophy *does not exist*.

the exception of Mehring who did not have the same erudition or source material, he is the only man to have made this indispensable effort. I confidently predict that he will be read for a long time, for there is no access to the Young Marx except by way of his real history.

I merely hope that I have been able to give some idea of the extraordinary relation between the enslaved thought of the Young Marx and the free thought of Marx by pointing out something which is generally neglected, that is, the *contingent beginnings* (in respect to his birth) that he had to start from and *the gigantic layer of illusions he had to break through before he could even see it*. We should realize that in a certain sense, if these beginnings are kept in mind, we cannot say absolutely that '*Marx's youth is part of Marxism*' unless we mean by this that, like all historical phenomena, the evolution of this young bourgeois intellectual can be illuminated by the application of the principles of historical materialism. Of course Marx's youth did *lead* to Marxism, but only at the price of a prodigious break with his origins, a heroic struggle against the illusions he had inherited from the Germany in which he was born, and an acute attention to the realities concealed by these illusions. If 'Marx's path' is an example to us, it is not because of his origins and circumstances but because of his ferocious insistence on freeing himself from the myths which presented themselves to him as the *truth*, and because of the role of the experience of real history which elbowed these myths aside.

Allow me to touch on one last point. If this interpretation does make possible a better reading of the Early Works, if the deeper unity of the thought (its problematic) casts light on their theoretical elements, and the acquisitions of Marx's actual experience (his history; his discoveries) illuminate the development of this problematic, and this makes it possible to settle those endlessly discussed problems of whether Marx was already Marx, whether he was still Feuerbachian or had gone beyond Feuerbach, that is, of the establishment at each moment of his youthful development of the internal and external meaning of the immediate elements of his thought, there is still *another question* that it leaves unanswered, or rather introduces: the question of the *necessity of Marx's beginnings*, from the vantage point of his *destination*.

It is as if Marx's necessity to *escape from his beginnings*, that is to

traverse and dissipate the extraordinarily dense ideological world
beneath which he was buried, had, as well as a *negative* significance
(escape from illusions), a significance in some sense *formative*,
despite these very illusions. We might even feel that the discovery
of historical materialism was 'in the air' and that in many respects
Marx expended a prodigious theoretical effort to arrive at a reality
and attain certain truths which had already in part been recognized
and accepted. So there ought to have been a 'short-cut' to the discovery (e.g. Engels's route via his 1844 article, or the one Marx admired
in Dietzgen) as well as the 'roundabout' route that Marx took himself.
What did he gain by this theoretical '*Long March*' that his beginnings
had forced on him? What profit was there in starting *so far from the
end*, in sojourning so long in philosophical abstraction and in crossing
such spaces on his way to reality? Probably the sharpening it gave
to his critical intelligence as an individual, the acquisition of that
historically incomparable 'clinical sense', ever vigilant for the struggles between classes and ideologies; but also, and in his contact with
Hegel *par excellence*, the feeling for and practice in *abstraction* that
is indispensable to the constitution of any scientific theory, the feeling for and practice in *theoretical synthesis* and *the logic of a process*
for which the Hegelian dialectic gave him a 'pure', abstract model. I
have not provided these reference points because I think I can answer
this question; but because they may perhaps make possible, subject to
certain scientific studies in progress, a definition of what might have
been the role of the German Ideology and even of German 'speculative philosophy' in Marx's formation. I am inclined to see this role
less as a *theoretical formation* than as a *formation for theory*, a sort of
education of the theoretical intelligence via the theoretical formations
of ideology itself. As if for once, in a form foreign to its *pretensions*,
the ideological overdevelopment of the German intellect had served
as a propaedeutic for the Young Marx, in two ways: both through the
necessity it imposed on him to criticize his whole ideology in order to
reach that point beneath (*en-deçà*) his myths; and through the training
it gave him in the manipulation of the abstract structure of its systems,
independently of their validity. And if we are prepared to stand back a
little from Marx's discovery so that we can see that he founded a new

scientific discipline and that this *emergence* itself was analogous to all the great *scientific discoveries* of history, we must also agree that no great discovery has ever been made without bringing to light a new object or a new domain, without a new horizon of meaning appearing, a new land in which the old images and myths have been abolished – but at the same time the inventor of this new world must of absolute necessity have prepared his intelligence *in the old forms* themselves, he must have learnt and practised them, and by criticizing them formed a taste for and learnt the art of manipulating abstract forms in general, without which familiarity he could never have conceived *new ones with which to think the new object*. In the general context of the human development which may be said to make urgent, if not inevitable, all great historical discoveries, the individual who makes himself the author of one of them is of necessity in the paradoxical situation of *having to learn the way of saying what he is going to discover in the very way he must forget*. Perhaps, too, it is this situation which gives Marx's Early Works that tragic imminence and permanence, that extreme tension between a beginning and an end, between a language and a meaning, out of which no philosophy could come without forgetting that the destiny they are committed to is irreversible.

December 1960

Part Three

Contradiction and Overdetermination

NOTES FOR AN INVESTIGATION

For Margritte and Gui

'With (Hegel) it is standing on its head. It must be turned right side up again, if you would discover the rational kernel within the mystical shell.'

Karl Marx, *Capital*

In an article devoted to the Young Marx,[1] I have already stressed the ambiguity of the idea of 'inverting Hegel'. It seemed to me that strictly speaking this expression suited Feuerbach perfectly; the latter did, indeed, 'turn speculative philosophy back onto its feet', but the only result was to arrive with implacable logic at an idealist *anthropology*. But the expression cannot be applied to Marx, at least not to the Marx who had grown out of this 'anthropological' phase.

I could go further, and suggest that in the well-known passage: '*With (Hegel, the dialectic) is standing on its head. It must be turned right side up again, if you would discover the rational kernel within the mystical shell*'[2], this 'turning right side up again' is merely gestural,

---

1   See the preceding chapter.
2   Karl Marx, *Das Kapital*, Afterword to the second edition. This is a literal translation of the German original. The Molitor translation also follows this text (Costes, *Le Capital*, t. I, p. XCV), not without fantasy. As for Roy, whose translation Marx inspected in proof, he edulcorates the text, for example, translating '*die mystifizierende Seite der h. Dialektik*' by '*le côté mystique*' – where he does not just cut it. For example, the original text says, 'With him (Hegel) it (the dialectic) is standing on its head. It must be turned right side up again if you would discover the rational kernel within the mystical shell'; but Roy has '*chez lui elle marche sur la tête; il suffit de la remettre sur les pieds pour lui trouver la physionomie tout à fait raisonnable*'! The kernel and its shell have been spirited away. Perhaps it is not without interest, but who can tell?, to add that with the Roy version Marx accepted a less 'difficult', or even less ambiguous, text than his own. Did he then admit after all the difficulty of certain of his original expressions?

Here is a translation of the important passages from the German text:

even metaphorical, and it raises as many questions as it answers.

How should we really understand its use in this quotation? It is no longer a matter of a general '*inversion*' of Hegel, that is, the inversion of speculative philosophy as such. From *The German Ideology* onwards we know that such an undertaking would be meaningless. Anyone who claims purely and simply to have inverted speculative philosophy (to derive, for example, materialism) can never be more than philosophy's Proudhon, its unconscious prisoner, just as Proudhon was the prisoner of bourgeois economics. We are now concerned with the *dialectic*, and the dialectic alone. It might be thought that when Marx writes that we must '*discover the rational kernel within the mystical shell*' he means that the '*rational kernel*' *is the dialectic itself*, while the '*mystical shell*' *is speculative philosophy*. Engels's time-honoured distinction between *method* and *system* implies precisely this.[3] The shell, the mystical wrapping (speculative philosophy),

---

'In principle (*der Grundlage nach*) my dialectical method is not only distinct from Hegel's but its direct opposite. For Hegel, the process of thought, which he goes so far as to turn into an autonomous subject under the name of the Idea, is the demiurge of the real, which only represents (*bildet*) its external phenomenon. For me, on the contrary, the ideal is nothing but the material transposed and translated in man's head. The mystificatory (*mystifizierende*) side of the Hegelian dialectic I criticized about thirty years ago while it was still fashionable . . . I then declared myself openly a disciple of that great thinker, and in my chapter on the theory of value I went so far as to flirt (*ich kokettierte . . . mit*) here and there with his peculiar mode of expression. The mystification the dialectic suffered at Hegel's hands does not remove him from his place as the first to expose (*darstellen*) consciously and in depth its general forms of movement. With him it is standing on its head. It must be turned right side up again if you would discover the rational kernel (*Kern*) within the mystical shell (*mystische Hülle*).

'In its mystified form the dialectic was a German fashion because it seemed to transfigure the given (*das Bestehende*). In its rational image (*Gestalt*) it is a scandal and abomination for the bourgeoisie. . . . As it includes in the understanding of the given (*Bestehende*) the simultaneous understanding of its negation and necessary destruction, as it conceives any mature (*gewordne*) form as in motion and thus equally in its ephemeral aspect it allows nothing to impose on it, and is in essence critical and revolutionary.'

3   'Feuerbach and the End of Classical German Philosophy', in Marx–Engels, *Selected Works*, Vol. II, pp. 360–402 (two-volume edition).

should be tossed aside and the precious kernel, the dialectic, retained. But in the same sentence Marx claims that this shelling of the kernel and the inversion of the dialectic are one and the same thing. How can an extraction be an inversion? or in other words, what is 'inverted' during this extraction?

Let us look a little closer. As soon as the dialectic is removed from its idealistic shell, it becomes '*the direct opposite of the Hegelian dialectic*'. Does this mean that for Marx, far from dealing with Hegel's sublimated, inverted world, it is applied to the real world? This is certainly the sense in which Hegel was '*the first consciously to expose its general forms of movement in depth*'. We could therefore take over the dialectic from him and apply it to life rather than to the Idea. The 'inversion' would then be an 'inversion' of the 'sense' of the dialectic. But such an inversion in sense would in fact leave the dialectic untouched.

Taking Young Marx as an example, in the article referred to above, I suggested that to take over the dialectic in *rigorous* Hegelian form could only expose us to dangerous ambiguities, for it is *impossible* given the principles of a Marxist interpretation of *any* ideological phenomenon, *it is unthinkable that the place of the dialectic in Hegel's system could be conceived as that of a kernel in a nut.*[4] By which I meant that it is inconceivable that the essence of the dialectic in Hegel's work should not be contaminated by Hegelian ideology, or, since such a

---

4   On the kernel, see Hegel: *The Philosophy of History*, Introduction (Sibree translation, New York: Dover, 1956, p. 30): Great men 'may be called Heroes, inasmuch as they have derived their purposes and their vocation, not from the calm, regular course of things, sanctioned by the existing order; but from a concealed fount – one which has not attained to phenomenal, present existence – from that inner Spirit, still hidden beneath the surface, *which, impinging on the outer world as on a shell, bursts it in pieces, because it is another kernel than that which belonged to the shell in question*'. A curious variant on the long history of the kernel, the pulp and the almond. Here the kernel plays the part of a shell containing the almond; the kernel is outside and the almond inside. The almond (the new principle) finally bursts the old kernel which no longer suits it (it was the kernel of the old almond); it wants a kernel *of its own*: new political and social forms, etc. This reference should be borne in mind whenever the problem of the Hegelian dialectic of history arises.

'contamination' presupposes the fiction of a pure pre-'contamination' dialectic, *that the Hegelian dialectic could cease to be Hegelian and become Marxist by a simple, miraculous 'extraction'.*

Even in the rapidly written lines of the Afterword to the second edition of *Das Kapital* Marx saw this difficulty clearly. By the accumulation of metaphors, and, in particular, in the remarkable encounter of the extraction and the inversion, he not only hints at something more than he *says*, but in other passages he puts it clearly enough, though Roy has half spirited them away.

A close reading of the German text shows clearly enough that the *mystical shell* is by no means (as some of Engels's later commentaries would lead one to think)[5] speculative philosophy, or its 'world

---

5   Cf. Engels: 'Feuerbach . . .', *op. cit.* Perhaps we should not take too literally all the formulations of a text on the one hand destined for wide popular diffusion, and therefore, as Engels himself admits, somewhat schematic, and on the other set down by a man who forty years previously had lived through the great intellectual adventure of the discovery of historical materialism, and himself passed through the *philosophical* forms of consciousness whose broad history he is writing. The essay does, in fact, contain a noteworthy critique of Feuerbach's ideology (Engels sees that for him 'nature and man remain mere *words*', p. 384) and a good sketch of the relations between Marxism and Hegelianism. For example, Engels demonstrates Hegel's extraordinary critical virtue as compared to Kant (this I think particularly important), and correctly declares in plain terms that '*in its Hegelian form this (dialectical) method was unusable*' (p. 386). Further, and basic: the development of philosophy is not philosophical; it was the 'practical necessities of (their) fight' in religion and politics that forced the neo-Hegelians to oppose Hegel's 'system' (p. 367); it is the progress of science and industry which overturns philosophies (p. 372). We should also note the recognition of the profound influence of Feuerbach on *The Holy Family* (p. 368), etc. But the same essay contains formulations which, if taken literally, can only lead to dead ends. For example, the theme of the 'inversion' is taken so seriously that Engels draws the unfortunately logical conclusion that 'ultimately, the Hegelian system represents merely a *materialism* idealistically *turned upside down* in method and content' (p. 372). If the inversion of Hegel into Marx is well founded, it follows that Hegel could only have been already a previously inverted materialism; two negations make an affirmation. Later (p. 387), we discover that the Hegelian dialectic was unusable in its Hegelian form precisely because it stands on its head (on the idea, not the real): 'Thereby the

outlook' or its 'system', that is, an element we can regard as *external* to its *method*, but refers directly to the dialectic itself. Marx goes so far as to talk of the '*mystification the dialectic suffered at Hegel's hands*', of its '*mystificatory side*', its '*mystified form*', and he opposes precisely to this *mystified form* (*mystifizierten Form*) of the Hegelian dialectic the *rational figure* (*rationelle Gestalt*) of his own dialectic. It would be difficult to indicate more clearly that *the mystical shell is nothing but the mystified form* of the dialectic itself: that is, not a relatively external element of the dialectic (e.g. the 'system') but an *internal* element, *consubstantial with the Hegelian dialectic*. It is not enough, therefore, to disengage it from its *first wrapping* (the system) to free it. It must also be freed from a *second*, almost inseparable skin, which is itself *Hegelian in principle* (*Grundlage*). We must admit that this extraction cannot be painless; in appearance an unpeeling, it is really a *demystification*, an operation which transforms what it extracts.

So I think that, in its approximation, this metaphorical expression – the 'inversion' of the dialectic – does not pose the problem of *the nature of the objects* to which a *single method* should be applied (the world of the Idea for Hegel – the real world for Marx), but rather the problem of the *nature of the dialectic* considered itself, that is, the problem of *its specific structures*; not the problem of the inversion of the 'sense' of the dialectic, but that of the *transformation of its structures*. It is hardly worth pointing out that, in the first case, the application of a method, the exteriority of the dialectic to its possible objects poses a *pre-dialectical question*, a question without any strict meaning for

---

dialectic of concepts itself becomes merely the conscious reflex of the dialectical motion of the real world and thus the dialectic of Hegel *was placed upon its head; or rather, turned off its head, on which it was standing, and placed upon its feet.*' Obviously these are only approximate formulations, but their very approximation points towards a difficulty. Also noteworthy is a singular affirmation of the necessity for all philosophers to construct a system (Hegel 'was compelled to make a system and, in accordance with traditional requirements, a system of philosophy must conclude with some sort of absolute truth' – p. 363), a necessity which 'springs from an imperishable desire of the human mind – the desire to overcome all contradictions' (p. 365); and another statement that explains the limitations of Feuerbach's materialism by his life in the country and his consequent rustication in isolation (p. 375).

Marx. The second problem on the other hand, raises a real question to which it is hardly likely that Marx and his disciples should not have given a concrete answer in theory and practice, in theory or in practice.

Let us say, to end this over-extended textual exposition, that if the Marxist dialectic is 'in principle' the opposite of the Hegelian dialectic, if it is rational and not mystical-mystified-mystificatory, this radical distinction must be manifest in its essence, that is, in its *characteristic determinations and structures*. To be clear, this means that *basic structures of the Hegelian* dialectic such as negation, the negation of the negation, the identity of opposites, 'supersession', the transformation of quantity into quality, contradiction, etc., *have for Marx (in so far as he takes them over, and he takes over by no means all of them) a structure different from the structure they have for Hegel*. It also means that *these structural differences* can be demonstrated, described, determined and thought. And if this is possible, it is therefore *necessary*, I would go so far as to say *vital*, for Marxism. We cannot go on reiterating indefinitely approximations such as the difference between system and method, the inversion of philosophy or dialectic, the extraction of the 'rational kernel', and so on, without letting these formulae think for us, that is, stop thinking ourselves and trust ourselves to the magic of a number of completely devalued words for our completion of Marx's work. I say *vital*, for I am convinced that *the philosophical development of Marxism currently depends on this task*.[6]

*

---

6   Mao Tse-tung's pamphlet *On Contradiction* (1937) contains a whole series of analyses in which the Marxist conception of contradiction appears in a quite un-Hegelian light. Its essential concepts would be sought in vain in Hegel: principal and secondary contradiction; principal and secondary aspect of a contradiction; antagonistic and non-antagonistic contradiction; law of the uneven development of a contradiction. However, Mao's essay, inspired by his struggle against dogmatism in the Chinese Party, remains generally *descriptive*, and in consequence it is in certain respects *abstract*. Descriptive: his concepts correspond to concrete experiences. In part abstract: the concepts, though new and rich in promise, are presented as *specifications* of the *dialectic* in general rather than as *necessary implications* of the Marxist conception of society and history.

As this is also a personal responsibility, whatever risks I shall run, I should like to attempt a moment's reflection on *the Marxist concept of contradiction*, in respect to a particular example: the Leninist theme of the '*weakest link*'.

Lenin gave this metaphor above all a practical meaning. A chain is as strong as its weakest link. In general, anyone who wants to control a given situation will look out for a weak point, in case it should render the whole system vulnerable. On the other hand, anyone who wants to attack it, even if the odds are apparently against him, need only discover this one weakness to make all its power precarious. So far there is no revelation here for readers of Machiavelli and Vauban, who were as expert in the arts of the defence as of the destruction of a position, and judged all armour by its faults.

But here we should pay careful attention: if it is obvious that the theory of the weakest link guided Lenin in his theory of the revolutionary party (it was to be faultlessly united in consciousness and organization to avoid adverse exposure and to destroy the enemy), it was also the inspiration for his reflections on the revolution itself. How was this revolution *possible* in Russia, why was it *victorious* there? It was *possible* in Russia for a reason that went beyond Russia: because with the unleashing of imperialist war humanity entered into an *objectively revolutionary* situation.[7] Imperialism tore off the 'peaceful' mask of the old capitalism. The concentration of industrial monopolies, their subordination to financial monopolies, had increased the exploitation of the workers and of the colonies. Competition between the monopolies made war *inevitable*. But this same war, which dragged vast masses, even colonial peoples from whom troops were drawn, into limitless suffering, drove its cannon-fodder not only into massacres, but also into history. Everywhere the experience, the horrors of war, were a revelation and confirmation of a whole century's protest

---

7   Lenin, *Collected Works*, Vol. XIII, pp. 370–71 (English translation): '*It was the objective conditions created by the imperialist war that brought the whole of humanity to an impasse, that placed it in a dilemma: either allow the destruction of more millions of lives and utterly ruin European civilization, or hand over power in all the civilized countries to the revolutionary proletariat, carry through the socialist revolution.*'

against capitalist exploitation; a focusing-point, too, for hand in hand with this shattering exposure went the effective means of action. But though this effect was felt throughout the greater part of the popular masses of Europe (revolution in Germany and Hungary, mutinies and mass strikes in France and Italy, the Turin soviets), *only in Russia*, precisely the '*most backward*' country in Europe, *did it produce a triumphant revolution*. Why this paradoxical exception? For this basic reason: in the 'system of imperialist states'[8] Russia represented the weakest point. The Great War had, of course, precipitated and aggravated this weakness, but it had not by itself created it. Already, even in defeat, the 1905 Revolution had demonstrated and measured the weakness of Tsarist Russia. This weakness was the product of this special feature: *the accumulation and exacerbation of all the historical contradictions then possible in a single State*. Contradictions of a regime of feudal exploitation at the dawn of the twentieth century, attempting ever more ferociously amid mounting threats to rule, with the aid of a deceitful priesthood, over an enormous mass of 'ignorant'[9] peasants (circumstances which dictated a singular association of the peasants' revolt with the workers' revolution).[10] Contradictions of large-scale capitalist and imperialist exploitation in the major cities and their suburbs, in the mining regions, oil-fields, etc. Contradictions of colonial exploitation and wars imposed on whole peoples. A gigantic contradiction between the stage of development of capitalist methods of production (particularly in respect to proletarian concentration: the largest factory in the world at the time was the Putilov works at Petrograd, with 40,000 workers and auxiliaries) and the medieval state of the countryside. The exacerbation of class struggles throughout the country, not only between exploiter and exploited, but even within the ruling classes themselves (the great feudal proprietors

---

8   Lenin, 'Report of the Central Committee to the Eighth Congress of the R.C.P.(B.)', *Collected Works*, Vol. XXIX, p. 153.

9   Lenin, 'Pages from a Diary', *Selected Works*, Vol. III, p. 809 (three-volume English edition).

10   Lenin, 'Left-Wing Communism, an Infantile Disorder', *Selected Works*, Vol. III, pp. 412–13; 'The Third International and its Place in History', *Collected Works*, Vol. XXIX, p. 311.

supporting autocratic, militaristic police Tsarism; the lesser nobility involved in constant conspiracy; the big bourgeoisie and the liberal bourgeoisie opposed to the Tsar; the petty bourgeoisie oscillating between conformism and anarchistic 'leftism'). The detailed course of events added other 'exceptional'[11] circumstances, incomprehensible outside the 'tangle' of Russia's internal and external contradictions. For example, the *'advanced'* character of the Russian revolutionary élite, exiled by Tsarist repression; in exile it became 'cultivated', it absorbed the whole heritage of the political experience of the Western European working classes (above all, Marxism); this was particularly true of the formation of the Bolshevik Party, *far ahead of any Western 'socialist' party in consciousness and organization;*[12] the *'dress rehearsal'* for the Revolution in 1905, which, in common with most serious crises, set class relations sharply into relief, crystallized them and made possible the 'discovery' of a new form of mass political organization: *the soviets.*[13] Last, but not the least remarkable, the unexpected 'respite' the exhausted imperialist nations allowed the Bolsheviks for them to make their 'opening' in history, the involuntary but effective support of the Anglo-French bourgeoisie, who, at the decisive moment, wishing to be rid of the Tsar, did everything to help the Revolution.[14] In short, as precisely these details show, the privileged situation of Russia with respect to the *possible* revolution was a matter of *an accumulation and exacerbation of historical contradictions* that would have been incomprehensible in any country which was not, as Russia was, *simultaneously at least a century behind the imperialist world, and at the peak of its development.*

Lenin said this time and time again,[15] and Stalin summarized it in

---

11   Lenin, 'Our Revolution', *Selected Works*, Vol. III, p. 821.

12   Lenin, 'Left-Wing Communism . . .', *op. cit.*, p. 379.

13   Lenin, 'The Third International . . .', *op. cit.*, p. 311.

14   Lenin, 'Report to the Petrograd City Conference of the RSDRP(B)', *Collected Works*, Vol. XXIV, p. 141.

15   See particularly: 'Left-Wing Communism . . .', *op. cit.*, pp. 379, 412, 435–6, 439, 444–5; 'The Third International . . .', *op. cit.*, p. 310; 'Our Revolution', *op. cit.*, pp. 820 ff; 'Letters from Afar (No. 1)', *Selected Works*, Vol. II, pp. 31 ff; 'Farewell letter to Swiss Workers', *Collected Works*, Vol. XXIII, pp. 367–73.

particularly clear terms in his April 1924 speeches.[16] The unevenness
of capitalist development led, via the 1914–18 War, to the Russian
Revolution because in the revolutionary situation facing the whole
of humanity Russia was *the weakest link in the chain of imperialist
states*. It had accumulated the largest sum of historical contradictions then possible; for it was at the same time *the most backward and
the most advanced nation*, a gigantic contradiction which its divided
ruling classes could neither avoid nor solve. In other words Russia
was overdue with its bourgeois revolution on the eve of its proletarian revolution; pregnant with two revolutions, it could not withhold
the second even by delaying the first. This exceptional situation was
'insoluble' (for the ruling classes)[17] and Lenin was correct to see in it
the *objective conditions* of a Russian revolution, and to forge its *subjective conditions*, the means of a decisive assault on this weak link in
the imperialist chain, in a Communist Party that was a chain without
weak links.

What else did Marx and Engels mean when they declared that
history always progresses by its *bad side*?[18] This obviously means
the worse side for the rulers, but without stretching the sense unduly
we can interpret the bad side as the bad side for those who expect
history *from another side*! For example, the German Social-Democrats
at the end of the nineteenth century imagined that they would shortly
be promoted to socialist triumph by virtue of belonging to the most
powerful capitalist State, then undergoing rapid economic growth,
just as they were experiencing rapid electoral growth (such coinci-
dences do occur . . .). They obviously saw History as progressing
by *the other side*, the 'good' side, the side with the greatest *economic
development*, the greatest growth, with *its contradiction reduced to*

Lenin's remarkable theory of *the conditions for a revolution* ('Left-Wing
Communism . . .', *op. cit.*, pp. 434–5, 444–6) deals thoroughly with the
decisive effects of Russia's specific situation.

16   Stalin, 'The Foundations of Leninism', *Problems of Leninism* (11th
English edition), pp. 13–93, particularly pp. 15–18, 29–32, 71–3. Despite
their 'pedagogical' dryness, these texts are excellent in many respects.

17   Lenin, 'Our Revolution', *op. cit.*, p. 821.

18   *The Poverty of Philosophy*, p. 121 (English translation).

the purest form (the contradiction between Capital and Labour), so they forgot that all this was taking place in a Germany armed with a powerful State machine, endowed with a bourgeoisie which had long ago given up 'its' political revolution in exchange for Bismarck's (and later Wilhelm's) military, bureaucratic and police protection, in exchange for the super-profits of capitalist and colonialist exploitation, endowed, too, with a chauvinist and reactionary petty bourgeoisie. They forgot that, in fact, this simple quintessence of *contradiction* was quite simply *abstract*: the real contradiction was so much one with its 'circumstances' that it was only discernible, identifiable and manipulable *through them and in them*.

What is the essence of this practical experience and the reflections it inspired in Lenin? It should be pointed out immediately that this was not Lenin's sole illuminating experience. Before 1917 there was 1905, before 1905 the great historical deceptions of England and Germany, before that the Commune, even earlier the German failure of 1848–9. These experiences had been *reflected en route* (Engels, *Revolution and Counter-revolution in Germany*; Marx, *The Class Struggles in France*, *The Civil War in France*, *The Eighteenth Brumaire*, *The Critique of the Gotha Programme*; Engels, *The Critique of the Erfurt Programme*, and so on), *directly* or *indirectly*, and had been related to even earlier revolutionary experience: to the bourgeois revolutions of England and France.

How else should we summarize these practical experiences and their theoretical commentaries other than by saying that the whole Marxist revolutionary experience shows that, if the general contradiction (it has already been specified: the contradiction between the forces of production and the relations of production, essentially embodied in the contradiction between two antagonistic classes) is sufficient to define the situation when revolution is the 'task of the day', it cannot of its own simple, direct power induce a 'revolutionary situation', nor *a fortiori* a situation of revolutionary rupture and the triumph of the revolution. If this contradiction is to become *'active'* in the strongest sense, to become a ruptural principle, there must be an accumulation of 'circumstances' and 'currents' so that whatever their origin and sense (and many of them will *necessarily* be paradoxically

foreign to the revolution in origin and sense, or even its 'direct opponents'), they '*fuse*' into a *ruptural unity*: when they produce the result
of the immense majority of the popular masses *grouped* in an assault
on a regime which its ruling classes are *unable to defend*.[19] Such a situation presupposes not only the 'fusion' of the two basic conditions into
a 'single national crisis', but each condition considered (abstractly)
by itself presupposes the 'fusion' of an 'accumulation' of contradictions. How else could the class-divided popular masses (proletarians,
peasants, petty bourgeois) throw themselves *together*, consciously
or unconsciously, into a general assault on the existing regime? And
how else could the ruling classes (aristocrats, big bourgeois, industrial bourgeois, finance bourgeois, etc.), who have learnt by long
experience and sure instinct to seal between themselves, despite their
class differences, a holy alliance against the exploited, find themselves
reduced to impotence, divided at the decisive moment, with neither
new political solutions nor new political leaders, deprived of foreign
class support, disarmed in the very citadel of their State machine, and
suddenly overwhelmed by the people they had so long kept in leash
and respectful by exploitation, violence and deceit? If, as in this situation, a vast accumulation of 'contradictions' comes into play *in the
same court*, some of which are radically heterogeneous – of different origins, different sense, different *levels* and *points* of application
– but which nevertheless 'merge' into a ruptural unity, we can no
longer talk of the sole, unique power of the general 'contradiction'.
Of course, the basic contradiction dominating the period (when the
revolution is 'the task of the day') is active in all these 'contradictions'

---

19   For the whole of this passage see (1) Lenin: 'Left-Wing Communism
. . .', *op. cit.*, pp. 430, 444–5; especially: 'Only when the "*lower classes*" *do
not want* the old way, and when the "*upper classes*" *cannot carry on in the old
way* – only then can revolution triumph' (p. 430); these formal conditions are
illustrated on pp. 444–5.

   (2) Lenin: 'Letters from Afar (No. 1)', *op. cit.*, pp. 35–6, notably: 'That
the revolution succeeded so quickly . . . is only due to the fact that, as
a result of an extremely unique historical situation, *absolutely dissimilar
currents*, *absolutely heterogeneous* class interests, *absolutely contrary* political and social strivings have *merged* . . . in a strikingly "harmonious"
manner . . .' (p. 35 – Lenin's emphasis).

and even in their 'fusion'. But, strictly speaking, it cannot be claimed that these contradictions and their fusion are merely the *pure phenomena* of the general contradiction. The 'circumstances' and 'currents' which achieve it are more than its phenomena pure and simple. They derive from the relations of production, which are, of course, one of the *terms* of the contradiction, but at the same time its *conditions of existence*; from the superstructures, instances which derive from it, but have their own consistency and effectivity, from the international conjuncture itself, which intervenes as a determination with a specific role to play.[20] This means that if the 'differences' that constitute each of the instances in play (manifested in the 'accumulation' discussed by Lenin) *'merge'* into a real unity, they are not *'dissipated'* as pure *phenomena* in the internal unity of a *simple* contradiction. The *unity* they *constitute* in this 'fusion' into a revolutionary rupture,[21] *is constituted by their own essence and effectivity*, by what they are, and according to the specific modalities of their action. In *constituting* this *unity*, they *reconstitute* and complete their basic animating unity, but at the same time they also bring out its *nature*: the 'contradiction' is inseparable from the total structure of the social body in which it is found, inseparable from its formal *conditions* of existence, and even from the *instances* it governs; it is radically *affected by them*, determining, but also determined in one and the same movement, and determined by the various *levels* and *instances* of the social formation it animates; it might be called *overdetermined in its principle*.[22]

I am not particularly taken by this term *overdetermination* (borrowed from other disciplines), but I shall use it in the absence of

---

20   Lenin goes so far as to include among the causes of the success of the Soviet Revolution the natural wealth of the country, its geographical extent, the shelter of the Revolution in its necessary military and political 'retreats'.
21   The 'crisis' situation, as Lenin remarked, has a *revelatory* role for the structure and dynamic of the social formation that lives it. What has been said for a revolutionary situation can therefore be referred cautiously to the social formation in a situation prior to the revolutionary crisis.
22   Cf. Mao's development of the theme of the distinction between *antagonistic* (explosive, revolutionary) contradictions and *non-antagonistic* contradictions ('On Contradiction', *Selected Works*, Vol. I, pp. 343 ff. – English translation, Peking, 1965).

anything better, both as an *index* and as a *problem*, and also because it enables us to see clearly why we are dealing with something *quite different from the Hegelian contradiction*.

Indeed, a Hegelian contradiction is never *really overdetermined*, even though it frequently has all the appearances of being so. For example, in the *Phenomenology of Mind*, which describes the 'experiences' of consciousness and their dialectic, culminating in Absolute Knowledge, contradiction does not *appear* to be *simple*, but on the contrary very complex. Strictly speaking, only the first contradiction – between sensuous consciousness and its knowledge – can be called simple. The further we progress in the dialectic of its production, the richer consciousness becomes, the more complex is its contradiction. However, it can be shown that this complexity is not the complexity of an *effective overdetermination*, but the complexity of a cumulative *internalization* which is only apparently an overdetermination. In fact, at each moment of its development consciousness lives and experiences its own essence (the essence corresponding to the stage it has attained) *through all the echoes* of the essence it has previously been, and through the *allusive presence* of the corresponding historical forms. Hegel, therefore, argues that every consciousness has a suppressed-conserved (*aufgehoben*) *past* even in its present, and *a world* (the world whose consciousness it could be, but which is marginal in the *Phenomenology*, its presence virtual and latent), and that therefore it also has as its past *the worlds of its superseded essences*. But these past *images* of consciousness and these latent *worlds* (corresponding to the images) never affect present consciousness as *effective determinations different from itself*: these images and worlds concern it only *as echoes* (memories, phantoms of its historicity) of what it has become, that is, *as anticipations of or allusions to itself*. Because the past is never more than the internal essence (in-itself) of the future it encloses, this presence of the past is the presence to consciousness of consciousness itself, *and no true external determination. A circle of circles, consciousness has only one centre*, which solely determines it; it would need circles *with another centre than itself – decentred circles –* for it to be affected at its centre by their effectivity, in short for its essence to be overdetermined by them. But this is not the case.

This truth emerges even more clearly from the *Philosophy of History*. Here again we encounter an *apparent* overdetermination: are not all historical societies constituted of an infinity of concrete determinations, from political laws to religion via customs, habits, financial, commercial and economic regimes, the educational system, the arts, philosophy, and so on? However, none of these determinations is essentially *outside* the others, not only because together they constitute an original, organic totality, but also and above all because this totality is *reflected in a unique internal principle*, which is *the truth* of all those concrete determinations. Thus Rome: its mighty history, its institutions, its crises and ventures, are nothing but the temporal manifestation of the internal principle of the *abstract legal personality*, and then its destruction. Of course, this internal principle contains *as echoes* the principle of each of the historical formations it has superseded, but as echoes of itself – that is why, too, it only has one centre, the centre of all the past worlds conserved in its memory; that is why *it is simple*. And its own *contradiction* appears in this very simplicity: in Rome, *the Stoic consciousness*, as consciousness of the contradiction inherent in the concept of the abstract legal personality, which *aims* for the concrete world of *subjectivity*, but *misses it*. This is the contradiction which will bring down Rome and produce its future: *the image of subjectivity* in medieval Christianity. So all Rome's complexity fails to overdetermine the contradiction in the simple Roman principle, which is merely the internal essence of this infinite historical wealth.

We have only to ask *why* Hegel thought the phenomena of historical mutation in terms of this *simple concept* of contradiction, to pose what is precisely *the* essential question. The simplicity of the Hegelian contradiction is made possible *only* by the simplicity of the *internal principle* that constitutes the essence of any historical period. If it is possible, *in principle*, *to reduce the totality*, the infinite diversity, of a historically given society (Greece, Rome, the Holy Roman Empire, England, and so on) to a *simple internal principle*, *this very simplicity* can be reflected in the contradiction *to which it thereby acquires a right*. Must we be even plainer? This reduction itself (Hegel derived the idea from Montesquieu), the reduction of *all* the elements that make up the concrete life of a historical epoch (economic, social, political and legal institutions, customs, ethics, art, religion, philosophy, and even historical *events*: wars, battles, defeats, and so on) to *one* principle of internal unity, is itself only possible on the *absolute condition* of taking the whole concrete life of a people for the externalization–alienation (*Entäusserung–Entfremdung*) of an *internal spiritual principle*, which can *never definitely be anything but the most abstract form of that epoch's consciousness of itself: its religious or philosophical consciousness, that is, its own ideology*. I think we can now see how the 'mystical shell' affects and contaminates the 'kernel' – for *the simplicity of Hegelian contradiction is never more than a reflection of the simplicity of this internal principle of a people, that is, not its material reality but its most abstract ideology*. It is also why Hegel could represent Universal History from the Ancient Orient to the present day as 'dialectical', that is, moved by the simple play of a principle of *simple* contradiction. It is why there is never for him any basic rupture, no actual end to any real history – nor any radical beginning. It is why his philosophy of history is garnished with uniformly 'dialectical' mutations. This stupefying conception is only defensible from the Spirit's topmost peak. From that vantage point what does it matter if a people die once it has embodied the determinate principle of a moment of the Idea (which has plenty more to come), once, having embodied it, it has cast it off to add it to that Self-Memory which is History, thereby delivering it to such and such *another* people (even if their historical relation is very tenuous!), who, reflecting it in their substance, will find in it the promise of their own internal principle, that is, as if by chance the logically consecutive moment of the Idea, etc., etc.? It must be clear that all these arbitrary decisions (shot through though they are with insights of genius) are not just *miraculously confined* to Hegel's 'world outlook', to his 'system', but are reflected *in the structure, in the very structures of his dialectic*, particularly in the '*contradiction*' whose task is the magical movement of the concrete contents of a historical epoch towards their ideological Goal.

Thus the Marxist 'inversion' of the Hegelian dialectic is something quite different from an extraction pure and simple. If we clearly perceive the *intimate and close relation* that the Hegelian structure of the dialectic has with Hegel's 'world outlook', that is, with his speculative philosophy, this 'world outlook' cannot really be cast aside *without our being obliged to transform profoundly the structures* of that dialectic. If not, whether we will or no, we shall drag along with us, one hundred and fifty years after Hegel's death and one hundred years after Marx, the shreds of the famous 'mystical wrapping'.

Let us return to Lenin and thence to Marx. If it is true, as Leninist practice and reflection prove, that the revolutionary situation in Russia was precisely a result of the *intense overdetermination* of the basic class contradiction, we should perhaps ask what is *exceptional* about this 'exceptional *situation*', and whether, like all exceptions, this one does not clarify its rule – is not, unbeknown to the rule, *the rule itself*. For, after all, *are we not always in exceptional situations?* The failure of the 1849 Revolution in Germany was an exception, the failure in Paris in 1871 was an exception, the German Social-Democratic failure at the beginning of the twentieth century pending the chauvinist betrayal of 1914 was an exception . . . exceptions, but *with respect to what?* To nothing but the *abstract*, but comfortable and reassuring idea of a pure, simple 'dialectical' schema, which in its very simplicity seems to have retained a memory (or rediscovered the style) of the Hegelian model and its faith in the resolving 'power' of the abstract contradiction as such: in particular, the 'beautiful' contradiction between Capital and Labour. I do not deny that the '*simplicity*' of this *purified* schema has answered to certain subjective necessities of the mobilization of the masses; after all, we know perfectly well that the utopian forms of socialism *also* played a historical part, and played it well because they took the masses at the word of their consciousness, because if they are to be led forward, even (and above all) this is how they must be taken. One day it will be necessary to do *what Marx and Engels did* for utopian socialism, but this time for those still schematic–utopian forms of mass consciousness influenced by *Marxism* (even the consciousness of certain of its theoreticians) in the first stage of its history: *a true historical study of the conditions and forms of that consciousness.*[23]

---

23   In 1890 Engels wrote (in a letter to J. Bloch, 21 September 1890), 'Marx and I are ourselves partly to blame for the fact that the younger people sometimes lay more stress on the economic side than is due to it. *We had to emphasize the main principle vis-à-vis our adversaries, who denied*

In fact we find that all the important historical and political articles written by Marx and Engels during this period give us precisely the material for a preliminary reflection on these so-called 'exceptions'. They draw from them the basic notion that *the Capital–Labour contradiction is never simple, but always specified by the historically concrete*

---

it, and we had not always the time, the place or the opportunity to allow the other elements involved in the interaction to come into their rights' (Marx–Engels, *Selected Works*, Vol. II, p.490). For Engels's view of determination 'in the last instance' see the *Appendix*, pp. 117–28.

In the context of these necessary investigations, I should like to quote the notes which *Gramsci* devoted to the mechanistic–fatalistic temptation in the history of nineteenth-century Marxism: '*the determinist, fatalist element has been an immediate ideological "aroma" of the philosophy of praxis, a form of religion and a stimulant (but like a drug) necessitated and historically justified by the "subordinate" character of certain social strata. When one does not have the initiative in the struggle and the struggle itself is ultimately identified with a series of defeats, mechanical determinism becomes a formidable power of moral resistance, of cohesion and of patient and obstinate perseverance. "I am defeated for the moment but the nature of things is on my side in the long run," etc. Real will is disguised as an act of faith, a sure rationality of history, a primitive and empirical form of impassioned finalism which appear as a substitute for the predestination, providence, etc., of the confessional religions. We must insist on the fact that even in such cases there exists in reality a strong active will. . . . We must stress the fact that fatalism has only been a cover by the weak for an active and real will. This is why it is always necessary to show the futility of mechanical determinism, which, explicable as a naïve philosophy of the masses, becomes a cause of passivity, of imbecile self-sufficiency, when it is made into a reflective and coherent philosophy on the part of the intellectuals . . .*' (Antonio Gramsci: *Opere*, Vol. II, *Il materialismo storico e la filosofia de Benedetto Croce*, pp. 13–14, *The Modern Prince*, pp. 69–70). This opposition (intellectuals / masses) might appear strange from the pen of a Marxist theoretician. But it should be realized that Gramsci's concept of the *intellectual* is infinitely wider than ours, that is, it is not defined by the idea intellectuals have of themselves, but by their social *role* as *organizers* and (more or less subordinate) *leaders*. In this sense, he wrote, '*The claim that all the members of a political party should be regarded as intellectuals lends itself to jokes and caricature; but on reflection, nothing could be more accurate. There must be a distinction of levels, with a party having more or less of the higher or lower level, but this is not what matters: what does matter is their function, which is to direct and to organize, that is, it is educational, which means intellectual*' (*Opere*, Vol. III, *Gli intellettuali e l'organizzazione della cultura*, p. 12).

forms and circumstances in which it is exercised. It is specified by the forms of the *superstructure* (the State, the dominant ideology, religion, politically organized movements, and so on); specified by *the internal and external historical situation* which determines it on the one hand as a function of the *national past* (completed or 'relapsed' bourgeois revolution, feudal exploitation eliminated wholly, partially or not at all, local 'customs', specific national *traditions*, even the 'etiquette' of political struggles and behaviour, etc.), and on the other as functions of the existing *world context* (what dominates it – competition of capitalist nations, or 'imperialist internationalism', or competition within imperialism, etc.), many of these phenomena deriving from the 'law of uneven development' in the Leninist sense.

What can this mean but that the apparently simple contradiction is *always overdetermined*? The exception thus dicovers in itself the rule, the rule of the rule, and the old 'exceptions' must be regarded as methodologically simple examples of the *new rule*. To extend the analysis to all phenomena using this rule, I should like to suggest that an *'overdetermined contradiction'* may either be *overdetermined* in the direction of a *historical inhibition*, a real 'block' for the contradiction (for example, Wilhelmine Germany), or in the direction of *revolutionary rupture*[24] (Russia in 1917), but in neither condition *is it ever found in the 'pure' state.* 'Purity' itself would be the exception, I agree, but I know of no example to refer to.

But if every contradiction appears in Marxist historical practice and experience as an *overdetermined contradiction*; if this overdetermination constitutes the *specificity* of Marxist contradiction; if the 'simplicity' of the Hegelian dialectic is inseparable from Hegel's 'world outlook', particularly the conception of history it reflects, we must ask *what is the content, the* raison d'être *of the overdetermination of* Marxist contradiction, and how can the Marxist conception of society

---

24   Cf. Engels (Letter to Schmidt, 27 October 1890, *Selected Works*, Vol. II, p. 493): '*The reaction of the state power upon economic development can be one of three kinds: it can run in the same direction, and then development is more rapid; it can oppose the line of development, in which case nowadays state power in every great people will go to pieces in the long run . . .*'. This well suggests the character of the two limit positions.

be reflected in this overdetermination. This is a crucial question, for it is obvious that if we cannot demonstrate the *necessary link* that unites the characteristic structure of contradiction for Marx to his conception of society and history, if this overdetermination is not based on the very concepts of the Marxist theory of history, the category will remain 'up in the air'. For however accurate and verified it may be in political practice, we have only so far used it *descriptively*, that is, *contingently*, and *like all descriptions* it is still at the mercy of any *philosophical* theory that happens to come along.

But this raises the ghost of the Hegelian model again – not of its abstract model of contradiction, but of the concrete model of the *conception of history* reflected in it. If we are to prove that the specific structure of Marxist contradiction is based on Marx's conception of history, we must first ensure that this conception is not itself a mere 'inversion' of the Hegelian conception pure and simple. It is true that we could argue as a first approximation that Marx 'inverted' the Hegelian conception of History. This can be quickly illustrated. The whole Hegelian conception is regulated by the dialectic of the internal principles of each society, that is, the dialectic of the moments of the idea; as Marx said twenty times, Hegel explains the material life, the concrete history of all peoples by a dialectic of consciousness (the people's consciousness of itself: its ideology). For Marx, on the other hand, the material life of men explains their history; their consciousness, their ideologies are then merely the phenomena of their material life. This opposition certainly unites all the appearances of an 'inversion'. To push this to extremes, almost to caricature: what do we find in Hegel? A conception of society which takes over the achievements of eighteenth-century political theory and political economy, and regards every society (every modern society of course; but the present reveals what was once only a germ) as constituted by *two societies*: the society of needs, or *civil society*, and the political society or State and everything embodied in the State: religion, philosophy, in short, the epoch's consciousness of itself. In other words, schematically, by material life on the one hand and spiritual life on the other. For Hegel, material life (civil society, that is, the economy) is merely a *Ruse of Reason*. Apparently autonomous, it is subject to a law outside itself: its own Goal, which is simultaneously its condition of possibility, the State, that is, spiritual life. So here again we have a way of inverting Hegel which would apparently give us Marx. It is simply to *invert the relation of the terms (and thus to retain them)*: civil society and State, economy and politics – ideology – but to transform the essence into the phenomena and the phenomena into an essence, or if you prefer, to make the Ruse of Reason work *backwards*. While for Hegel, the politico-ideological was the essence of the economic, for Marx, the economic will be the essence of the politico-ideological. The political and the ideological will therefore be merely pure phenomena of the economic which will be their 'truth'. For Hegel's 'pure' principle of consciousness (of the epoch's consciousness of itself), for the simple internal principle which he conceived as the principle of the intelligibility of all the determinations of a historical people, we have substituted *another simple principle*, its opposite: material life, the economy – a simple principle which in turn becomes the sole principle of the universal intelligibility of all the determinations of a historical people.[25] *Is this a caricature?* If we take Marx's famous comments on the hand-mill, the water-mill and the steam-mill literally or out of context, this is their meaning. The logical destination of this temptation is the *exact mirror image of the Hegelian dialectic* – the only difference being that it is no longer a question of deriving the successive moments from the Idea, but from the Economy, by virtue of the same internal contradiction. This temptation results in the radical reduction of the dialectic of history to the dialectic generating the successive *modes of production*, that is, in the last analysis, the different production *techniques*. There are names for these temptations in the history of Marxism: *economism* and even *technologism*.

But these terms have only to be mentioned to evoke the memory of the theoretical and practical struggles of Marx and his disciples against these 'deviations'. And how many peremptory attacks on economism there are to counterbalance that well-thumbed piece on the steam engine! Let us abandon this caricature, not so as to oppose the official

---

25 Of course, as with all 'inversions' this one retains the terms of the Hegelian conception: *civil society* and *the State*.

condemnations to economism, but to examine *what authentic princi-ples* are active in these condemnations and in Marx's actual thought.

For all its apparent rigour, the fiction of the '*inversion*' is now clearly untenable. We know that *Marx did not retain the terms of the Hegelian model of society and 'invert' them.* He substituted other, only distantly related terms for them. Furthermore, he overhauled the *connexion* which had previously ruled over the terms. For Marx, *both terms* and *relation* changed in nature and sense.

Firstly, *the terms* are no longer the same.

Of course, Marx still talks of '*civil society*' (especially in *The German Ideology*: the term is often mistranslated as 'bourgeois soci-ety') but as an allusion to the past, to denote *the site* of his discoveries, not to re-utilize the *concept*. The formation of this concept requires closer examination. Beneath the abstract forms of the political philosophy of the eighteenth century and the more concrete forms of its political economy, we discover, not a true theory of economic history, nor even a true economic theory, but *a description and foun-dation of economic behaviour*, in short, a sort of *philosophico-economic Phenomenology*. What is remarkable in this undertaking, as much in its philosophers (Locke, Helvetius, etc.) as in its economists (Turgot, Smith, etc.), is that this description of civil society acts as if it were the description (and foundation) of what Hegel, aptly summariz-ing its spirit, called '*the world of needs*'; a world related immediately, as if to its internal essence, *to the relations of individuals* defined by their particular wishes, personal interests, in short, their 'needs'. We know that Marx's whole conception of political economy is based on a critique of this presupposition (the *homo œconomicus* and its ethical and legal abstraction, the '*Man*' of philosophy); how then could he take over a concept which is *its direct product*? Neither this (abstract) *description* of economic behaviour nor its supposed *foundation* in the mythical *homo œconomicus* interested Marx – his concern was rather the '*anatomy*' of this world, and *the dialectic of the mutations* of this 'anatomy'. Therefore the concept of '*civil society*' – the world of indi-vidual economic behaviour and its ideological origin – disappears from Marx's work. He understands *abstract economic reality* (which Smith, for example, *rediscovers* in the laws of the market as a *result* of his work of foundation) as the effect of a deeper, more concrete real-ity: *the mode of production* of a determinate social formation. Thus for the first time individual economic behaviour (which was the pretext for this economico-philosophical Phenomenology) is measured according to its *conditions of existence*. The degree of development of the *forces of production*, the state of the *relations of production*: these are from now on the basic Marxist concepts. 'Civil society' may well have gestured towards the *site* of the new concepts ('dig here'), but we must admit that it did not even contribute to their material. But where in Hegel would you find all that?

As for the State, it is only too easy to show that it no longer has the same content for Marx as it had for Hegel. Not just because the State can no longer be the 'reality of the Idea', but also and primarily because it is systematically thought as an *instrument* of coercion in the service of the ruling, exploiting class. Beneath the 'description' and sublimation of the attributes of the State, Marx finds here also *a new concept*, foreshadowed in the eighteenth century (Linguet, Rousseau, etc.), taken up even by Hegel in his *Philosophy of Right* (making it into a 'phenomenon' of the Ruse of Reason which triumphs in the State: the opposition of wealth and poverty), and abundantly used by the historians of the 1830s: *the concept of social class*, in direct relation with *the relations of production*. The intervention of this new concept and its interconnexion with one of the basic concepts of the economic struc-ture transforms the *essence of the State* from top to toe, for the latter is no longer above human groups, but at the service of the ruling class; it is no longer its mission to consummate itself in art, religion and philosophy, but to set them to serve the interests of the ruling class, or rather to force them to base themselves on ideas and themes which it renders *ruling*; it therefore ceases to be the 'truth of' civil society, to become, not the 'truth of' something else, not even of the economy, but the means of action and domination of a social class, etc.

But it is not just *the terms* which change, it is also *their relations themselves*.

We should not think that this means a new technical distribution of roles imposed by the multiplication of new terms. How are these new terms arranged? On the one hand, the *structure* (the economic base: the forces of production and the relations of production); on the other, the *superstructure* (the State and all the legal, political and ideological forms). We have seen that one could nevertheless attempt to maintain *a Hegelian relation* (the relation Hegel imposed between civil society and the State) between these two groups of categories: *the relation between an essence and its phenomena*, sublimated in the concept of the '*truth of . . .*'. For Hegel, the State is the '*truth of*' civil society, which, thanks to the action of the Ruse of Reason, is merely its own phenomenon *consummated* in it. For a Marx thus relegated to the rank of a Hobbes or a Locke, civil society would be nothing but the '*truth of*' its phenomenon, the State, nothing but a Ruse which Economic Reason would then put at the service of a class: the ruling class. Unfortunately for this neat schema, this is not Marx. For him, this tacit identity (phenomenon-essence-truth-of . . .) of the economic and the political disappears in favour of a *new conception* of the relation between *determinant instances* in the structure–superstructure complex which constitutes the essence of any social formation. Of course, these specific *relations* between structure and superstructure still deserve theoretical elaboration and investigation. However, Marx has at least given us the 'two ends of the chain', and has told us to find out what goes on between them: on the one hand, *determination in the last instance by the* (*economic*) *mode of production*; on the other, *the relative autonomy of the superstructures and their specific effectivity*. This clearly breaks with the Hegelian principle of explanation by consciousness of self (ideology), but also with the Hegelian theme of *phenomenon-essence-truth-of*. We really are dealing with a *new relationship* between *new terms*.

Listen to the old Engels in 1890, taking the young 'economists' to task for not having understood that this was a *new relationship*.[26] Production is the determinant factor, but only '*in the last instance*': '*More than this neither Marx nor I have ever asserted.*' Anyone who '*twists this*' so that it says that the economic factor is *the only* determinant factor, '*transforms that proposition into a meaningless, abstract,*

26   Letter from Engels to J. Bloch, 21 September 1890 (Marx–Engels, *Selected Works*, Vol. II, pp. 488–9).

empty phrase'. And as explanation: '*The economic situation is the basis, but the various elements of the superstructure – the political forms of the class struggle and its results: to wit constitutions established by the victorious class after a successful battle, etc., juridical forms, and then even the reflexes of all these actual struggles in the brains of the participants, political, juristic, philosophical theories, religious views and their further development into systems of dogmas – also exercise their influence upon the course of the historical struggles, and in many cases preponderate in determining their form . . .*' The word '*form*' should be understood in its strongest sense, designating something quite different from the formal. As Engels also says: '*The Prussian State also arose and developed from historical, ultimately economic causes. But it could scarcely be maintained without pedantry that among the many small states of North Germany, Brandenberg was specifically determined by economic necessity to become the great power embodying the economic, linguistic and, after the Reformation, also the religious difference between North and South, and not by other elements as well (above all by the entanglement with Poland, owing to the possession of Prussia, and hence with international political relations – which were indeed also decisive in the formation of the Austrian dynastic power).*'[27]

Here, then, are the two ends of the chain: the economy is determinant, but *in the last instance*, Engels is prepared to say, in the long run, the run of History. But History 'asserts itself' through the multiform world of the superstructures, from local tradition[28] to international circumstance. Leaving aside the *theoretical solution* Engels proposes for the problem of the relation between determination *in the last instance* – the economic – and those determinations imposed by the superstructures – national traditions and international events – it is sufficient to retain from him what should be called the *accumulation of effective determinations* (deriving from the superstructures and

---

27 Engels adds: '*Marx hardly wrote anything in which this theory did not play a part. But especially* The Eighteenth Brumaire of Louis Bonaparte *is a most excellent example of its application. There are also many allusions in* Capital' (*ibid.*, p. 489). He also cites *Anti-Dühring* and *Ludwig Feuerbach*.

28 Engels, '*Political conditions . . . and even the traditions which haunt human minds also play a part*' (*ibid.*, p. 488).

from special national and international circumstances) *on the determination in the last instance by the economic*. It seems to me that this clarifies the expression *overdetermined contradiction*, which I have put forward, *this* specifically because the existence of overdetermination is no longer *a fact* pure and simple, for in its essentials we have related it *to its bases*, even if our exposition has so far been merely gestural. This *overdetermination* is inevitable and thinkable as soon as the real existence of the forms of the superstructure and of the national and international conjuncture has been recognized – an existence largely specific and autonomous, and therefore irreducible to a pure *phenomenon*. We must carry this through to its conclusion and say that this overdetermination does not just refer to apparently unique and aberrant historical situations (Germany, for example), but is *universal*; the economic dialectic is never active *in the pure state*; in History, these instances, the superstructures, etc. – are never seen to step respectfully aside when their work is done or, when the Time comes, as his pure phenomena, to scatter before His Majesty the Economy as he strides along the royal road of the Dialectic. From the first moment to the last, the lonely hour of the 'last instance' never comes.

In short, the idea of a 'pure and simple' non-overdetermined contradiction is, as Engels said of the economist turn of phrase, 'meaningless, abstract, senseless'. That it can serve as a pedagogical model, or rather that it did serve as a polemical and pedagogical instrument at a certain point in history does not fix its destiny for all time. After all, pedagogic systems do change in history. It is time to make the effort to raise pedagogy to the level of circumstances, that is, of historical needs. But we must all be able to see that this pedagogical effort *presupposes* another purely theoretical effort. For if Marx has given us the general principles and some concrete examples (*The Eighteenth Brumaire*, *The Civil War in France*, etc.), if all political practice in the history of Socialist and Communist movements constitutes an inexhaustible reservoir of concrete 'experiential protocol', it has to be said that *the theory of the specific effectivity of the superstructures and other 'circumstances' largely remains to be elaborated*; and before the theory of their effectivity or simultaneously (for it is by formulating their effectivity that their *essence* can be attained) there must be elaboration of *the theory of the particular essence of the specific elements of the superstructure*. Like the map of Africa before the great explorations, this theory remains a realm sketched in outline, with its great mountain chains and rivers, but often unknown in detail beyond a few well-known regions. Who has *really* attempted to follow up the explorations of Marx and Engels? I can only think of Gramsci.[29] But this task is indispensable if we are to be able to express even propositions more precise than these approximations on the character of the *overdetermination* of Marxist contradiction, based primarily on the existence and nature of the superstructures.

Allow me one last example. Marxist political practice is constantly coming up against that reality known as '*survivals*'. There can be no doubt that these survivals exist – they cling tenaciously to life. Lenin struggled with them inside the Russian Party even before the Revolution. We do not need to be reminded that after the Revolution and from then till now they have been the source of constant difficulties, battles and commentaries. What is a '*survival*'? What is its theoretical status? Is it essentially social or 'psychological'? Can it be reduced to the survival of certain economic *structures* which the Revolution was unable to destroy with its first decrees: for example, the small-scale production (primarily peasant production in Russia) which so preoccupied Lenin? Or does it refer as much to *other structures*, political, ideological structures, etc.: *customs*, *habits*, even '*traditions*' such as the '*national tradition*' with its specific traits? The term '*survival*' is constantly invoked, but it is still virtually uninvestigated, not in *its*

---

29 *Lukács*'s attempts, which are limited to the history of literature and philosophy, seem to me to be tainted by a guilty Hegelianism: as if Lukács wanted to absolve through Hegel his upbringing by Simmel and Dilthey. *Gramsci* is of another stature. The jottings and developments in his *Prison Notebooks* touch on all the basic problems of Italian and European history: economic, social, political and cultural. There are also some completely original and in some cases genial insights into the problem, basic today, of the superstructures. Also, as always with true discoveries, there are *new concepts*, for example, *hegemony*: a remarkable example of a theoretical solution in outline to the problems of the interpenetration of the economic and the political. Unfortunately, at least as far as France is concerned, who has taken up and followed through Gramsci's theoretical effort?

name (it has one!), but *in its concept*. The concept it deserves (and has fairly won) must be more than a vague Hegelianism such as '*supersession*' – the *maintenance-of-what-has-been-negated-in-its-very-negation* (that is, the negation of the negation). If we return to Hegel for a second we see that the survival of the past as the '*superseded*' (*aufgehoben*) is simply reduced to the modality of a *memory*, which, furthermore, is merely the inverse of (that is, the same thing as) an *anticipation*. Just as at the dawn of Human History the first stammerings of the Oriental Spirit – joyous captive of the giants of the sky, the sea and the desert, and then of its own stone bestiary – already betrayed the unconscious presage of the future achievements of the Absolute Spirit, so in each instant of Time the past survives in the form of a memory of what it has been; that is, as the whispered promise of its present. That is why *the past is never opaque on an obstacle*. It must always be digestible as it has been *pre-digested*. Rome lived happily in a world impregnated by Greece: Greece 'superseded' survived as objective memories: its reproduced temples, its assimilated religion, its rethought philosophy. Without knowing it, as at last it died to bring forth its Roman future, it was already Rome, so it never shackled Rome in Rome. That is why the present can feed on the shades of its past, or even project them before it, just as the great effigies of Roman Virtue opened up the road to Revolution and Terror for the Jacobins. Its past is never anything more than itself and only recalls to it that law of interiority which is the destiny of the whole Future of Humanity.

I think this is enough to show that, though the word is still meaningful (in fact, not *rigorously* meaningful), Marx's conception of 'supersession' has nothing to do with this dialectic of historical comfort; his past was no shade, not even an 'objective' shade – it is a terribly positive and active structured reality, just as cold, hunger and the night are for his poor worker. How, then, are we *to think these survivals?* Surely, with a number of *realities*, which are precisely *realities* for Marx, whether superstructures, ideologies, 'national traditions' or the customs and 'spirit' of a people, etc? Surely, with *the overdetermination of any contradiction and of any constitutive element of a society which means*: (1) that a revolution in the *structure* does not *ipso facto* modify the existing superstructures and particularly the *ideologies* at one blow (as it would if the economic was the *sole determinant factor*), for they have sufficient of their own consistency *to survive beyond their immediate life context*, even to recreate, to 'secrete' substitute conditions of existence temporarily; (2) that the new society produced by the Revolution may itself *ensure the survival, that is, the reactivation, of older elements* through both the forms of its new superstructures and specific (national and international) 'circumstances'. Such a reactivition would be totally inconceivable for a dialectic deprived of overdetermination. I shall not evade the most burning issue: it seems to me that either the whole logic of 'supersession' must be rejected, or we must give up any attempt to explain how the proud and generous Russian people bore Stalin's crimes and repression with such resignation; how the Bolshevik Party could tolerate them; not to speak of the final question – how a Communist leader could have ordered them. But there is obviously much *theoretical* work needed here as well. By this I mean more than the historical work which has priority – precisely because of this priority, priority is given to one essential of any Marxist historical study: *rigour; a rigorous conception of Marxist concepts, their implications and their development; a rigorous conception and investigation of what appertains to them in particular, that is, what distinguishes them once and for all from their phantoms.*

One phantom is more especially crucial than any other today: the shade of Hegel. To drive this phantom back into the night we need *a little more light on Marx*, or what is the same thing, *a little more Marxist light on Hegel himself.* We can then escape from the ambiguities and confusions of the 'inversion'.

June–July 1962

Appendix[*]

I should like to stop here for a moment to examine a passage from Engels's letter to Bloch that I deliberately ignored in the preceding article. For this passage, containing Engels's theoretical *solution* to the problem of the basis for the determination 'in the last instance' by the economy, is, in fact, *independent* of the Marxist theses that Engels was counterposing to 'economist' dogmatism.

No doubt this is only a letter. But as it constitutes a *decisive* theoretical document for the refutation of schematism and economism, and as it has already played a *historical* role as such and may well do so again, we should not conceal the fact that his argument for this *basis* will no longer answer to our critical needs.

In his solution, Engels resorts to *a single model* at two different levels of analysis:

First Level

Engels has just shown that the superstructures, far from being pure phenomena of the economy, have their own effectivity: '*The various elements of the superstructure . . . in many cases preponderate in determining their* (the historical struggles') *form.*' But this poses the question as to how, under these conditions, we should think the *unity* of this real, but relative effectivity of the superstructures – and of the determinant

[*] This *Appendix* to the article 'Contradiction and Overdetermination' is published here for the first time. Engels's letter to Bloch is dated 21 September 1890 (Marx–Engels, *Selected Works*, Vol. II, pp. 488–90).

principle '*in the last instance*' of the economy? How should we think the relation between these distinct effectivities? What *basis* is there within this unity for the *role* of the economic as a 'last instance'? Engels's reply is that '*There is an interaction of all these elements (the superstructures) in which, amid all the endless host of accidents (that is, of things and events, whose inner connexion is so remote or so impossible of proof that we can regard it as non-existent, as negligible) the economic movement finally asserts itself as necessary.*' So the explanatory model goes like this: '*the various elements of the superstructure*' act and react on one another to produce an *infinity* of effects. These effects can be assimilated to an infinity of *accidents* (infinite in number and with an *inner connexion* so remote and therefore so difficult to discover that it is *negligible*), amid which '*the economic movement*' asserts itself. These effects are *accidents*, the economic movement is *necessity*, *their necessity*. For the moment I shall ignore the accidents–necessity *model* and its presuppositions. What is remarkable in this text is *the role it attributes* to the different elements of the superstructure. It is just as if, once the *action–reaction* system was set in motion between them, they were charged with finding a *basis for the infinite diversity of effects* (things and events, as Engels puts it) between which, as if between so many accidents, the economy picks its sovereign way. In other words, the elements of the superstructure do have an effectivity, but this effectivity is *in some way dispersed into an infinity*, into the infinity of effects, of accidents, whose inner connexion may, once this extremity in the infinitesimal has been reached, be regarded as *non-existent*. So the effect of this infinitesimal dispersion is to *dissipate* the effectivity granted the superstructures in their *macroscopic* existence *into a microscopic non-existence*. Of course, this non-existence is *epistemological* ('*we can regard*' the microscopic connexion '*as non-existent*' – it is not said to be non-existent, but it is non-existent for *knowledge*). But whatever the case, within this infinitesimal microscopic diversity the macroscopic necessity '*finally asserts itself*', that is, finally prevails.

Two comments should be made here.

First comment: This schema does not give us a *true solution*, but an elaboration of *one part* of the solution. We learn that in their mutual action–reaction the superstructures cash their effectivity as

infinitesimal '*things and events*', that is, as so many 'accidents'. We
see that the solution must be *based at the level* of these accidents, since
their object is to introduce the counter-concept of the (economic)
necessity which is determinant in the last instance. But this is only a
half-solution since the relation between *these accidents* and *this necessity* is neither established nor made explicit; since (in what is really a
denial of the relation and the problem posed by it) Engels presents
even *this necessity* as completely *external* to these accidents (as a
movement which finally asserts itself *amid* an infinity of accidents).
But if this is so then we do not know *whether this necessity is really the
necessity of these accidents, and, if it is, why it is*. This question is left
unanswered.

   Second comment: It is astonishing to find Engels in this text presenting the *forms of the superstructure* as the source of a microscopic
infinity of events whose inner connexion is unintelligible (and therefore negligible). For, on the one hand, we could say exactly the same
of the forms of the infrastructure (and it is quite true that the detail of
microscopic economic events might be said to be unintelligible and
negligible!). But, more important, these *forms* as such are certainly
forms as *principles of reality*, but they are also forms as *principles of
the intelligibility of their effects*. For their part they are perfectly *knowable*, and in this respect they are the transparent reason of the *events*
that derive from them. How could Engels pass so rapidly over these
forms, their essence and their role, and only consider the negligible
and unintelligible microscopic dust of their effects? More precisely,
is this *reduction* to a dust of accidents not *absolutely opposed* to the
real and *epistemological* function of these forms? And since Engels
invokes it, what else did Marx do in the *Eighteenth Brumaire* than give
an analysis of the action and reaction of these 'different factors'? a
perfectly intelligible analysis of *their effects*? But Marx was only able
to perform this 'proof' because he did not confuse the *historical effects*
of these factors with *their microscopic effects*. The forms of the superstructures are indeed the cause of an infinity of events, but not all
these events are *historical* (cf. Voltaire's remark that all children have
fathers, but not all 'fathers' have children), only those of them that
the said 'factors' *retain*, *select* from among the others, in short, *produce*

as such (to take just one case: every politician in government makes a *choice* among events according to his *policies* and also his *means*, and *promotes the chosen ones to the rank of historical events*, even if it is only, for example, by suppressing a demonstration!). So, to sum up, on this *first level*: (1) we have not yet been given a true solution; (2) 'cashing' the effectivity of the forms of the *superstructure* (which is all that is in question here) as an infinity of microscopic effects (unintelligible accidents) does not correspond to the Marxist conception of the *nature* of the superstructures.

Second Level

And, in fact, at the second level of his analysis we find Engels *abandoning* the case of the superstructures and applying his model to another object which *does* this time correspond to it: the combination of individual wills. We also find that he answers the question by giving us *the relation* between the accidents and the necessity, that is *by finding a basis for it. 'History is made in such a way that the final result always arises from conflicts between many individual wills, of which each again has been made what it is by a host of particular conditions of life. Thus there are innumerable intersecting forces, an infinite series of parallelograms of forces which give rise to one resultant – the historical event. This may again itself be viewed as the product of a power which works as a whole, unconsciously and without volition. For what each individual wills is obstructed by everyone else, and what emerges is something that no one willed. Thus past history proceeds in the manner of a natural process and is essentially subject to the same laws of motion. But from the fact that individual wills – of which each desires what he is impelled to by his physical constitution and external, in the last resort economic, circumstances (either his own personal circumstances or those of society in general) – do not attain what they want, but are merged into a collective mean, a common resultant, it must not be concluded that their value is equal to zero. On the contrary, each contributes to the resultant and is to this degree involved in it.'*

I apologize for this long quotation, but I had to give it in full as it provides the answer to our question. Here indeed, the necessity is *established at the level of the accidents themselves, on the accidents them-selves,* as *their* global resultant: so it really is *their necessity.* The answer missing from the first analysis *we really are given here.* But on what condition do we get it? On condition that we *change objects,* that our starting-point is no longer the superstructures, their interaction and ultimately their microscopic effects – but *individual wills, confronted and combined in relations of forces.* So it is as if the *model* applied to the effectivity of the superstructures had really been *borrowed* from its *true* object, the object we are now dealing with: *the play of individual wills.* It is now clear why it failed with its first object, for that was not its real object, and why it should go on to a second, *which is its real object.*

How, then, does this proof work? It relies on the model of a *paral-lelogram of forces* derived from physics: the wills are so many forces; if they confront one another by twos in a simple situation their result-ant is a *third force,* different from either but none the less common to both, and such that though neither can *recognize itself* in the third, each is none the less a party to it, that is, its co-author. So one basic phenomenon appears straightaway, the *transcendence of the resultant* with respect to the component forces: a double transcendence, in relation to the respective size of the component forces – and in rela-tion to the reflection of these forces on themselves (that is, to their consciousness, since we are dealing with *wills*). Which implies: (1) that the resultant is quite different in size from each force by itself (higher if they add together, lower if they oppose each other); (2) that the resultant is, in essence, *unconscious* (it does not correspond to the consciousness of each will – and at the same time, it is a *force without a subject,* an objective force, but, from the outset *nobody's force*). That is why it immediately becomes the global resultant that may be '*viewed as the product of a power which works as a whole, unconsciously and with-out volition*'. It is clear that we have now found a *basis* and an *origin* for this force that triumphs *in the last* instance: determination by the economy is no longer external to the accidents amid which it asserts itself, it is the *internal essence* of these accidents.

I hope to be able to show: (1) that we are now dealing with the *true object* of Engels's *model*; (2) that thanks to this readjustment, Engels has really provided *the* solution to *the* problem he raised; (3) that problem and solution only exist as a function of the adequacy of the model to its *object*; (4) that, as this object does not exist, neither *the problem* nor *the solution* exist; (5) that we must find some reason for this whole futile construction.

I am quite prepared to ignore Engels's reference to *nature*. As the model he has used is itself *physical* (the earliest example of the type can be found in Hobbes and then in innumerable later versions, of which Holbach's is noteworthy as a particularly pure case), there is nothing surprising in the fact that it refers us from history to *nature*. This is not a proof, it is a tautology. (Note that this is merely a matter of the *model* used and that the *dialectic of nature* is obviously not at stake in this exposition, for the very good reason that it arises in a quite different context.) Epistemologically, a tautology is null and void; but it may nevertheless have a *heuristic* role. It is reassuring to be able to refer directly to *nature*, to be sure. (Hobbes said it long ago: men tear out their hair or their lives over politics, but they are as thick as thieves over the hypotenuse or falling bodies.)

It is Engels's argument itself that I should like to examine very closely, the argument which seems at first sight to achieve such a perfect harmony between *the model and its object*. But what do we find? A harmony between model and object at the *immediate* level. But beneath (*en deça*) this level and beyond (*au dela*), this harmony is *postulated*, not *proved*, and in its place we find an *indeterminancy*, that is, from the point of view of knowledge, a void.

Beneath the level of individual wills. The transparency of content which strikes us when we imagine the parallelogram of forces (of individual wills) disappears once we ask (as Engels does himself!) about the origin (and therefore about the cause) of the *determinations* of these individual wills. For we are *referred to infinity*. '*Each . . . has been made what it is by a host of particular conditions of life.*' Each individual will may be simple when it is considered as an absolute beginning, but it becomes the product of an infinity of microscopic circumstances arising from its '*physical constitution*' and '*external circumstances*', its '*own personal circumstances*' '*or*' '*those of society in general*', the external circumstances which are '*in the last resort economic*', and all these thrown together so that side by side with

purely contingent and peculiar determinations we *also* find general
determinations (in particular, *the one we are discussing*: the economic
circumstances which are determinant in the last resort). It is clear that
here Engels is mixing up two types of explanation.

The First Type: a non-Marxist type, but one *adapted to its present
object* and to its hypotheses, viz., explanation by *the infinity of
circumstances* or accidents (this form can be found in Helvetius and
Holbach): such explanation may have a critical value (to the extent
that it is destined, as was already the case in the eighteenth century,
to refute divine intervention, among other things), but from the point
of view of knowledge it is *empty*. It puts forward an infinity without
content, an abstract and hardly even programmatic generalization.

The Second Type: However, *at the same time*, Engels introduces a
Marxist type of *explanation*, when he ranks among the infinite circumstances (which are in essence microscopic) those determinations
which are at once both *general* and *concrete*, viz., *social* circumstances
and *economic* circumstances (which are determinant in the last resort).
But this type of explanation *does not answer to its object*, since it represents at the beginning *the very solution* which it is supposed to be
producing and *establishing* (the generation of this determination in
the last resort). To sum up: either we stay with the object and the
problem which Engels has posed, in which case we come face to face
with the infinite, the indeterminate (and therefore with an epistemological void); or from this moment we take as the beginning itself the
(content-ful) solution which is precisely what is *in question*. But then
we are no longer *either in the object or in the problem*.

Beyond the level of individual wills. We find ourselves confronted
by the same alternatives. For, once the first parallelogram is given, we
only have a formal resultant, which is not equivalent to the definitive
resultant. The definitive resultant will be the resultant of an infinity
of resultants, that is, the product of an infinite proliferation of parallelograms. Once again, either we trust to the infinite (that is, the
indeterminate, epistemological void) for the production in the final
resultant of *the* resultant we are hoping to *deduce*: the one that will
coincide with economic determination in the last instance, etc., that is,
we trust a void to produce a fullness (for example, within the limits of the

purely *formal* model of the composition of forces, it does not escape Engels that the said forces present might cancel one another out, or oppose one another . . . under such conditions, what is there to prove that the global resultant might not be *nothing*, for example, or at any rate, what is there to prove that *it will be what we want, the economic*, and not something else, politics, or religion? At this formal level *there is no assurance of any kind as to the content of the resultant, of any* result-ant). Or we surreptitiously *substitute the result we expect for the final resultant*, and duly rediscover in it, along with other, microscopic determinations, the macroscopic determinations which were secreted in the conditioning of the individual at the outset; this expected result, these macroscopic determinations will be the economy. I am obliged to repeat what I have just said of what was beneath the immediate level: either we stay within the *problem* Engels poses for his object (individual wills), in which case we fall into the epistemological void of the infinity of parallelograms and their resultants; or else, quite simply, we *accept* the Marxist solution, but then we have found no *basis* for it, and it was not worth the trouble of *looking for it*.

So the problem we face now is this: why is everything so clear and harmonious at the level of *individual wills*, whereas *beneath this level* or *beyond it*, it all becomes either empty or tautological? How is it that this problem, so *well posed*, corresponding so well to *the object* in which it is posed, should become incapable of solution as soon as we *move away* from its initial object? A question which must remain the riddle of riddles until we realize that it is *this initial object* which commands both *the transparency of the problem and the impossibility of its solution*.

Indeed, Engels's whole proof hangs by that very particular *object, individual wills* interrelated according to the physical model of the parallelogram of forces. *This is his real presupposition, both in method and in theory*. In this respect the model does have meaning: it can be given a *content*, it can be *manipulated*. It 'describes' apparently 'elementary' bilateral human relations of rivalry, competition or co-operation. At this level what was previously the infinite diversity of microscopic causes might seem to be organized in real, and discrete, and visible unities. At this level accident becomes man, what

was movement above becomes conscious will. This is where everything really begins, and it is from this point that *deduction* must begin.
But unfortunately this so secure basis establishes nothing at all, this
so clear principle merely leads to darkness – unless it withdraws into
itself, reiterating *its own transparency* as a fixed proof of all that is
expected of it. Precisely what is *this transparency*? We must recognize
that *this transparency is nothing but the transparency of the presuppositions
of classical bourgeois ideology and bourgeois political economy*. What is
the starting-point for this classical ideology, whether it is Hobbes on
the composition of the conatus, Locke and Rousseau on the generation
of the general will, Helvetius and Holbach on the production of the
general interest, Smith and Ricardo (the texts abound) on atomistic
behaviour, what is the starting-point if not precisely the confrontation
of these famous *individual wills* which are by no means the starting-
point for reality, but for a *representation* of reality, for a *myth* intended
to provide a *basis* (for all eternity) in nature (that is, for all eternity)
for *the objectives* of the bourgeoisie? When Marx had so thoroughly
criticized *the myth of the* homo œconomicus *in this explicit presupposition*, how could Engels return to it so naïvely on his own account?
How, if not by a fiction quite as optimistic as the fiction of bourgeois
economics, a fiction closer to Locke and Rousseau than to Marx,
could he suggest to us that the resultant of all the individual wills, and
the resultant of these resultants, actually has a *general content*, really
embodies determination *by the economy in the last instance* (I am thinking of Rousseau, whose dearest wish was that the particular wills, cut
off from one another, might come together in a fair vote, producing
that miraculous Minerva, the general will!). The ideologues of the
eighteenth century (with the exception of Rousseau) did not demand
that their presupposition should produce *anything but itself*. They just
asked that it should provide a basis for *the values already embodied* in
the presupposition, and that is why *the tautology did have a meaning
for them*, but one obviously denied Engels, who, for his part, hoped to
discover the exact opposite of the presupposition.

   This is why, in his own text, Engels ultimately reduces his own
claims almost to nothing. What is there left of his schema, his 'proof'?
Just the one expression, that given the whole system of resultants,

the final resultant does contain something of the original individual wills: '*each contributes to the resultant and is to this degree involved in it*'. This is a thought which *in a quite different context* might *reassure* minds uncertain of their grasp on history, or, given that God is dead, uncertain of the recognition of their historical personality. I would go so far as to say that it is a desperate, honest thought which nourishes despair, that is, hopes. (It is no accident that Sartre, basing himself on Engels's 'question', on the question of the 'basis' for and genesis of the necessity of history, should *pursue the same object*, with arguments which are equally philosophical, *while of quite different inspiration*.)

What have we left now? One sentence in which *the final result-ant* is no longer long-term economic determination, but '*the historical event*'. So individual wills produce *historical events*! But a closer look shows that strictly speaking we can only admit that the schema gives us *the possibility of an event* (some men confront one another: some-thing must *happen*, or nothing, which is also an event – waiting for Godot), but *absolutely not the possibility of a historical event*, absolutely not the reason that will distinguish a *historical* event as such from the infinity of things which *happen* to men day and night, things which are as anonymous as they are unique. The problem must be put the *other way round* (for once!), or rather, *in a different way*. It is never possible to explain a *historical* event – not even by invoking the law which makes quantity pass over into quality – *if one proposes to derive it from the (indefinite) possibility of non-historical events*. What makes *such and such* an event *historical* is not the fact that it is an *event*, but precisely its *insertion into forms which are themselves historical*, into forms which have nothing to do with the bad infinity which Engels retains even when he has left the vicinity of his original model, forms which, on the contrary, are perfectly *definable* and *knowable* (knowable, Marx insisted, and Lenin after him, through empirical, that is, non-philo-sophical, scientific disciplines). An event falling within one of these forms, which has the wherewithal to fall within one of these forms, *which is a possible content for one of these forms*, which affects them, concerns them, reinforces or disturbs them, which provokes them or which they provoke, or even choose or select, that is a *historical event*. So it is these forms which command the whole, which already contained the answer to Engels's *false* problem — whose solution, it must be admitted, he could never have reached, since there was never any *other problem* than the one he posed on the basis of purely *ideological* presuppositions — since it never was *a problem*!

Of course, once again, there had certainly been the semblance of a problem for *bourgeois ideology*: to rediscover the world of history on the basis of *principles* (the *homo œconomicus* and his *political* and *philosophical* avatars) which, far from being principles of scientific explanation, were, on the contrary, merely a projection of its own *image of the world*, its own aspirations, its own *ideal* programme (a world which would be reducible to its essence: the conscious will of individuals, their actions and their private undertakings ...). But once this ideology, without which *this* particular problem could not have been posed, had been swept aside by Marx, how could this problem still remain *the* problem posed by this ideology, that is, how could it still remain *a problem*?

To close this too lengthy commentary, allow me two more remarks: one epistemological; the other historical.

It should be noted, *vis-à-vis* Engels's *model*, that every scientific discipline is based *at a certain level*, precisely that level at which *its concepts find a content* (without which they are the concepts of nothing, that is, they are not concepts). Such is the level of Marx's *historical theory*: the level of the concepts of *structure, superstructure and all their specification*. But if *the same scientific discipline* should set out from *another level than its own*, from a level which is not the object of *any scientific knowledge* (such as, in our case, the genesis of individual wills from the infinity of circumstances and the genesis of the final resultant from the infinity of parallelograms ...), to produce *the possibility of its own object and of the concepts corresponding to it*, then it will fall into an *epistemological void*, or, and this is what gives it its vertigo, into a *philosophical fullness*. This is the fate of the search for a *basis* Engels undertook in his letter to Bloch: and we find it impossible to distinguish in it between the epistemological void and the philosophical vertigo, since they are nothing but *one and the same thing*. Precisely this passage, with its arguments borrowed from the kinds of model used in the natural sciences (and ultimately this is their only *precaution*, a purely *moral* one), Engels is merely a *philosopher*. His use of a reference 'model' is philosophical. I insist on this point deliberately, for there is a more recent example of the same kind, that of Sartre, who also tries to find a *philosophical* basis for the epistemological concepts of historical materialism (he has one advantage over Engels in this respect, he *knows* it and *says so*). It is enough to refer to certain pages from the *Critique de la raison dialectique* (for example, pp. 68–9) to see that if Sartre rejects Engels's answer and his arguments, he basically approves of the *attempt itself*. All that separates them is a quarrel over the means employed, but on this point they are united in the same *philosophical* task. It is only possible to bar Sartre from his path by closing the one Engels opened for him.

But this makes it necessary to pose the problem of the philosophical leanings which can be detected in certain of Engels's writings. Why beside genial theoretical intuitions do we find in Engels examples of this step backwards from the Marxist critique of all '*philosophy*'? This question could only be answered by a history of the relations between Marxist thought and 'philosophy', and of the new philosophical theory (in the non-ideological sense) which Marx's discovery brought with it. Obviously, I cannot enter into this problem here. But perhaps we have to be convinced of the existence of the problem before we will find either the will or the way to *pose* it correctly and then resolve it.

Part Four

The 'Piccolo Teatro': Bertolazzi and Brecht

NOTES ON A MATERIALIST THEATRE

I should like to make amends to the *Piccolo Teatro* of Milan and their extraordinary production at the *Théatre des Nations* in July 1962. Amends for the condemnation and disappointment that Bertolazzi's *El Nost Milan* drew so copiously from Parisian criticism,[1] depriving it of the audiences it deserved. Amends, because, far from diverting our attention from the problems of modern dramaturgy with tired, anachronistic entertainment, Strehler's choice and his production take us to the heart of these problems.

*

Readers will forgive me if I give a brief summary of the plot of Bertolazzi's play, so that what follows can be understood.[2]

The first of its three acts is set in the Milan Tivoli in the 1890s: a cheap, poverty-stricken fun-fair in the thick fog of an autumn evening. With this fog we already find ourselves in an Italy unlike the Italy of our myths. And the people strolling at day's end from booth to booth, between the fortune-tellers, the circus and all the attractions of the

---

1 'Epic melodrama' . . . 'Poor popular theatre' . . . 'Noxious Central European Miserabilism' . . . 'Tear jerker' . . . 'detestable sentimentalism' . . . 'Worn out old shoe' . . . 'A Piaf croon' . . . 'Miserabilist melodrama, realist excess' (comments drawn from *Parisien-libéré*, *Combat*, *Figaro*, *Libération*, *Paris-Presse*, *Le Monde*).

2 Bertolazzi was a late nineteenth-century Milanese playwright who achieved no more than moderate success – no doubt because of his obstinate persistence in '*verismo*' of a style odd enough to displease the public which then set 'theatrical taste': the bourgeois public.

fairground: unemployed, artisans, semi-beggars, girls on the look-out, old men and women on the watch for the odd halfpenny, soldiers on a spree, pickpockets chased by the cops ... neither are these people the people of our myths, they are a sub-proletariat passing the time as best they can before supper (not for all of them) and rest. A good thirty characters who come and go in this empty space, waiting for who knows what, for something to happen, the show perhaps? – no, for they stop at the doorway, waiting for something of some sort to happen in their lives, in which nothing happens. They wait. However, at the end of the act, in a flash a 'story' is sketched out, the image of a destiny. A girl, Nina, stands transfixed by the lights of the circus, staring with all her heart through a rent in the canvas at the clown performing his peril- ous act. Night has fallen. For one moment, time is in suspense. But she is already being watched by the Togasso, the good-for-nothing who hopes to seduce her. A quick defiance, retreat, departure. Now an old man appears, the 'fire-eater', her father, and he has seen everything. Something has taken shape, which might turn into a tragedy.

A tragedy? It is completely forgotten in the second act. It is broad day in the spacious premises of a cheap eating-house. Here again we find a whole crowd of poor people, the same people but different char- acters: the same poverty and unemployment, the flotsam of the past, the tragedies and comedies of the present: small craftsmen, beggars, a cabman, a Garibaldian veteran, some women, etc. Also a few workers who are building a factory, in sharp contrast with their lumpenpro- letarian surroundings: they are already discussing industry, politics, and, almost, the future, but only just and with difficulty. This is Milan from below, twenty years after the conquest of Rome and the deeds of the Risorgimento: King and Pope are on their thrones, the masses are in poverty. Yes, the day of the second act is indeed the truth of the night of the first: these people have no more history in their lives than they had in their dreams. They survive, that is all: they eat (only the workers depart, called by the factory hooter), they eat and wait. A life in which nothing happens. Then, just at the end of the act, Nina re- appears on the stage, for no apparent reason, and with her the tragedy. We learn that the clown is dead. The men and women leave the stage little by little. The Togasso appears, he forces the girl to kiss him and give him what little money she has. Hardly more than a few gestures. Her father arrives. (Nina is weeping at the end of the long table.) He does not eat: he drinks. After a terrible struggle he succeeds in killing the Togasso with a knife and then flees, haggard, overwhelmed by what he has done. Once again a lightning flash after a long grind.

In the third act it is dawn in the women's night shelter. Old women, blending into the walls, sitting down, talk or stay silent. One stout peasant woman, bursting with health, will certainly return to the country. Some women pass; as always, we do not know them. The lady warden leads her whole company to Mass when the bells ring. When the stage has emptied, the tragedy begins again. Nina was sleeping in the shelter. Her father comes to see her for the last time before prison: she must realize at least that he killed for her sake, for her honour ... but suddenly everything is reversed: Nina turns on her father, on the illusions and lies he has fed her, on the myths which will kill him. But not her; for she is going to rescue herself, all alone, for that is the only way. She will leave this world of night and poverty and enter the other one, where pleasure and money reign. The Togasso was right. She will pay the price, she will sell herself, but she will be on the other side, on the side of freedom and truth. The hooters sound. Her father has embraced her and departed, a broken man. The hooters still sound. Erect, Nina goes out into the daylight.

*

There are the themes of this play and the order in which they appear, pressed into a few words. Altogether not much. Enough, however, to foster misunderstandings, but also enough to clear them up, and discover beneath them an astonishing depth.

The first of these misunderstandings is, of course, the accusation that the play is a '*mélodrame misérabiliste*'. But anyone who has 'lived' the performance or studied its economy can demolish this charge. For if it does contain melodramatic elements, as a whole, the drama is simply a criticism of them. Nina's father does indeed live his daughter's story in the melodramatic mode, and not just his daughter's adventure, but above all his own life in his relations with his daughter. He has invented for her the fiction of an imaginary condition, and encouraged her in

her romantic illusions; he tries desperately to give flesh and blood to
the illusions he has fostered in his daughter: as he wishes to keep her
free from all contact with the world he has hidden from her, and as,
desperate that she will not listen to him, he kills the source of Evil, the
Togasso. So he lives intensively and really the myths he has constructed
to spare his daughter from the law of this world. So the father is the
very image of melodrama, of the 'law of the heart' deluding itself as
to the 'law of the world'. It is precisely this deliberate unconsciousness
that Nina rejects. She makes her own real trial of the world. With the
clown's death her adolescent dreams have died too. The Togasso has
opened her eyes and dispatched her childhood myths along with her
father's. His violence itself has freed her from words and duties. She has
at last seen this naked, cruel world where morality is nothing but a lie;
she has realized that her safety lies in her own hands and that she can
only reach the other world by selling the only goods at her disposal: her
young body. The great confrontation at the end of the third act is more
than a confrontation between Nina and her father, it is the confrontation of a world without illusions with the wretched illusions of the
'heart', it is the confrontation of the real world with the melodramatic
world, the dramatic access to consciousness that destroys the myths of
melodrama, the very myths that Bertolazzi and Strehler are charged
with. Those who make this charge could quite easily have found in the
play the criticism they tried to address to it from the stalls.

But there is another, deeper reason that should clear up this misunderstanding. I was trying to hint at it in my summary of the play's
'sequence', when I pointed out its strange 'temporal' rhythm.

For this is, indeed, a play remarkable for its internal dissociation.
The reader will have noted that its three acts have the same structure,
and almost the same content: the coexistence of a long, slowly-pass-
ing, empty time and a lightning-short, full time; the coexistence of
a space populated by a crowd of characters whose mutual relations
are accidental or episodic – and a short space, gripped in mortal
combat, inhabited by three characters: the father, the daughter and
the Togasso. In other words, this is a play in which about forty characters appear, but the tragedy concerns only three of them. Moreover,
there is no *explicit* relationship between these two times or between

these two spaces. The characters of the time seem strangers to the characters of the lightning: they regularly give place to them (as if the thunder of the storm had chased them from the stage), only to return in the next act, in other guises, once the instant foreign to their rhythm has passed. If we deepen the latent meaning of this dissociation it will lead us to the heart of the play. For the spectator actually lives this deepening as he moves from disconcerted reserve to astonishment and then passionate involvement between the first and the third acts. My aim here is merely to reflect this lived deepening, to make explicit this latent meaning which affects the spectator despite himself. But the decisive question is this: why is it that this dissociation is so expressive, and what does it express? What is this absence of relations to suggest a latent relation as its basis and justification? How can there coexist two forms of temporality, apparently foreign to one another and yet united by a lived relationship?

The answer lies in a paradox: the true relationship is constituted precisely by the absence of relations. The play's success in illustrating this absence of relations and bringing it to life gives it its originality. In short, I do not think we are dealing with a melodramatic veneer on a chronicle of Milanese popular life in 1890. We are dealing with a melodramatic consciousness criticized by an existence: the existence of the Milanese sub-proletariat in 1890. With out this existence it would be impossible to tell what the melodramatic consciousness was; without this critique of the melodramatic consciousness it would be impossible to grasp the tragedy latent in the existence of the Milanese sub-proletariat: its powerlessness. What is the significance of the chronicle of wretched existence that makes up the essential part of the three acts? Why is this chronicle's time a march-past of purely typed, anonymous and interchangeable beings? Why is this time of vague meetings, brief exchanges and broached disputes precisely an empty time? In its progress from the first act through the second to the third, why does this time tend towards silence and immobility? (In the first act there is still a semblance of life and movement on the stage; in the second, everyone is sitting down and some are already lapsing into silence; in the third, the old women blend into the walls.) Why – if not to suggest the actual content of this wretched time: it is a time in which nothing happens, a time without hope or future, a time in which even the past is fixed in repetition (the Garibaldian veteran) and the future is hardly groped for in the political stammerings of the labourers building the factory, a time in which gestures have no continuation or effect, in which everything is summed up in a few exchanges close to life, to 'everyday life', in discussions and disputes which are either abortive or reduced to nothingness by a consciousness of their futility.[3] In a word, a stationary time in which nothing resembling History can yet happen, an empty time, accepted as empty: the time of their situation itself.

I know of nothing so masterly in this respect as the setting for the second act, because it gives us precisely *a direct perception of this time*. In the first act it was still possible to wonder whether the waste land of the Tivoli only harmonized with the nonchalance of the unemployed and idlers who saunter between the few illusions and few fascinating lights at the end of the day. In the second act it is overwhelmingly obvious that the empty, closed cube of this cheap restaurant is an image of time in these men's situation. At the bottom of the worn surface of an immense wall, and almost at the limit of an inaccessible ceiling covered with notices of regulations half effaced by the years but still legible, we see two enormously long tables, parallel to the footlights, one downstage, the other mid-stage; behind them, up against the wall, a horizontal iron bar dividing off the entrance to the restaurant. This is the way the men and women will come in. Far right, a high partition perpendicular to the line of the tables separates the hall from the kitchens. Two hatches, one for alcohol, the other for food. Behind the screen, the kitchens, steaming pots, and the imperturbable cook. The bareness of this immense field, created by the parallel tables against the interminable background of the wall, constitutes an unbearably austere and yawning location. A few men are seated at the tables. Here and there. Facing the audience, or with their backs to them. They will talk face on or backwards, just as they are sitting. In a space which is too large for them, a space they will

---

3   There is a whole tacit conspiracy among these poor folk to separate quarrellers, to circumvent unbearable pains, such as those of the unemployed young couple, to reduce all the troubles and disturbances of this life to its truth: to silence, immobility and nothingness.

never be able to fill. Here they will make their derisory exchanges, but however often they leave their places in an attempt to join some chance neighbour, who has tossed them a proposal across tables and benches, they will never abolish tables or benches, which will always cut them off from each other, under the inalterable, silent regulation that dominates them. This space is really the time they live in. One man here, another there. Strehler has scattered them around. They will stay where they are. Eating, pausing in their meal, eating again. At these times, the gestures themselves reveal all their meaning. The character seen face-on at the beginning of the scene, his head hardly higher than the plate he would prefer to carry between his two hands. The time it takes him to fill his spoon, to lift it up to his mouth and over it, in an interminable movement designed to ensure that not one scrap is lost, and when at last he has filled his mouth, he lingers over his portion weighing it up before swallowing it. Then we see that the others with their backs to us are making the same movements: their raised elbows compensating for their unstable backs – we see them eating, absently, like all the other absent people, making the same holy movements in Milan and in all the world's great cities, because that is the whole of their lives, and there is nothing which would make it possible for them to live out their time otherwise. (The only ones with an air of haste are the labourers, their life and work punctuated by the hooters.) I can think of no comparable representation in spatial structure, in the distribution of men and places, of the deep relations between men and the time they live.

Now for the essential point: this temporal structure – that of the 'chronicle' – is opposed to another temporal structure: that of the 'tragedy'. For the tragedy's time (Nina) is full: a few lightning-flashes, an articulated time, a 'dramatic' time. A time in which some history must take place. A time moved from within by an irresistible force, producing its own content. It is a dialectical time *par excellence*. A time that abolishes the other time and the structure of its spatial representation. When the men have left the restaurant, and only Nina, her father and the Togasso are left, something has suddenly disappeared: as if the diners had taken the whole *décor* with them (Strehler's stroke of genius: to have made two acts one, and played two different acts *in the same décor*), the very space of walls and tables, the logic and meaning of these locations; as if conflict alone substituted for this visible and empty space another dense, invisible, irreversible space, with one dimension, the dimension that propels it towards tragedy, ultimately, the dimension that had to propel it into tragedy if there was really to be any tragedy.

It is precisely this opposition that gives Bertolazzi's play its depth. On the one hand, a non-dialectical time in which nothing happens, a time with no internal necessity forcing it into action; on the other, a dialectical time (that of conflict) induced by its internal contradiction to produce its development and result. The paradox of *El Nost Milan* is that the dialectic in it is acted marginally, so to speak, in the wings, somewhere in one corner of the stage and at the ends of the acts: this dialectic (although it does seem to be indispensable to any theatrical work) is a long time coming: the characters could not care less about it. It takes its time, and never arrives until the end, initially at night, when the air is heavy with the renowned night-owls, then as midday strikes, with the sun already on its descent, finally as dawn rises. This dialectic always appears after everyone has departed.

How is the 'delay' of this dialectic to be understood? Is it delayed in the way consciousness is for Marx and Hegel? But can a dialectic be delayed? Only on condition that it is another name for consciousness.

If the dialectic of *El Nost Milan* is acted in the wings, in one corner of the stage, it is because it is nothing but the dialectic of a consciousness: the dialectic of Nina's father and his consciousness. And that is why its destruction is the precondition for any real dialectic. Here we should recall Marx's analyses in *The Holy Family* of Eugène Sue's personages.[4] The motor of their dramatic conduct is their

---

4   Marx's book (*The Holy Family*, English translation, Moscow, 1956) contains no explicit definition of melodrama. But it does tell us its genesis, with Sue as its eloquent witness.

(*a*)   The *Mystères de Paris* present morality and religion as a *veneer* on 'natural' beings ('natural' despite their poverty or disgrace). What efforts have gone into this veneer! It needed Rodolphe's cynicism, the priest's moral blackmail, the paraphernalia of police, prison, internment, etc. Finally 'nature' gives in: a foreign consciousness will henceforth govern it (and catastrophes multiply to guarantee its salvation).

(*b*)   The origin of this 'veneer' is obvious: it is Rodolphe who imposes this borrowed consciousness on these 'innocents'. Rodolphe neither comes

identification with the myths of bourgeois morality: these unfortunates live their misery within the arguments of a religious and moral conscience; in borrowed finery. In it they disguise their problems and even their condition. In this sense, melodrama is a foreign consciousness as a veneer on a real condition. The dialectic of the melodramatic consciousness is only possible at this price: this consciousness must be borrowed from outside (from the world of alibis, sublimations and lies of bourgeois morality), and it must still be lived as *the* consciousness of a condition (that of the poor) even though this condition is radically foreign to the consciousness. It follows that between the melodramatic consciousness on the one hand, and the existence of the characters of the melodrama on the other, there can exist no *contradiction* strictly speaking. The melodramatic consciousness is not

---

from the 'people', nor is he 'innocent'. But (naturally) he wants to 'save' the people, to teach them that they have souls, that God exists, etc. – in other words, whether they will or no he gives them bourgeois morality to parrot so as to keep them quiet.

(*c*) It can be inferred (cf. *The Holy Family*, p. 242; 'Eugène Sue's personages ... must express as the result of their *own* thoughts the conscious motive of their acts, the reason why the writer makes them behave in a certain way and no other') that Sue's novel is the admission of his own project: to give the 'people' a literary myth which will be both the propaedeutic for the consciousness they must have, and the consciousness they must have to be the people (i.e. 'saved', i.e. subordinate, paralysed and drugged, in a word moral and religious). It could not be more bluntly put that it was the bourgeoisie itself that invented for the people the popular myth of the melodrama, that proposed or imposed it (serials in the popular Press, cheap 'novels') just as it was the bourgeoisie that 'gave' them night shelters, soup-kitchens, etc.: in short, a fairly deliberate system of preventive charities.

(*d*) All the same, it is entertaining to witness the majority of established critics pretending to be disgusted by melodrama! As if in them the bourgeoisie had *forgotten* that melodrama was its own invention! But, in all honesty, we must admit that the invention dated quickly: the myths and charities handed out to the 'people' are otherwise organized today, and more ingeniously. We must also accept that at heart it was an invention for others, and it is certainly very disconcerting to see your own works sitting squarely at your right hand for all to see – or parading unashamedly on your own stages! Is it conceivable, for example, that the romantic Press (the popular 'myth' of recent times) should be invited to the spiritual concert of ruling ideas? We must not mix ranks.

contradictory to these conditions: it is a quite different consciousness, imposed from without on a determinate condition but without any dialectical relation to it. That is why the melodramatic consciousness can only be dialectical if it ignores its real conditions and barricades itself inside its myth. Sheltered from the world, it unleashes all the fantastic form of a breathless conflict which can only ever find peace in the catastrophe of someone else's fall: it takes this hullabaloo for destiny and its breathlessness for the dialectic. In it, the dialectic turns in a void, since it is only the dialectic of the void, cut off from the real world for ever. This foreign consciousness, without contradicting its conditions, cannot emerge from itself by itself, by its own 'dialectic'. It has to make a rupture – and recognize this nothingness, discover the non-dialecticity of this dialectic.

This never happens with Sue: but it does in *El Nost Milan*. In the end the last scene does give an answer to the paradox of the play and of its structure. When Nina turns on her father, when she sends him back into the night with his dreams, she is breaking both with her father's melodramatic consciousness and with his 'dialectic'. She

---

(*e*) It is also true that one can allow oneself what one would forbid others (it used to be what marked out the 'great' in their own consciousness): an exchange of roles. A Person of Quality can use the back stairs for fun (borrow from the people what he has given it, or left over for it). Everything depends on the double-meaning of this surreptitious exchange, on the short terms of the loan, and on its conditions: in other words, on the irony of the game in which one proves to oneself (so this proof is necessary?) that one is not to be fooled by anything, not even by the means that one is using to fool others. In other words one is quite prepared to borrow from the 'people' the myths, the trash that one has fabricated and handed out (or sold) to them, on condition that they are suitably accommodated and 'treated'. Good or mediocre 'treaters' (such as Bruant and Piaf, and the Frères Jacques, respectively) may arise from their ranks. One makes oneself 'one of the people' through a delight in being above one's own methods; that is why it is essential to play at being (not being) the people that one forces the people to be, the people of popular 'myth', people with a flavour of melodrama. This melodrama is not worthy of the stage (the real, theatrical stage). It is savoured in small sips in the cabaret.

(*f*) My conclusion is that neither amnesia, nor disgust, nor irony produce even the shadow of a critique.

has finished with these myths and the conflicts they unleash. Father, consciousness, dialectic, she throws them all overboard and crosses the threshold of the other world, as if to show that it is in this poor world that things are happening, that everything has already begun, not only its poverty, but also the derisory illusions of its consciousness. This dialectic which only comes into its own at the extremities of the stage, in the aisles of a story it never succeeds in invading or dominating, is a very exact image for the quasi-null relation of a false consciousness to a real situation. The sanction of the necessary rupture imposed by real experience, foreign to the content of consciousness, is to chase this dialectic from the stage. When Nina goes through the door separating her from the daylight she does not yet know what her life will be; she might even lose it. At least *we* know that she goes out into the real world, which is undoubtedly the world of money, but also the world that produces poverty and imposes on poverty even its consciousness of 'tragedy'. And this is what Marx said when he rejected the false dialectic of consciousness, even of popular consciousness, in favour of experience and study of the other world, the world of Capital.

At this point someone will want to stop me, arguing that what I am drawing from the play goes beyond the intentions of the author – and that I am, in fact, attributing to Bertolazzi what really belongs to Strehler. But I regard this statement as meaningless, for at issue here is the play's latent structure and nothing else. Bertolazzi's explicit intentions are unimportant: what counts, beyond the words, the characters and the action of the play, is the internal relation of the basic elements of its structure. I would go further. It does not matter whether Bertolazzi consciously wished for this structure, or unconsciously produced it: it constitutes the essence of his work; it alone makes both Strehler's interpretation and the audience's reaction comprehensible.

Strehler was acutely aware of the implications of this remarkable structure,[5] and his production and direction of the actors were

---

5 'The principal feature of the work is precisely the sudden appearances in it of a truth as yet hardly defined . . . *El Nost Milan* is a drama *sotto voce*, a drama continually referred back, reconsidered, a drama which is focused

determined by it; that is why the audience was bowled over by it. The spectators' emotion cannot be explained merely by the 'presence' of this teeming popular life – nor by the poverty of these people, who still manage to keep up a hand-to-mouth existence, accepting their fate, taking their revenge, on occasion with a laugh, at moments by solidarity, most often by silence – nor by the lightning tragedy of Nina, her father and the Togasso; but basically by their unconscious perception of this structure and its profound meaning. The structure is nowhere exposed, nowhere does it constitute the object of a speech or a dialogue. Nowhere can it be perceived directly in the play as can the visible characters or the course of the action. But it is there, in the tacit relation between the people's time and the time of the tragedy, in their mutual imbalance, in their incessant 'interference' and finally in their true and delusive criticism. It is this revealing latent relation, this apparently insignificant and yet decisive tension that Strehler's production enables the audience to perceive without their being able to translate this presence directly into clearly conscious terms. Yes, the audience applauded in the play something that was beyond them, which may even have been beyond its author, but which Strehler provided him: a meaning buried deeper than words and gestures, deeper than the immediate fate of the characters who live this fate without ever being able to reflect on it. Even Nina, who is for us the rupture and the beginning, and the promise of another world and another consciousness, does not know what she is doing. Here we can truly say that consciousness is delayed – for even if it is still blind, it is a consciousness aiming at last at a real world.

*

---

from time to time only to be deferred once again, a drama which is made up of a long grey line broken by the cracks of a whip. This is no doubt the reason why Nina and her Father's few decisive cries stand out in particularly tragic relief. . . . We have decided to make some rearrangements in the construction of the play so as to stress this secret structure. Bertolazzi's four acts have been reduced to three by the fusion of the second and third acts. . . .' (Programme Notes).

If this reflection on an 'experience' is acceptable, we might use it to illuminate other experiences by an investigation into their meaning. I am thinking of the problems posed by Brecht's great plays, problems which recourse to such concepts as the alienation effect or the epic theatre has perhaps not in principle perfectly solved. I am very struck by the fact that a latent asymmetrical–critical structure, the dialectic-in-the-wings structure found in Bertolazzi's play, is in essentials also the structure of plays such as *Mother Courage* and (above all) *Galileo*. Here again we also find forms of temporality that do not achieve any mutual integration, which have no relation to one another, which coexist and interconnect, but never meet each other, so to speak; with lived elements which interlace in a dialectic which is localized, separate and apparently ungrounded; works marked by an internal dissociation, an unresolved alterity.

The dynamic of this specific latent structure, and in particular, the coexistence without any explicit relation of a dialectical temporality and a non-dialectical temporality, is the basis for a true critique of the illusions of consciousness (which always believes itself to be dialectical and treats itself as dialectical), the basis for a true critique of the false dialectic (conflict, tragedy, etc.) by the disconcerting reality which is its basis and which is waiting for recognition. Thus, the war in *Mother Courage*, as opposed to the personal tragedies of her blindness, to the false urgency of her greed; thus, in *Galileo* the history that is slower than consciousness impatient for truth, the history which is also disconcerting for a consciousness which is never able to 'take' durably onto it within the period of its short life. This silent confrontation of a consciousness (living its own situation in the dialectical–tragic mode, and believing the whole world to be moved by its impulse) with a reality which is indifferent and strange to this so-called dialectic – an apparently undialectical reality, makes possible an immanent critique of the illusions of consciousness. It hardly matters whether these things are said or not (they are in Brecht, in the form of fables or songs): in the last resort it is not the words that produce this critique, but the internal balances and imbalances of forces between the elements of the play's structure. For there is no true critique which is not immanent and already real and material before it is conscious. I wonder whether this asymmetrical, decentred structure should not be regarded as essential to any theatrical effort of a materialist character. If we carry our analysis of this condition a little further we can easily find in it Marx's fundamental principle that it is impossible for any form of ideological consciousness to contain in itself, through its own internal dialectic, an escape from itself, that, *strictly speaking, there is no dialectic of consciousness*: no dialectic of consciousness which could reach reality itself by virtue of its own contradictions; in short, there can be no 'phenomenology' in the Hegelian sense: for consciousness does not accede to the real through its own internal development, but by the radical discovery of what is *other than itself*.

It was in precisely this sense that Brecht overthrew the problematic of the classical theatre – when he renounced the thematization of the meaning and implications of a play in the form of a consciousness of self. By this I mean that, to produce a new, true and active consciousness in his spectators, Brecht's world must necessarily exclude any pretensions to exhaustive self-recovery and self-representation in the form of a consciousness of self. The classical theatre (though Shakespeare and Molière must be excepted, and this exception explained) gave us tragedy, its conditions and its 'dialectic', completely reflected in the speculative consciousness of a central character – in short, reflected its total meaning in a consciousness, in a talking, acting, thinking, developing human being: what tragedy is for us. And it is probably no accident that this formal condition of 'classical' aesthetics (the central unity of a dramatic consciousness, controlling the other, more famous 'unities') is closely related to its material content. I mean that the material, or the themes, of the classical theatre (politics, morality, religion, honour, 'glory', 'passion', etc.) are precisely ideological themes, and they remain so, without their ideological nature ever being questioned, that is, criticized ('passion' itself, opposed to 'duty' or 'glory' is no more than an ideological counterpoint – never the effective dissolution of the ideology). But what, concretely, is this uncriticized ideology if not simply the 'familiar', 'well-known', transparent myths in which a society or an age can recognize itself (but not know itself), the mirror it looks into for self-recognition, precisely the mirror it must break if it is to know itself? What is the ideology of a society or a period if it is not that society's or period's consciousness of itself, that is, an immediate material which spontaneously implies, looks for and naturally finds its forms in the image of a consciousness of self living the totality of its world in the transparency of its own myths? I am not asking why these myths (the ideology as such) were not *generally* questioned in the classical period. I am content to be able to infer that a time without real self-criticism (with neither the means nor the need for a real theory of politics, morality and religion) should be inclined to represent itself and recognize itself in an uncritical theatre, that is, a theatre whose (ideological) material presupposed the formal conditions for an aesthetic of the consciousness of self. Now Brecht can only break with these formal conditions because he has already broken with their material conditions. His principal aim is to produce a critique of the spontaneous ideology in which men live. That is why he is inevitably forced to exclude from his plays this formal condition of the ideology's aesthetics, the consciousness of self (and its classical derivations: the rules of unity). For him (I am still discussing the 'great plays'), no character consciously contains in himself the totality of the tragedy's conditions. For him, the total, transparent consciousness of self, the mirror of the whole drama is never anything but an image of the ideological consciousness, which does include the whole world in its own tragedy, save only that this world is merely the world of morals, politics and religion, in short, of myths and drugs. In this sense these plays are decentred precisely because they can have no centre, because, although the illusion-wrapped, naïve consciousness is his starting-point, Brecht refuses to make it that centre of the world it would like to be. That is why in these plays the centre is always to one side, if I may put it that way, and in so far as we are considering a demystification of the consciousness of self, the centre is always deferred, always in the beyond, in the movement going beyond illusion towards the real. For this basic reason the critical relation, which is a real production, cannot be thematized for itself: that is why no character is in himself 'the morality of history' – except when one of them comes down to the footlights, takes off his mask and, the play over, 'draws the lessons' (but then he is only a spectator reflecting on it from the outside, or rather prolonging its movement: 'we have done our best, now it is up to you').

It should now be clear why we have to speak of the dynamic of the play's latent structure. It is the structure that we must discuss in so far as the play cannot be reduced to its actors, nor to their explicit relations – only to the dynamic relation existing between consciousnesses of self alienated in spontaneous ideology (Mother Courage, her sons, the cook, the priest, etc.) and the real conditions of their existence (war, society). This relation, abstract in itself (abstract with respect to the consciousness of self – for this abstract is the true concrete) can only be acted and represented as characters, their gestures and their acts, and their 'history' only as a relation which goes beyond them while implying them; that is, as a relation setting to work abstract structural elements (e.g. the different forms of temporality in *El Nost Milan* – the exteriority of dramatic crowds, etc.), their imbalance and hence their dynamic. This relation is necessarily latent in so far as it cannot be exhaustively thematized by any 'character' without ruining the whole critical project: that is why, even if it is implied by the action as a whole, by the existence and movements of all the characters, it is their deep meaning, beyond their consciousness – and thus hidden from them; visible to the spectator in so far as it is invisible to the actors – and therefore visible to the spectator in the mode of a perception which is not given, but has to be discerned, conquered and drawn from the shadow which initially envelops it, and yet produced it.

Perhaps these remarks give us a more precise idea of the problem posed by the Brechtian theory of the alienation-effect. By means of this effect Brecht hoped to create a new relation between the audience and the play performed: a critical and active relation. He wanted to break with the classical forms of identification, where the audience hangs on the destiny of the 'hero' and all its emotional energy is concentrated on theatrical catharsis. He wanted to set the spectator at a distance from the performance, but in such a situation that he would be incapable of flight or simple enjoyment. In short, he wanted to make the spectator into an actor who would complete the unfinished play, but in real life. This profound thesis of Brecht's has perhaps been too often interpreted solely as a function of the technical elements of alienation: the abolition of all 'impressiveness' in the acting, of all lyricism and all 'pathos': *al fresco* acting; the austerity of the set, as if to eliminate any eye-catching relief (cf. the dark ochre and ash colours in *Mother Courage*); the 'flat' lighting; the commentary-placards to direct the readers' attention to the external context of the conjuncture (reality), etc. The thesis has also given rise to psychological interpretations centred around the phenomenon of identification and its classical prop: the hero. The disappearance of the hero (whether positive or negative), the object of identification, has been seen as the very precondition of the alienation-effect (no more hero, no more identification – the suppression of the hero being also linked to Brecht's 'materialist' conception – it is the masses who make history, not 'heroes'). Now, I feel that these interpretations are limited to notions which may well be important, but which are not determinant, and that it is essential to go beyond the technical and psychological conditions to an understanding that this very special critique must be constituted in the spectator's consciousness. In other words, if a distance can be established between the spectator and the play, it is essential that in some way this distance should be produced within the play itself, and not only in its (technical) treatment, or in the psychological modality of the characters (are they really heroes or non-heroes? Take the dumb daughter on the roof in *Mother Courage*, shot because she beat her infernal drum to warn the unknowing city that an enemy was about to fall on it, is she not, in fact, a 'positive hero'? Surely we do temporarily 'identify' with this secondary character?). It is within the play itself, in the dynamic of its internal structure, that this distance is produced and represented, at once criticizing the illusions of consciousness and unravelling its real conditions.

This – that the dynamic of the latent structure produces this distance within the play itself – must be the starting-point from which to pose the problem of the relation between the spectator and the performance. Here again Brecht reverses the established order. In the classical theatre it was apparently quite simple: the hero's temporality was the sole temporality, all the rest was subordinate to it, even his opponents were made to his measure, they had to be if they were to be *his* opponents; they lived *his* time, *his* rhythm, they were dependent on him, they were merely his dependants. The opponent was really *his* opponent: in the struggle the hero belonged to the opponent as much as the opponent did to the hero, the opponent was the hero's double, his reflection, his opposite, his night, his temptation, his own unconscious turned against him. Hegel was right, his destiny was consciousness of himself as of an enemy. Thereby the content of the struggle was identified with the hero's consciousness of himself. And quite naturally, the spectator seemed to 'live' the play by 'identifying' himself with the hero, that is, with his time, with his consciousness, the only time and the only consciousness offered him. In Bertolazzi's play and in Brecht's great plays this confusion becomes impossible, precisely because of their dissociated structure. I should say, not that the heroes have disappeared because Brecht has banished them from his plays, but that even as the heroes they are, and in the play itself, the play makes them impossible, abolishes them, their consciousness and its false dialectic. This reduction is not the effect of the action alone, nor of the demonstration which certain popular figures are fated to make of it (on the theme: neither God nor Caesar); it is not even merely the result of the play appreciated as an unresolved story; it is not produced at the level of detail or of continuity, but at the deeper level of the play's structural dynamic.

At this point close attention is essential: up till now only the play has been discussed – now we must deal with the spectator's consciousness. I should like to show in a few words that this is not, as might have been thought, a new problem, but really the same one. However, if this is to be accepted, two classical models of the spectatorial consciousness which cloud our reflection must first of all be relinquished. The first of these misleading models is once again a consciousness of self, this time the spectator's. It accepts that the spectator should not identify with the 'hero'; he is to be kept at a distance. But is he not then outside the play judging, adding up the score and drawing the conclusions? *Mother Courage* is presented to you. It is for her to act. It is for you to judge. On the stage the image of blindness – in the stalls the image of lucidity, led to consciousness by two hours of unconsciousness. But this division of roles amounts to conceding to the house what has been rigorously excluded from the stage. Really, the spectator has no claim to this absolute consciousness of self which the play cannot tolerate.

The play can no more contain the 'Last Judgement' on its own 'story' than can the spectator be the supreme Judge of the play. He also sees and lives the play in the mode of a questioned false consciousness. For what else is he if not the brother of the characters, caught in the spontaneous myths of ideology, in its illusions and privileged forms, as much as they are? If he is kept at a distance from the play by the play itself, it is not to spare him or to set him up as a Judge – on the contrary, it is to take him and enlist him in this apparent distance, in this 'estrangement' – to make him into this distance itself, the distance which is simply an active and living critique.

But then, no doubt, we must also reject the second model of the spectatorial consciousness – a model that will haunt us until it has been rejected: the identification model. I am unable to answer this question fully here, but I shall try to pose it clearly: surely the invocation of a conception of identification (with the hero) to deal with the status of the spectatorial consciousness is to hazard a dubious correlation? Rigorously speaking, the concept of identification is a psychological or, more precisely, a psychoanalytic concept. Far be it from me to contest the effectivity of psychological processes in the spectator seated in front of the stage. But it must be said that the phenomena of projection, sublimation, etc., that can be observed, described and defined in controlled psychological situations cannot by themselves account for complex behaviour as specific as that of the spectator-attending-a-performance. This behaviour is primarily social and cultural-aesthetic, and as such it is also ideological. Certainly, it is an important task to elucidate the insertion of concrete psychological processes (such as identification, sublimation, repression, etc., in their strict psychological senses) in behaviour which goes beyond them. But this first task cannot abolish the second – the definition of the specificity of the spectatorial consciousness itself – without lapsing into psychologism. If the consciousness cannot be reduced to a purely psychological consciousness, if it is a social, cultural and ideological consciousness, we cannot think its relation to the performance solely in the form of a psychological identification. Indeed, before (psychologically) identifying itself with the hero, the spectatorial consciousness recognizes itself in the ideological content of the play, and in the forms characteristic of this content. Before becoming the occasion for an identification (an identification with self in the species of another), the performance is, fundamentally, the occasion for a cultural and ideological recognition.[6] This self-recognition presupposes as its principle an essential identity (which makes the processes of psychological identification themselves possible, in so far as they are psychological): the identity uniting the spectators and actors assembled in the same place on the same evening. Yes, we are first united by an institution – the performance, but more deeply, by the same myths, the same themes, that govern us without our consent, by the same spontaneously lived ideology. Yes, even if it is the ideology of the poor *par excellence*, as in *El Nost Milan*, we still eat of the same bread, we have the same rages, the same rebellions, the same madness (at least in the memory where stalks this ever-imminent possibility), if not the same prostration before a time unmoved by any History. Yes, like Mother Courage, we have the same war at our gates, and a

---

6   We should not imagine that this self-recognition escapes the exigencies which, in the last instance, command the destiny of the ideology. Indeed, it is as much the desire for self-recognition as self-recognition itself. So, from the beginning, the unity I have assumed to be (in essentials) achieved so as to restrict the analysis, the stock of common myths, themes and aspirations which makes representation possible as a cultural and ideological phenomenon – this unity is as much a desired or rejected unity as an achieved unity. In other words, in the theatrical world, as in the aesthetic world more generally, ideology is always in essence the site of a competition and a struggle in which the sound and fury of humanity's political and social struggles is faintly or sharply echoed. I must say that it is very odd to put forward purely psychological processes (such as identification) as explanations of spectatorial behaviour, when we know that the effects of these processes are sometimes radically absent – when we know that there are professional and other spectators who do not want to understand anything, even before the curtain rises, or who, once the curtain has been raised, refuse to recognize themselves in the work presented to them, or in its interpretation. We need not look far for a wealth of examples. Was not Bertolazzi rejected by the late nineteenth-century Italian bourgeoisie and forced into failure and poverty? And here in Paris, June 1962, was he not condemned – along with Strehler – without a hearing, a real hearing, by the leaders of 'Parisian' public consciousness? Whereas a large popular audience now accepts and recognizes him in Italy?

handsbreadth from us, if not in us, the same horrible blindness, the same dust in our eyes, the same earth in our mouths. We have the same dawn and night, we skirt the same abysses: our unconsciousness. We even share the same history – and that is how it all started. That is why we were already ourselves in the play itself, from the beginning – and then what does it matter whether we know the result, since it will never happen to anyone but ourselves, that is, still in our world. That is why the false problem of identification was solved from the beginning, even before it was posed, by the reality of recognition. The only question, then, is what is the fate of this tacit identity, this immediate self-recognition, what has the author already done with it? What will the actors set to work by the Dramaturg, by Brecht or Strehler, do with it? What will become of this ideological self-recognition? Will it exhaust itself in the dialectic of the consciousness of self, deepening its myths without ever escaping from them? Will it put this infinite mirror at the centre of the action? Or will it rather displace it, put it to one side, find it and lose it, leave it, return to it, expose it from afar to forces which are external – and so drawn out – that like those wine-glasses broken at a distance by a physical resonance, it comes to a sudden end as a heap of splinters on the floor.

To return finally to my attempt at definition, with the simple aim of posing the question anew and in a better form, we can see that the play itself *is* the spectator's consciousness – for the essential reason that the spectator has no other consciousness than the content which unites him to the play in advance, and the development of this content in the play itself: the new result which the play *produces* from the self-recognition whose image and presence it is. Brecht was right: if the theatre's sole object were to be even a 'dialectical' commentary on this eternal self-recognition and non-recognition – then the spectator would already know the tune, it is his own. If, on the contrary, the theatre's object is to destroy this intangible image, to set in motion the immobile, the eternal sphere of the illusory consciousness's mythical world, then the play is really the development, the production of a new consciousness in the spectator – incomplete, like any other consciousness, but moved by this incompletion itself, this distance achieved, this inexhaustible work of criticism in action; the play is really the production of a new spectator, an actor who starts where the performance ends, who only starts so as to complete it, but in life.

I look back, and I am suddenly and irresistibly assailed by *the* question: are not these few pages, in their maladroit and groping way, simply that unfamiliar play *El Nost Milan*, performed on a June evening, pursuing in me its incomplete meaning, searching in me, despite myself, now that all the actors and sets have been cleared away, for the *advent* of its silent discourse?

August 1962

Part Five

The '1844 Manuscripts' of Karl Marx

POLITICAL ECONOMY AND PHILOSOPHY

The publication of the *1844 Manuscripts* is a real *event*, one I should like to draw to the attention of the readers of *La Pensée*.[1]

It is, first of all, a *literary* and *critical* event. Up till now, the *Manuscripts* have only been accessible to French readers in the Costes edition (Molitor, Vol. VI of the *Œuvres Philosophiques*). Anyone who had to use it knows from experience that this partial text, with important arguments cut out and afflicted with errors and inaccuracies, could not serve as a tool for serious work. Thanks to E. Bottigelli, who is to be highly praised, we now have an *up-to-date* version (the most up to date there is, for Bottigelli has made use of the latest readings and emendations, sent him from the Marx–Engels Institute, Moscow) presented in the most reasonable order (that of the M.E.G.A.) and in a translation remarkable for its rigour, its attention to detail, its critical annotations, and may I add – and this is particularly important – for its *theoretical reliability*. (It should be obvious that it is impossible to conceive of a good translator except on the express condition that he be *much more than a translator*, in fact, an expert, steeped not only in the work of his author but also in the conceptual and historical universe in which the latter was brought up. On this occasion this condition has been fulfilled.)

But it is also a *theoretical* event. This is the text which has for thirty years been in the front line of the polemics between defenders of Marx and his opponents. Bottigelli gives a good account of the way

---

1   Presented, translated and annotated by Emile Bottigelli (Editions Sociales).

the roles were shared out in this great debate. First Social-Democrats (initially its first editors, Landshut and Mayer), then spiritualist philosophers, existentialist philosophers, phenomenological philosophers, etc., ensured this great text's success; but, as might be expected, in a spirit foreign to an understanding of Marx or even to the simple comprehension of his *formation*. The Economic-Philosophic manuscripts have nourished a whole ethical or (what amounts to the same thing) anthropological interpretation of Marx – making *Capital*, with its sense of perspective and apparent 'objectivity', merely the development of a youthful intuition which finds its major philosophical expression in this text and in its concepts: above all in the concepts of *alienation*, of *humanism*, of the *social essence of man*, etc. As we know, Marxists did not think to react until very late, and their reaction was often of the same order as their fears and haste: they have tended to defend Marx *in toto*, and to take over their opponents' thesis, thereby overestimating the *theoretical* prestige of the 1844 writings, but *to the profit of Capital*. On this point Bottigelli has some noteworthy comments (pp. IX, XXXIX). They are a prelude to a demand which no serious commentator can avoid: the demand for a definition of a new and rigorous *method* of investigation, *'another method'* (p. X) than that of a simple prospective or retrospective assimilation. So we *can* and *must* now deal with these *Manuscripts*, which have been the argument of a struggle, the pretext for a prosecution, or the defence's redoubt, by an assured method: as a *moment* in the formation of Marx's thought, which, like all the moments in an intellectual development, does obviously contain a promise for the future, but also pin-points an irreducible and *singular present*. It is no exaggeration to say that in this irreproachable translation Bottigelli has given us a *privileged object* which has a dual theoretical order of interest for Marxists: because it concerns the *formation*, or rather the *transformation* of Marx's thought, but also because it provides the Marxist theory of ideology with an excellent opportunity to exercise and test its method.

Finally, I should like to add that this translation is introduced by an important historical and theoretical *Presentation*, which not only brings us to the essential problems, but also situates and clarifies them.

What, in fact, is the *specific* feature of the *1844 Manuscripts* if they are compared with Marx's earlier writings? What is there in them which is radically new? The answer is given by the *fact* that the *Manuscripts* were the result of *Marx's discovery of political economy*. Naturally, this was not the first time that, as he put it himself, he experienced the 'embarrassment' of having to give an opinion on questions of an *economic* order (as early as 1842, the question of wood thefts evoked all the conditions of feudal agrarian property; similarly, also in 1842, an article on censorship and the freedom of the Press came up against the reality of 'industry', etc., etc.), but these encounters with Economics only concerned *some* economic questions, and from the angle of *political* debates: in other words, these were not encounters with political economy, but with particular effects of an economic *policy*, or the particular economic conditions of social conflicts (*The Critique of Hegel's Philosophy of Right*). But in 1844 Marx was confronted with political economy *as such*. Engels had prepared the way with his 'brilliant sketch' of England. But Marx had been impelled in this direction, as had Engels himself, by the need to look beyond politics for the reasons for its insoluble internal conflicts. It is difficult to understand the *Manuscripts* without taking into account this *encounter*, this *first* encounter. In his Parisian period (February to May 1844), decisive in this respect, Marx gave himself over to the classical economists (Say, Skarbek, Smith, Ricardo), he took copious notes which leave their mark in the body of the *Manuscripts* themselves (the first part contains long quotations) – as if he wanted *to take into account a fact*. But while recognizing it, he states that *this fact rests on nothing*, at least in the economists he has read, it is ungrounded and lacks its own *principle*. So, in one and the same movement, the encounter with political economy is a *critical reaction* to political economy and a thorough investigation of its *foundations*.

What is the source of Marx's conviction that Political Economy is unfounded? The contradictions it states and registers, or even accepts and traduces: and before all else, the major contradiction opposing the increasing *pauperization* of the workers and the remarkable *wealth* whose arrival in the modern world is celebrated by political economy. This is the crux, the stumbling-block of the optimistic science which is built upon this feeble argument, just as the wealth of the proprietors is on the poverty of the workers. This is also its disgrace, which

Marx wants to suppress by giving economics the principle it lacks, the principle which will be its light and its verdict.

Here we come upon the other aspect of the *Manuscripts*: their *philosophy*. For this encounter of Marx's with political economy is, as Bottigelli correctly points out (pp. XXXIX, LIV, LXVII, etc.), an encounter of *philosophy* with Political Economy. Naturally, not of any philosophy: of the philosophy erected by Marx through all his practico-theoretical experiments (Bottigelli sketches out the essential moments: the idealism of the very first writings, closer to Kant and Fichte than to Hegel; Feuerbach's anthropology), modified, corrected and amplified by this encounter itself. But a *philosophy* still, for all that, profoundly coloured by the Feuerbachian problematic (Bottigelli, p. XXXIX) and leaning hesitantly towards a return from Feuerbach to Hegel. This is the philosophy which resolves the contradiction of Political Economy by *thinking it*, and through it, by thinking the whole of Political Economy and all its categories, with a key-concept as starting-point, the concept of *alienated labour*. This brings us to the real heart of the problem, and close to all the temptations both of idealism and of a hasty materialism. . . . For, *at first sight*, we are in familiar territory, I mean in that conceptual landscape in which we can identify private property, capital, money, the division of labour, the alienation of the labourer, his emancipation and the humanism which is his promised future. These are all, or *nearly all*, categories we shall meet again in *Capital*, and on this basis we might accept them as anticipations of *Capital*, or better, as a project for *Capital*, or even as *Capital* crayoned, already outlined, but only as a sketch, which, if it has the genius of the completed work, has not yet been filled in as it is in the latter. Painters do pencil sketches of this kind, drawn in one movement, new-born, and precisely because of this emergence, greater than the works they contain. There is something of this glitter in the fascination of the *Manuscripts*, in the irresistibility of their *logic* (Bottigelli correctly notes their '*rigorous reasoning*', pp. XXXIII, LXII, LIV, and their 'implacable logic') and the conviction of their dialectic. But there is also the conviction, the *meaning* conferred by this logic and rigour on the concepts we recognize in it, and therefore the very *meaning* of this logic and rigour: *a meaning which is still philosophical*, and when I say philosophical I am using it in *the same sense* as that to which Marx later linked *an absolute condemnation*. For rigour and dialectic are worth no more than the meaning they serve and add lustre to. One day we shall have to study this text in detail and give a word-by-word explanation of it; discuss the theoretical status and theoretical role assigned to the key concept of *alienated labour*; examine this notion's conceptual field; and recognize that it does fill the role Marx then assigned it, the role of *original basis*; but also that it can only fill this role so long as it *receives it* as a mandate and commission from a whole *conception of Man* which can derive from the *essence of Man* the necessity and content of the familiar *economic concepts*. In short, we shall have to discover beneath these terms imminently awaiting a future meaning, the meaning that still keeps them prisoners of a philosophy that is exercising its last prestige and power over them. And except that I would rather not abuse my freedom to anticipate this proof, I should almost say that *beneath this relation*, that is, beneath philosophy's relation of *radical domination* over a content soon to become *radically independent*, the Marx *furthest from Marx* is this Marx, the Marx on the brink, on the eve, on the threshold – as if, before the rupture, in order to achieve it, he had to give philosophy every chance, its last, this absolute empire over its opposite, this boundless theoretical triumph, that is, *its defeat*.

Bottigelli's presentation takes us to the heart of these problems. Among the most remarkable sections are the pages where he discusses the theoretical status of alienated labour, where he compares the economic concepts of the *Manuscripts* with the economic concepts of *Capital*, where he raises the basic question of the theoretical *nature* (for Marx in 1844) of the *just encountered* political economy. The simple sentence: 'Bourgeois political economy appeared to Marx as a *kind of phenomenology*' (p. XLI) seems to me to be decisive, also, the fact that Marx accepts political economy precisely *as it presents itself* (p. LXVII) without questioning the content of its concepts or their systematicity as he was to do later on: it is this 'abstraction' of the *Economy* that authorizes the other 'abstraction': that of the *Philosophy* which is used *to give it a basis*. So a recognition of the *philosophy* at work in the *Manuscripts* necessarily returns us to *our point of departure*: the *encounter* with political economy, forcing us to ask the question: what is the *reality* that Marx *encountered* in the terms of *this* economics? The economy itself? Or more likely an *economic ideology* inseparable from the economists' theories, that is, in the powerful expression quoted above, *a 'phenomenology'*?

I have only one more remark to make before closing. If some people find this interpretation disconcerting, it is because they give credence to a *confusion* (a confusion difficult for our contemporaries to avoid, be it said, for a whole historical past spares them a distinction between these roles) between what have been called *the political positions* and *the theoretical positions* adopted by Marx in his formative period. Bottigelli has seen this difficulty very well and he takes it by the horns when, for example, he writes (p. XXXIII) that the *Critique of Hegel's Philosophy of Right* (1843) 'signals Marx's adhesion to the cause of the proletariat, that is, to Communism. *This does not mean that historical materialism had already been worked out.*' So it is a *political* and *theoretical* reading of the writings of Marx's youth. A text such as *On the Jewish Question*, for instance, is a text *politically committed* to the struggle for Communism. But it is a profoundly 'ideological' text: so *it cannot, theoretically, be identified with the later texts which were to define historical materialism*, and which were to be capable of illuminating even the basis of that real Communist movement of 1843 which was born before them and independently of them, and to whose side Marx had rallied at that time. Anyway, even our own experience should remind us that it is possible to be 'Communist' without being 'Marxist'. This distinction is essential if we are to avoid the *political trap* of confusing Marx's theoretical positions with his *political* positions, and justifying the former from the latter. But this illuminating distinction brings us back to the demand formulated by Bottigelli: we must conceive of *'another method'* to explain Marx's *formation*, that is, his *moments*, his *stages*, his *'presents'*, in short, his *transformation*: to explain this *paradoxical dialectic* whose most extraordinary episode this is, the *Manuscripts* that Marx never published, but which, no doubt precisely for that reason, show him naked in his triumphant and vanquished thoughts, on the threshold of becoming himself at last by a *radical* realignment, the last: that is, the *first*.

December 1962

Part Six

On the Materialist Dialectic

ON THE UNEVENNESS OF ORIGINS

'All mysteries which lead theory to mysticism find their rational solution in human practice and in the comprehension of this practice.'

Karl Marx, *Eighth Thesis on Feuerbach*

This article proposes the term *Theory* (with a capital T) to designate Marxist 'philosophy' (dialectical materialism) – and reserves the term *philosophy* for *ideological* philosophies. It was in this sense of an *ideological* formation that the term *philosophy* had already been used in the article 'Contradiction and Overdetermination'.

This terminology, distinguishing between (ideological) philosophy and Theory (or Marxist philosophy constituted in rupture with philosophical ideology) is authorized by several passages from the works of Marx and Engels. In *The German Ideology*, Marx always uses philosophy to mean ideology pure and simple. And Engels writes, in the earlier preface to his *Anti-Dühring*, 'If theoreticians are semi-initiates in the sphere of natural science, then natural scientists today are actually just as much so in *the sphere of theory, in the sphere of what hitherto was called philosophy*' (English translation, Moscow, 1959, p. 454).

This remark proves that Engels felt the need to encapsulate the difference between ideological philosophies and Marx's absolutely new philosophical project in a terminological distinction. He proposed to register this difference by designating Marxist philosophy by the term *theory*.

However, the fact that a new terminology is well founded does not mean that it can really be manipulated and diffused. It seems difficult to go against familiar usage by designating the scientific philosophy founded by Marx as Theory. Also, the capital T which distinguishes it from other uses of the word *theory* obviously cannot be perceived aurally. For these reasons, since writing the article 'On the Materialist Dialectic', I have reverted to the terminology in current use, and speak of *philosophy* to refer to Marx himself, therefore using the term *Marxist philosophy*.

If I had to sum up in one sentence all the criticisms I have received, I should say that, while acknowledging the interest of my articles, they regard them as theoretically and politically dangerous.

These critics formulate two essential grounds for objection, with various modifications:

(1) That I have stressed the discontinuity between Marx and Hegel. The result: what remains of the 'rational kernel' of the Hegelian dialectic, of the dialectic itself, and, in consequence, of Capital itself and the basic law of our age?[1]

(2) That by proposing the concept of 'overdetermined contradiction', I have substituted a 'pluralist' conception of history for the Marxist 'monist' conception. The result: what remains of historical necessity, of its unity, of the determinant role of the economy – and, in consequence, of the basic law of our age?[2]

---

1   R. Garaudy: 'We should realize how much we risk throwing overboard if we underestimate the Hegelian heritage in Marx: not only his youthful works, Engels and Lenin, but also *Capital* itself.' R. Garaudy, '*A propos des manuscrits de 44*', *Cahiers du Communisme*, March 1963, p. 118.

2   G. Mury: 'It would hardly be reasonable to suppose that he [L.A.] should have introduced with such a fanfare a new concept to express a truth known since Marx and Engels. It is more likely that he thought it essential to insist on the existence of an unbridgeable gulf between the determinations coming from the infrastructure and those coming from the superstructure. This must be why he refuses to invert the poles of the contradiction between civil society and the State that Hegel proposed by following Marx in making civil society the dominant pole and the State the phenomenon of this essence. But this solution by continuity artificially introduced into the dialectic of history

Two problems are at issue in these objections, and in my essays. The first concerns the Hegelian dialectic: what is the 'rationality' that Marx attributes to it? The second concerns the Marxist dialectic: what is the *specificity* that distinguishes it rigorously from the Hegelian dialectic? Two problems which are in fact only two parts of a single problem, since in its two aspects it always remains a matter of a more rigorous and clearer understanding of Marx's thought.

I shall return later to the 'rationality' of the Hegelian dialectic. For the moment, I should like to examine more closely the second aspect of the problem (which governs the other): the *specificity* of the Marxist dialectic.

The reader should realize that I am doing all I can to give the *concepts* I use a *strict* meaning, and that if he wants to understand these concepts he will have to pay attention to this rigour, and, in so far as it is not imaginary, he will have to adopt it himself. Need I remind him that without the rigour demanded by its object there can be no question of *theory*, that is, of theoretical practice in the strict sense of the term?

Practical Solution and Theoretical Problem. Why Theory?

The problem posed by my last study – what constitutes Marx's 'inversion' of the Hegelian dialectic, what is the specific difference that distinguishes the Marxist dialectic from the Hegelian dialectic? – is a theoretical problem.

---

prevents him from seeing how the internal principle of capitalism itself in its own specific contradiction engenders by its own development the highest stage of imperialism, the unevenness of progress and the necessity for the weakest link' (*La Pensée*, April 1963, '*Matérialisme et Hyperempirisme*', p. 49). R. Garaudy: 'Whatever the complexity of the mediations, human practice is one, and it is the dialectic of human practice that constitutes the motor of history. To blur this with the (real) multiplicity of "overdeterminations" is to obscure the essence of Marx's *Capital* which is above all a study of this major contradiction, this basic law of the development of bourgeois society. Once this is obscured, how is it possible to conceive the objective existence of a basic law of development of our own epoch, the epoch of the transition to socialism?' (*op. cit.*, p. 119).

To say that it is a *theoretical* problem implies that its theoretical solution should give us a new knowledge, organically linked to the other knowledges of Marxist theory. To say that it is a theoretical *problem* implies that we are not dealing merely with an imaginary difficulty, but with a really existing difficulty posed us in the form of a *problem*, that is, in a form governed by imperative conditions: definition of the field of (theoretical) knowledges in which the problem is posed (situated), of the exact *location* of its posing, and of the concepts required to pose it.

Only the position, examination and resolution of the problem, that is, the *theoretical practice* we are about to embark on, can provide the *proof* that these conditions have been respected.

Now, in this particular case, what has to be expressed in the form of a theoretical problem and its solution *already exists in Marxist practice*. Not only has Marxist practice come up against this 'difficulty', confirmed that it was indeed real rather than imaginary, but what is more, it has, within its own limits, 'settled' it and surmounted it in fact. In the practical state, the solution to our theoretical problem has already existed for a long time in Marxist practice. So to pose and resolve our theoretical problem ultimately means to express theoretically the '*solution*' existing in the practical state, that Marxist practice has found for a real difficulty it has encountered in its development, whose existence it has noted, and, according to its own submission, settled.[3]

So we are merely concerned with filling in a 'gap' between theory and practice on a particular point. We are not setting Marxism any imaginary or subjective problem, asking it to 'resolve' the 'problems' of 'hyperempiricism', nor even what Marx called the difficulties a philosopher has in his *personal* relations with a concept. No. The

---

3 *Settled*: this is the very word Marx used in the Preface to the *Contribution* (1858), when, reviewing his past and evoking his meeting with Engels in Brussels, spring 1845, and the drafting of *The German Ideology*, he speaks of *settling accounts* (*Abrechnung*) with 'our erstwhile philosophical conscience'. The Afterword to the second edition of *Capital* openly records this settlement, which, in good accounting style, includes the acknowledgement of a debt: the acknowledgement of the 'rational side' of the Hegelian dialectic.

problem posed[4] exists (and has existed) in the form of a difficulty signalled by Marxist practice. Its solution exists in Marxist practice. So we only have to express it theoretically. But this simple theoretical *expression* of a solution that exists in the practical state cannot be taken for granted: it requires a real theoretical labour, not only to work out the specific *concept* or *knowledge* of this practical resolution – but also for the real destruction of the ideological confusions, illusions or inaccuracies that may exist, by a radical critique (a critique which takes them by the root). So this *simple* theoretical 'expression' implies both the *production* of a knowledge and the *critique* of an illusion, in one movement.

And if I am asked: but why take all this trouble to express a 'truth' 'known' for such a long time?[5] – my answer is that, if we are still using the term in its strictest sense, the existence of this truth has been *signalled*, *recognized* for a long time, but it has not been *known*. For the (practical) *recognition* of an existence cannot pass for a *knowledge* (that is, for *theory*) except in the imprecision of a confused thought. And if I am then asked: but what use is there in posing this problem *in theory* if its solution has already existed for a long time in the practical state? why give a theoretical expression to this practical solution, a theoretical expression it has so far done quite well without? what do we gain by this 'speculative' investigation that we do not possess already?

One sentence is enough to answer this question: Lenin's 'Without revolutionary theory, no revolutionary practice'. Generalizing it: theory is essential to practice, to the forms of practice that it helps bring to birth or to grow, as well as to the practice it is the theory of. But the transparency of this sentence is not enough; we must also know its *titles to validity*, so we must pose the question: what are we to understand by *theory*, if it is to be essential to *practice*?

---

4   Of course, this is not the first time this problem has been posed! It is at the moment the object of important works by Marxist investigators in the U.S.S.R. and, to my knowledge, in Rumania, Hungary and Democratic Germany, as well as in Italy, where it has inspired historical and theoretical studies of great scientific interest (Della Volpe, Rossi, Colletti, Merker, etc.).
5   G. Mury quite correctly says: '. . . it would hardly be reasonable to suppose that he [L.A.] should have introduced . . . a new concept to express a truth known since Marx and Engels' (*op. cit.*).

I shall only discuss the aspects of this theme that are indispensable to our investigation. I propose to use the following definitions, as essential preliminary hypotheses.

By *practice* in general I shall mean any process of *transformation* of a determinate given raw material into a determinate *product*, a transformation effected by a determinate human labour, using determinate means (of 'production'). In any practice thus conceived, the *determinant* moment (or element) is neither the raw material nor the product, but the practice in the narrow sense: the moment of the *labour of transformation* itself, which sets to work, in a specific structure, men, means and a technical method of utilizing the means. This general definition of practice covers the possibility of particularity: there are different practices which are really distinct, even though they belong organically to the same complex totality. Thus, 'social practice', the complex unity of the practices existing in a determinate society, contains a large number of distinct practices. This complex unity of 'social practice' is structured, we shall soon see how, in such a way that in the last resort the determinant practice in it is the practice of transformation of a given nature (raw material) into useful *products* by the activity of living men working through the *methodically organized* employment of determinate *means of production* within the framework of determinate relations of production. As well as production social practice includes other essential levels: political practice – which in Marxist parties is no longer spontaneous but organized on the basis of the scientific theory of historical materialism, and which transforms its raw materials: social relations, into a determinate product (new social relations); ideological practice (ideology, whether religious, political, moral, legal or artistic, also transforms its object: men's 'consciousness'): and finally, *theoretical practice*. Ideology is not always taken seriously as an existing practice: but to recognize this is the indispensable prior condition for any theory of ideology. The existence of a *theoretical practice* is taken seriously even more rarely: but this prior condition is indispensable to an understanding of what theory itself and its relation to 'social practice' are for Marxism.

Here we need a second definition. By theory, in this respect, I shall mean a *specific form of practice*, itself belonging to the complex unity of the 'social practice' of a determinate human society. Theoretical practice falls within the general definition of practice. It works on a raw material (representations, concepts, facts) which it is given by other practices, whether 'empirical', 'technical' or 'ideological'. In its most general form theoretical practice does not only include *scientific* theoretical practice, but also prescientific theoretical practice, that is, 'ideological' theoretical practice (the forms of 'knowledge' that make up the prehistory of a science, and their 'philosophies'). The theoretical practice of a science is always completely distinct from the ideological theoretical practice of its prehistory: this distinction takes the form of a 'qualitative' theoretical and historical discontinuity which I shall follow Bachelard in calling an 'epistemological break'. This is not the place to discuss the dialectic in action in the advent of this 'break': that is, the labour of specific theoretical transformation which installs it in each case, which establishes a science by detaching it from the ideology of its past and by revealing this past as ideological. Restricting myself to the essential point as far as our analysis is concerned, I shall take up a position beyond the 'break', within the constituted science, and use the following nomenclature: I shall call *theory* any theoretical practice of a *scientific* character. I shall call 'theory' (in inverted commas) the determinate *theoretical system* of a real science (its basic concepts in their more or less contradictory unity at a given time): for example, the theory of universal attraction, wave mechanics, etc. . . . or again, the '*theory*' of historical materialism. In its 'theory' any determinate science reflects within the complex unity of its concepts (a unity which, I should add, is more or less problematic) the results, which will henceforth be the conditions and means, of its own theoretical practice. I shall call Theory (with a capital T), general theory, that is, the Theory of practice in general, itself elaborated on the basis of the Theory of existing theoretical practices (of the sciences), which transforms into 'knowledges' (scientific truths) the ideological product of existing 'empirical' practices (the concrete activity of men). This Theory is the materialist *dialectic* which is none other than dialectical materialism. These definitions are necessary for us to be able to give an answer to this question: what is the use of a theoretical expression of a solution which already exists in the practical state? – an answer with a theoretical basis.

When Lenin said 'without theory, no revolutionary action', he meant one particular theory, the theory of the Marxist science of the development of social formations (historical materialism). The proposition is to be found in *What is to be Done?*, where Lenin examined the organizational methods and objectives of the Russian Social-Democratic Party in 1902. At that time he was struggling against an opportunist policy that tagged along behind the 'spontaneity' of the masses; his aim was to transform it into a revolutionary practice based on 'theory', that is, on the (Marxist) science of the development of the social formation concerned (Russian society at that time). But in expressing this thesis, Lenin was doing more than he said: by reminding Marxist political practice of the necessity for the 'theory' which is its basis, he was in fact expressing a thesis of relevance to Theory, that is, to the Theory of practice in general – the materialist dialectic.

So theory is important to practice in a double sense: for 'theory' is important to its own practice, directly. But the *relation* of a 'theory' to its practice, in so far as it is at issue, on condition that it is reflected and expressed, is also relevant to the general Theory (the dialectic) in which is theoretically expressed the essence of theoretical practice in general, through it the essence of practice in general, and through it the essence of the transformations, of the 'development' of things in general.

To return to our original problem: we find that the theoretical expression of a practical solution involves Theory, that is, the dialectic. The exact theoretical expression of the dialectic is relevant first of all to those practices in which the Marxist dialectic is active; for these practices (Marxist 'theory' and politics) need the concept of their practice (of the dialectic) in their development, if they are not to find themselves defenceless in the face of qualitatively new forms of this development (new situations, new 'problems') – or to lapse, or relapse, into the various forms of opportunism, theoretical or practical. These 'surprises' and deviations, attributable in the last resort to 'ideological errors', that is, to a *theoretical* deficiency, are always costly, and may be very costly.

But Theory is also essential for the transformation of domains in which a Marxist theoretical practice does not yet really exist. In most of these domains the question has not yet been 'settled' as it has in *Capital*. The Marxist theoretical practice of *epistemology*, of the history of science, of the history of ideology, of the history of philosophy, of the history of art, has yet in large part to be constituted. Not that there are not Marxists who are working in these domains and have acquired much real experience there, but they do not have behind them the equivalent of *Capital* or of the revolutionary practice of a century of Marxists. Their practice is largely *in front of them*, it still has to be developed, or even founded, that is, it has to be set on correct theoretical bases so that it corresponds to a *real* object, not to a presumed or ideological object, and so that it is a truly theoretical practice, not a technical practice. It is for this purpose that they need Theory, that is, the materialist dialectic, as the sole method that can anticipate their theoretical practice by drawing up its formal conditions. In this case, the utilization of Theory is not a matter of *applying* its formulae (the formulae of the dialectic, of materialism) to a pre-existing content. Lenin himself criticized Engels and Plekhanov for having *applied* the dialectic externally to 'examples' from the natural sciences.[6] The external application of a concept is never equivalent to a *theoretical practice*. The application changes nothing in the externally derived truth but its *name*, a re-baptism incapable of producing any real transformation of the truths that receive it. The application of the 'laws' of the dialectic to such and such a result of physics, for example, makes not one iota of difference to the structure or development of

---

6   V. I. Lenin, 'Philosophical Notebooks' (*Collected Works*, Vol. XXXVIII), p. 266: 'Hegel's Logic cannot be *applied* in its given form, it cannot be *taken* as given. One *must separate out* from it the logical (epistemological) nuances, after purifying them from *Ideenmystik*: that is still a big job.'

Ibid., p. 359: 'The correctness of this aspect of the content of dialectics (the "identity of opposites", L.A.) must be tested by the history of science. This aspect of dialectics (e.g. in Plekhanov) usually receives inadequate attention: the identity of opposites is taken as the sum-total of *examples* ("for example, a seed", "for example, primitive communism". The same is true of Engels. But it is "in the interests of popularisation . . .") and not as a *law of cognition* (*and* as a law of the objective world).' (Lenin's emphasis.)

the theoretical *practice* of physics; worse, it may turn into an ideological fetter.

However, and this is a thesis essential to Marxism, it is not enough to reject the dogmatism of the *application* of the forms of the dialectic in favour of the *spontaneity* of existing theoretical practices, for we know that there is no *pure* theoretical practice, no perfectly transparent science which throughout its history as a science will always be preserved, by I know not what Grace, from the threats and taints of idealism, that is, of the *ideologies* which besiege it; we know that a 'pure' science only exists on condition that it continually frees itself from the ideology which occupies it, haunts it, or lies in wait for it. The inevitable price of this purification and liberation is a continuous struggle against ideology itself, that is, against idealism, a struggle whose reasons and aims can be clarified by Theory (dialectical materialism) and guided by it as by no other method in the world. What, then, should we say for the *spontaneity* of those triumphant *avant-garde* disciplines devoted to precise pragmatic interests; which are not strictly sciences but claim to be since they use methods which are 'scientific' (but defined independently of the specificity of their presumed objects); which think, like every true science, that they have an *object*, when they are merely dealing with a certain given reality that is anyway disputed and torn between several competing 'sciences': a certain domain of phenomena not yet constituted into scientific facts and therefore not *unified*; disciplines which in their present form cannot constitute true theoretical practices because most often they only have the unity of a *technical practice* (*examples*: social psychology, and sociology and psychology in many of their branches)?[7]

---

7   Theoretical practice produces knowledges which can then figure as *means* that will serve the ends of a technical practice. Any technical practice is defined by its ends: such and such effects to be produced in such and such an object in such and such a situation. The means depend on the ends. Any theoretical practice uses among other means knowledges which intervene as procedures: either knowledges borrowed from outside, from existing sciences, or 'knowledges' produced by the technical practice itself in pursuance of its ends. In every case, the relation between technique and knowledge is an *external*,

The only Theory able to raise, if not to pose, the essential question of the status of these disciplines, to criticize ideology in all its guises, including the disguises of technical practice as sciences, is the Theory of theoretical practice (as distinct from ideological practice): the materialist dialectic or dialectical materialism, the conception of the Marxist dialectic in its *specificity*.

For we are all agreed that where a really existing science has to be defended against an encroaching ideology, where what is truly science's and what is ideology's has to be discerned without a really scientific element being taken by chance for ideology, as occasionally happens, or, as often happens, an ideological element being taken for a scientific element . . ., where (and this is very important politically) the claims of the ruling technical practices have to be criticized and the true theoretical practices that socialism, communism and our age will need more and more established, where these tasks which all demand the intervention of the *Marxist* dialectic are concerned, it is very obvious that there can be no question of making do with a formulation of Theory, that is, of the materialist dialectic, which has the disadvantage of being *inexact*, in fact of being very inexact, as inexact as the Hegelian dialectic. Of course, even this imprecision may correspond to a certain degree of reality and as such be endowed with a certain *practical* meaning, serving as a reference point or index

---

unreflected relation, radically different from the internal, reflected relation between a science and its knowledges. It is this exteriority which justifies Lenin's thesis of the necessity to *import* Marxist theory into the spontaneous political practice of the working class. Left to itself, a spontaneous (technical) practice produces only the 'theory' it needs as a means to produce the ends assigned to it: this 'theory' is never more than the reflection of this end, uncriticized, unknown, in its means of realization, that is, it is a *by-product* of the reflection of the technical practice's end on its means. A 'theory' which does not question the end whose *by-product* it is remains a prisoner of this end and of the 'realities' which have imposed it as an end. Examples of this are many of the branches of psychology and sociology, and of Economics, of Politics, of Art, etc. . . . This point is crucial if we are to identify the most dangerous ideological menace: the creation and success of so-called theories which have nothing to do with real theory but are mere *by-products* of technical activity. A belief in the 'spontaneous' theoretical virtue of technique lies at the root of this ideology, the ideology constituting the essence of Technocratic Thought.

(as Lenin says, 'The same is true of Engels. But it is "in the interests of popularisation",' *Philosophical Notebooks*, p. 359), not only in education, but also in struggle. But if a practice is to be able to make use of imprecise formulations, it is absolutely essential that this practice should at least be 'true', that on occasion it should be able to do without the expression of Theory and recognize itself globally in an imprecise Theory. But if a practice *does not really exist*, if it must be *constituted*, then imprecision becomes an obstacle in itself.

Those Marxist investigators working in *avant-garde* domains such as the theory of ideologies (law, ethics, religion, art, philosophy), the theory of the history of the sciences and of their ideological prehistory, epistemology (theory of the theoretical practice of mathematics and other natural sciences), etc. . . ., these risky but existing *avant-garde* domains; those who pose themselves difficult problems even in the domain of Marxist theoretical practice (the domain of history); not to speak of those other revolutionary 'investigators' who are confronted by political difficulties in radically new forms (Africa, Latin America, the transition to communism, etc.); if all these investigators had only the Hegelian dialectic instead of the Marxist dialectic, even if the former were purged of Hegel's ideological *system*, even if it were declared to have been 'inverted' (if this inversion amounts to applying the Hegelian dialectic to the real instead of to the Idea), they would certainly not get very far in its company! So, whether we are dealing with a confrontation with something new in the domain of a real practice, or with the foundation of a real practice we all need the materialist dialectic *as such*.

A Theoretical Revolution in Action

So we shall start by considering practices in which the Marxist dialectic as such is in action: Marxist theoretical practice and Marxist political practice.

Marxist Theoretical Practice

So a practice of theory does exist; theory is a specific practice which acts on its own object and ends in its own *product*: a knowl-*edge*. Considered in itself, any theoretical work presupposes a given raw material and some 'means of production' (the concepts of the 'theory' and the way they are used: the method). The raw material worked by theoretical labour may be very 'ideological' if the science is just coming into being; where an already constituted and developed science is concerned, it may be material that has already been elaborated theoretically, concepts which have already been formed. Very schematically, we may say that the means of theoretical labour, which are an absolute condition of its existence – 'theory' and method – represent the 'active side' of theoretical practice, the determinant moment of the process. The knowledge of the process of this theoretical practice in its generality, that is, as the specified form or real difference of the practice, itself a specified form of the general process of transformation, of the 'development of things', constitutes a first theoretical elaboration of Theory, that is, of the materialist dialectic.

Now, a real theoretical practice (one that produces knowledges) may be well able to do its duty as theory without necessarily feeling the need to make the Theory of its own practice, of its process. This is the case with the majority of sciences; they do have a 'theory' (their corpus of concepts), but it is not a Theory of their theoretical practice. The moment of the Theory of theoretical practice, that is, the moment in which a 'theory' feels the need for the Theory of its own practice – the moment of the Theory of method in the general sense – always occurs *post festum*, to help it surmount practical or 'theoretical' difficulties, resolve problems insoluble for the movement of practice immersed in its activities and therefore theoretically blind, or face up to even deeper crises. But the science can do its duty, that is, produce knowledges, for a long time before it feels the need to make the Theory of what it is doing, the theory of its practice, of its 'method'. Look at Marx. He wrote ten books as well as the monument that is *Capital* without ever writing a *Dialectics*. He talked of writing it, but never started. He never found the time. Which means that he never took the time, for at that period the Theory of his own theoretical practice was not *essential* to the development of his theory, that is, to the fruitfulness of his own practice.

However, Marx's *Dialectics* would have been very relevant to us today, since it would have been the Theory of Marx's theoretical practice, that is, exactly a determinant theoretical form of the solution (that exists in the practical state) to the problem we are dealing with: the problem of the specificity of the Marxist *dialectic*. This practical solution, this *dialectic*, exists in Marx's theoretical practice, and we can see it in action there. The method Marx used in his theoretical practice, in his scientific work on the 'given' that he transformed into knowledge, this method is precisely the *Marxist dialectic*; and it is precisely *this dialectic* which contains inside it in a practical state the solution to the problem of the relations between Marx and Hegel, of the reality of that famous 'inversion' which is Marx's gesture to us, in the Afterword to the Second Edition of *Capital*, warning us that he has settled his relations with the Hegelian dialectic. That is why today we so miss the *Dialectics* which Marx did not need and which he refused us, even though we know perfectly well that we have it, and where it is: in Marx's theoretical works, in *Capital*, etc. – yes, and of course this is the main thing, we can find it there, but *not in a theoretical state*! [8]

Engels and Lenin knew this. [9] They knew that the Marxist dialectic existed in *Capital*, *but only* in a practical state. They *also* knew that Marx did not give us a 'dialectic' in a *theoretical* state. So they did not, could not – except in extremely general expositions or in historically defined situations of theoretical urgency – confuse the *gesture* with which Marx indicated that he had *settled* his relations with Hegel with the *knowledge* of this solution, that is, with the theory of this solution. Marx's '*gestures*' as to the 'inversion' might well serve as *reference points* whereby we can situate and orient ourselves in the ideological domain: they do represent a gesture towards, a practical recognition of the existence of the solution, but they do not represent a rigorous knowledge of it. That is why Marx's gestures

---

8   With one remarkable exception which I shall discuss later.
9   Cf. Lenin: 'If Marx did not leave behind him a "*Logic*" (with a capital letter), he did leave the *logic* of *Capital*, and this ought to be utilized to the full in this question. In *Capital*, Marx applied to a single science logic, dialectics and the theory of knowledge of materialism (three words are not needed: it is one and the same thing) which has taken everything valuable in Hegel and developed it further' (*Philosophical Notebooks*, *op. cit.*, p. 319).

can and must *provoke* us into theory: into as rigorous as possible an expression of the practical solution whose existence they indicate.

Marxist Political Practice

The same is true of the Marxist political practice of the class struggle. In my last essay I took as an example the 1917 Revolution, but a hundred others from close at hand or far afield would have done just as well, as everyone must know very well. In this example, we see the 'dialectic' we obtained from Marx in action and under test (the two are one and the same thing), and in it the 'inversion' that distinguishes him from Hegel – but again, *in a practical state*. This dialectic comes from Marx, for the practice of the Bolshevik Party was based on the dialectic in *Capital*, on Marxist 'theory'. In the practice of the class struggle during the 1917 Revolution, and in Lenin's reflections on it, we do have the Marxist dialectic, but in a practical state. And here again we can see that this political *practice*, which has its defined raw material, its tools and its method, which, like any other practice, also produces transformations (which are not *knowledges*, but a revolution in *social relations*), this practice *also* may exist and develop, at least for a time, without feeling the need to make the theory of its own practice, the Theory of its 'method'. It may exist, survive and even progress without it; just like any other practice – until the moment in which its object (the existing world of the society that it is transforming) opposes enough resistance to it to *force* it to fill in this gap, to question and think its own method, so as to produce the adequate solutions, the *means* of producing them, and, in particular, so as to produce in the '*theory*' which is its basis (the theory of the existing social formation) the *new knowledges* corresponding to the content of the new 'stages' of its development. An example of these 'new knowledges': what have been called the contributions of 'Leninism' for the period of imperialism in the phase of inter-imperialist wars; and what will later be called by a name which does not exist as yet, the theoretical contributions necessary for the present period, when, in the struggle for peaceful coexistence the first *revolutionary* forms are appearing in certain so-called 'underdeveloped' countries out of their struggles for national independence.

After this, it may come as a surprise to read that the practice of the class struggle has not been reflected in the theoretical form of *method* or *Theory*,[10] when we seem to have ten decisive texts by Lenin, the most famous of which is *What is to be Done?*. But while this last text, for example, may define the theoretical and historical bases for Russian Communist practice, and prepare the way for a programme of action, it does not constitute a theoretical reflection on political practice as such. It does not, and did not intend to, constitute the theory of its own method in the general sense of Theory. So it is not a text on the dialectic, although the dialectic is certainly active in it.

For a better understanding of this point, let us take as an example the texts by Lenin on the 1917 Revolution that I quoted or gave precise references to previously.[11] The status of these texts should be made clear. They are not the texts of a historian, but of a political leader tearing himself away from the struggle for an hour or two so as to speak of the struggle to the men involved in it, and give them an understanding of it. So they are texts for direct political use, written down by a man involved in the revolution who is reflecting on his practical experience within the field of his experience itself. I regard it as a great honour to have been criticized for what amounts to having respected the form of Lenin's reflections down to the details and even the expression, presenting them for what they are without any attempt to 'supersede' them straightaway with a real historical analysis.[12] Yes, some of Lenin's reflections do have all the appearances of what might be called a 'pluralism' or a 'hyperempiricism', 'the theory of factors', etc., in their invocation of the multiple and exceptional circumstances which induced and made possible the triumph of the revolution.[13] I

---

10   With one remarkable exception which I shall discuss later.

11   It would have been better had I quoted all my texts verbatim and not been content in the majority of cases to give just a reference, even a precise one.

12   Cf. Mury, *op. cit.*, p. 47.

13   'That the revolution succeeded so quickly . . . is only due to the fact that, as a result of an extremely unique historical situation, *absolutely dissimilar currents*, *absolutely heterogeneous* class interests, *absolutely contrary* political and social strivings have *merged* . . . in a strikingly "harmonious" manner . . .' (Lenin: 'Letter from Afar (No. 1)', *Selected Works*, Vol. II, p. 35). Lenin himself stressed

took them as they were, not in their appearance but in their essence, not in their apparent 'pluralism' but in the deeply theoretical significance of this 'appearance'. Indeed, the meaning of these texts of Lenin's is not a simple description of a given situation, an empirical enumeration of various paradoxical or exceptional elements: on the contrary, it is an *analysis* of theoretical scope. They deal with a reality absolutely essential to political practice, a reality that we must *think* if we are to attain the specific essence of this practice. These texts are an analysis of the structure of the field, of the object, or (to return to our earlier terminology) of the specific raw material of political practice in general, via a precise example: the political practice of a Marxist leader in 1917.

Thus conceived, Lenin's analysis is a practical response (his analysis is this response in a practical state) to the general theoretical question: what is political practice? what distinguishes it from other practices? or, if you prefer a more classical formulation: what is political action? Through Lenin, and against the speculative thesis (a Hegelian thesis, but one that Hegel inherited from an older ideology since it is already supreme in Bossuet) which regards the concrete of a political situation as 'the contingency' in which 'necessity is realized', we come to the beginning of a theoretical answer to this real question. We can see that the object of Lenin's political practice is obviously not Universal History, nor even the general History of Imperialism. The History of Imperialism is certainly at issue in his practice, but it does not constitute its particular object. The History of Imperialism as such is the particular object of other activities: the activity of the Marxist theoretician or of the Marxist historian – but in such cases it is the object of a theoretical practice. Lenin meets Imperialism

---

certain words in this passage. A little later he declares: 'This, and this only, is the way *the situation developed*. This, and this only, is the view that should be taken by a politician who does not fear the truth, who soberly weighs the balance of social forces in the revolution, who appraises every "current situation" not only from the point of view of all its present, current peculiarities, but also from the point of view of the deeper-lying springs, the deeper relations between the interests of the proletariat and bourgeoisie, both in Russia and throughout the world' (p. 36 – this time the stress is mine. L.A.).

in his political practice in the modality of a *current* existence: in a concrete present. The theoretician of history or the historian meet it in another modality, the modality of non-currency and abstraction. So the particular object of political practice does belong to the history which is also discussed by the theoretician and the historian; but it is *another* object. Lenin knew perfectly well that he was acting on a social present which was the product of the development of imperialism, otherwise he would not have been a Marxist, but in 1917 he was not acting on Imperialism in general; he was acting on the concrete of the Russian situation, of the Russian conjuncture, on what he gave the remarkable name, 'the current situation', the situation whose currency defined his political practice as such. In the world that a historian of Imperialism is forced to see in section, if he wants to see it as Lenin lived it and understood it – because it was, as the existing world is, the sole concrete world in existence, in the sole concrete possible, the concrete of its currency, in the 'current situation' – Lenin analysed what constituted the characteristics of its structure: the essential articulations, the interconnexions, the strategic nodes on which the possibility and the fate of any revolutionary practice depended; the disposition and relations typical of the contradictions in a determinate country (semi-feudal and semi-colonialist, and yet imperialist) in the period in which the principal contradiction was approaching explosion. This is what is irreplaceable in Lenin's texts: the analysis of the structure of a *conjuncture*, the displacements and condensations of its contradictions and their paradoxical unity, all of which are the very existence of that 'current situation' which political action was to transform, in the strongest sense of the word, between February and October, 1917.

And if anyone opposes or offers these texts the irreproachable lesson of a long-term historical analysis[14] in which Lenin's 'current situation' is no more than an instant absorbed in a process which began long before it and which will supersede it in the realization of its own future – one of those historical analyses in which imperialism explains everything, which is true, but in which the unfortunate

---

14   Cf. Mury, *op. cit.*, pp. 47–8.

Lenin, struggling with the problems and analyses of revolutionary practice, is usually literally overtaken, swept off his feet and carried away by the avalanche of historical proof – then that person will never make any headway with them. As if Lenin did not regard *Imperialism* as precisely such and such current contradictions, their current structure and relations; as if this structured currency did not constitute the sole object of his political action! As if a single word could thus magically dissolve the reality of an irreplaceable practice, the revolutionaries' practice, their lives, their sufferings, their sacrifices, their efforts, in short, their concrete history, by the use made of another practice, based on the first, the practice of a historian – that is, of a scientist, who necessarily reflects on necessity's *fait accompli*; as if the theoretical practice of a classical historian who analyses the past could be confused with the practice of a revolutionary leader who reflects on the present in the present, on the necessity to be achieved, on the means to produce it, on the strategic application points for these means; in short, on his own action, for *he* does act on concrete history! and his mistakes and successes do not just feature between the covers of a *written*, 8vo 'history' in the *Bibliothèque Nationale*; their names will always be remembered, in concrete life: 1905, 1914, 1917, Hitler, Franco, Stalingrad, China, Cuba. To distinguish between the two practices, this is the heart of the question. For Lenin knew better than anyone else that the contradictions he analysed arose from one and the same Imperialism, the Imperialism that even produced their paradoxes. But knowing this, he was concerned with something else in them than this general historical knowledge, and it was because a tested science had taught him the latter that he could really concern himself with something else, with what it was that constituted the structure of his practical object: with the typicality of the contradictions, with their displacements, their condensations and the 'fusion' in revolutionary rupture that they produced; in short, with the 'current situation' that they constituted. That is why the theory of the 'weakest link' is identical with the theory of the 'decisive link'.

Once we have realized this we can return to Lenin with a quiet mind. However much any ideologue tries to bury him beneath a proof by historical analysis, there is always this one man standing there in the plain of History and of our lives, in the eternal 'current situation'. He goes on talking, calmly or passionately. He goes on talking to us about something quite simple: about his revolutionary practice, about the practice of the class struggle, in other words, about what makes it possible to act on History from within the sole history present, about what is specific in the contradiction and in the dialectic, about the specific difference of the contradiction which quite simply allows us, not to demonstrate or explain the 'inevitable' revolutions *post festum*, but to 'make' them in our unique present, or, as Marx profoundly formulated it,[15] to make the dialectic into a revolutionary method, rather than the theory of the *fait accompli*.[16]

To sum up, the problem posed – what constitutes Marx's 'inversion' of the Hegelian dialectic? what is the specific difference which distinguishes the Marxist dialectic from the Hegelian? – has already been resolved by Marxist practice, whether this is Marx's theoretical practice or the political practice of the class struggle. So its solution does exist, in the works of Marxism, but only in a practical state. We have to express it in its theoretical form, that is, to move from what, in most of the 'famous quotations',[17] is a practical recognition of an existence, to a theoretical knowledge of it.

This distinction should keep us clear of one last blind alley. It would be very easy – and is therefore tempting – to take the recognition of the existence of an object for the *knowledge* of it. Because of this facility, I might have found part or the whole of the list of 'famous quotations' used against me as a total argument, or as the equivalent of a theoretical argument. However, these quotations are precious because they say that the problem exists and that it has been resolved! They say that Marx has resolved it by 'inverting' Hegel's dialectic. But the 'famous quotations' do not give us the theoretical knowledge

---

15   In the Afterword to the second edition of *Capital*: 'In its mystified form, dialectic ... seemed to transfigure ... the existing state of things (*das Bestehende*). In its rational form ... it is in its essence critical and revolutionary' (*Capital*, Vol. I, p. 20).

16   Which can also be the *fait accompli* of a superseded revolution.

17   For convenience, I have given this name to the well-known texts from the Marxist classics which serve as guide-lines for our problem.

of this inversion. And the proof of this is, as clear as day, that we have
to make a very serious theoretical effort if we are to succeed in thinking this inversion which seems so obvious. Indeed, too many of the
'explanations' that we have been given have restricted themselves to
repeating the 'famous quotations' in paraphrase (but a paraphrase is
not an explanation) to mingling the (gestural but enigmatic) concepts
of 'inversion', 'rational kernel' with authentic and rigorous Marxist
concepts, as if the theoretical clarity of the latter could illuminate
the obscurity of the former by contagion, as if knowledge could be
born merely of the cohabitation of the known and the little known or
unknown,[18] as if the contiguity of one or two scientific concepts was
enough to transfigure our recognition of the existence of the 'inversion' or the 'kernel' into the knowledge of them! It would be more
honest to take full responsibility for one's position, for example, to
declare that Marx's remark about the 'inversion' is a *true knowledge*,
to take that risk, and put the thesis to the test of theoretical practice –
and to examine the results. Such a trial is interesting since it is a real
experiment and because it leads to a *reductio ad absurdum*, demonstrating that Marx's thought would be profoundly weakened if it had to
admit that he did give us a knowledge with the 'inversion'.[19]

   In their own way, these temptations and this experiment prove
that the theory of the solution is not to be found in a gesture towards
its existence. The existence of the solution in a practical state is one
thing. The knowledge of this solution is something else.

*

I said that Marx left us no *Dialectics*. This is not quite accurate. He
did leave us one first-rate methodological text, unfortunately without finishing it: the *Introduction to the Critique of Political Economy*,
1859. This text does not mention the 'inversion' by name, but it does

---

18   Cf. Marx, *Critique of the Gotha Programme*, 1875: 'The question then
arises: what transformation will the State undergo in communist society?
. . . This question can only be answered scientifically, and one does not get
a flea-hop nearer to the problem by a thousandfold combination of the word
people with the word State' (Marx–Engels, *Selected Works*, Vol. II, p. 32).
19   G. Mury tries to prove this in *La Pensée*, no. 108, *op. cit*.

discuss its reality: the validating conditions for the scientific use of the concepts of Political Economy. A reflection on this use is enough to draw from it the basic elements of a Dialectics, since this use is nothing more nor less than the Dialectics in a practical state.

I said that Lenin left us no *Dialectics* that would be the theoretical expression of the dialectic in action in his own political practice; more generally, that the theoretical labour of expressing the dialectic in action in the Marxist practice of the class struggle had still to be performed. This is not quite accurate. In his *Notebooks* Lenin did leave us some passages which are the sketch for a *Dialectics*. Mao Tse-tung developed these notes in the midst of a political struggle against dogmatic deviations inside the Chinese party in 1937, in an important text *On Contradiction*.[20]

I hope to be able to show how we can find in these texts – in a form which has already been considerably elaborated and which it is only necessary to develop, to relate to its basis and to reflect on continually – the theoretical answer to our question: what is the specificity of the Marxist dialectic?

The Process of Theoretical Practice

'The concrete totality as a totality of thought, as a thought concretum, is in fact a product of thought and conception; but in no sense a product of the concept thinking and engendering itself outside or over intuitions or conceptions, but on the contrary, a product of the elaboration of intuitions and conceptions into concepts.'

Karl Marx, *Introduction to the Critique of Political Economy*

Mao Tse-tung begins with contradiction in its 'universality', but his only serious discussion centres around the contradiction in the practice of the class struggle, by virtue of another 'universal' principle, the principle that the universal only exists in the particular, a principle which Mao reflects, *vis-à-vis* contradiction, in the following universal form: contradiction is always specific and specificity

---

20   Cf. *La Pensée*, December 1962, p. 7, no. 6.

universally appertains to its essence. We may be tempted to smile at this preliminary 'labour' of the universal, which seems to need a supplement of universality if it is to give birth to specificity, and to regard this 'labour' as the labour of the Hegelian 'negativity'. But a real understanding of materialism reveals that this 'labour' is not a labour of the universal, but a labour *on* a pre-existing universal, a labour whose aim and achievement is precisely to refuse this universal the abstractions or the temptations of 'philosophy' (ideology), and to bring it back to its condition by force; to the condition of a scientifically specified universality. If the universal has to be this specificity, we have no right to invoke a universal which is not the universal of this specificity.

This point is essential to dialectical materialism, and Marx discusses an illustration of it in the *Introduction* when he demonstrates that although the use of general concepts – for example, 'production', 'labour', 'exchange', etc. – is indispensable to a scientific theoretical practice, this first generality does not coincide with the product of the scientific labour: it is not its achievement, it is its prior condition. This first generality (which I shall call *Generality I*) constitutes the raw material that the science's theoretical practice will transform into specified 'concepts', that is, into that other 'concrete' generality (which I shall call *Generality III*) which is a knowledge. But what, then, is Generality I, that is, the raw material on which the labour of science is expended? Contrary to the ideological illusions – illusions which are not 'naïve', not mere 'aberrations', but necessary and well founded as ideologies – of empiricism or sensualism, a science never works on an existence whose essence is pure immediacy and singularity ('sensations' or 'individuals'). It always works on something 'general', even if this has the form of a 'fact'. At its moment of constitution, as for physics with Galileo and for the science of the evolution of social formations (historical materialism) with Marx, a science always works on existing concepts, '*Vorstellungen*', that is, a preliminary Generality I of an ideological nature. It does not 'work' on a purely objective 'given', that of pure and absolute 'facts'. On the contrary, its particular labour consists of *elaborating its own scientific facts* through a critique of the *ideological 'facts'* elaborated by an earlier ideological theoretical practice. To elaborate its own specific 'facts' is simultaneously to elaborate its own 'theory', since a scientific fact – and not the self-styled pure phenomenon – can only be identified in the field of a theoretical practice. In the development of an already constituted science, the latter works on a raw material (Generality I) constituted either of still ideological concepts, or of scientific 'facts', or of already scientifically elaborated concepts which belong nevertheless to an earlier phase of the science (an ex-Generality III). So it is by transforming this Generality I into a Generality III (knowledge) that the science works and produces.

But *who* or *what* is it that works? What should we understand by the expression: the science works? As we have seen, every transformation (every practice) presupposes the transformation of a raw material into products by setting in motion determinate means of production. What is the moment, the level or the instance which corresponds to the means of production, in the theoretical practice of science? If we abstract from men in these means of production for the time being, it is what I shall call the *Generality II*, constituted by the corpus of concepts whose more or less contradictory unity constitutes the 'theory' of the science at the (historical) moment under consideration,[21] the 'theory' that defines the field in which all the problems of the science must necessarily be posed (that is, where the

21   This Generality II, designated by the concept of 'theory', obviously deserves a much more serious examination than I can embark on here. Let us simply say that the unity I am calling 'theory' rarely exists in a science in the reflected form of a unified theoretical system. In the experimental sciences at least, besides concepts in their purely theoretical existence, it includes the whole field of technique, in which the theoretical concepts are in large part invested. The explicitly theoretical part proper is very rarely unified in a non-contradictory form. Usually it is made up of regions locally unified in regional theories that coexist in a complex and contradictory whole with a theoretically unreflected unity. This is the extremely complex and contradictory unity which is in action, in each case according to a specific mode, in the labour of theoretical production of each science. For example, in the experimental sciences, this is what constitutes the 'phenomena' into 'facts', this is what poses an existing difficulty in the form of problem, and 'resolves' this problem by locating the theoretico-technical dispositions which make up the real corpus of what an idealist tradition calls 'hypotheses', etc., etc.

'difficulties' met by the science in its object, in the confrontation of its 'facts' and its 'theory', of its previous 'knowledges' and its 'theory', or of its 'theory' and its new knowledges, will be posed in the form of a problem by and in this field). We must rest content with these schematic gestures and not enter into the dialectic of this theoretical labour. They will suffice for an understanding of the fact that theoretical practice produces *Generalities III* by the work of *Generality II* on *Generality I*.

So they will suffice for an understanding of the two following important propositions:

(1) There is never an identity of essence between Generality I and Generality III, but always a real transformation, either by the transformation of an ideological generality into a scientific generality (a mutation which is reflected in the form Bachelard, for example, calls an 'epistemological break'); or by the production of a new scientific generality which rejects the old one even as it 'englobes' it, that is, defines its 'relativity' and the (subordinate) limits of its validity.

(2) The work whereby Generality I becomes Generality III, that is – abstracting from the essential differences that distinguish Generality I and Generality III – whereby the 'abstract' becomes the 'concrete', only involves the process of theoretical practice, that is, it all takes place 'within knowledge'.

Marx is expressing this second proposition when he declares that 'the correct scientific method' is to start with the abstract to produce the concrete in thought.[22] We must grasp the precise meaning of this

---

22   Cf. Marx, *Introduction*: 'It would appear to be correct to start with the real and concrete. . . . However, a closer look reveals that this is false. . . . The latter (the method of those economic systems which move from general notions to concrete ones) is decidedly the correct scientific method. The concrete is concrete because it is the synthesis of many determinations, and therefore a unity of diversity. That is why it appears in thought as a process of synthesis, as a result, not as a point of departure . . . (in scientific method) abstract determinations lead to the reproduction of the concrete via the path of thought . . . the method which consists of rising from the abstract to the concrete is merely the way thought appropriates the concrete and repro-duces it as a concrete in thought' (Marx–Engels, *Werke*, Berlin, Vol. XIII, pp. 631–2).

thesis if we are not to slide into the ideological illusions with which these very words are only too often associated, that is, if we are not to believe that the *abstract* designates theory itself (science) while the *concrete* designates the real, the 'concrete' realities, knowledge of which is produced by theoretical practice; if we are to confuse *two different concretes*: the *concrete-in-thought* which is a knowledge, and the *concrete–reality* which is its object. The process that produces the concrete–knowledge takes place wholly in the theoretical practice: of course, it does concern the concrete–real, but this concrete–real 'survives in its independence after as before, outside thought' (Marx), without it ever being possible to confuse it with that other 'concrete' which is the knowledge of it. That the concrete-in-thought (Generality III) under consideration is the knowledge of its object (the concrete–real) is only a 'difficulty' for the ideology which transforms this reality into a so-called 'problem' (the Problem of Knowledge), and which therefore thinks as problematic what has been produced precisely as a non-problematic solution to a real problem by scientific practice itself: the non-problematicity of the relation between an object and the knowledge of it. So it is essential that we do not confuse the real distinction between the abstract (Generality I) and the concrete (Generality III) which affects theoretical practice only, with another, ideological, distinction which opposes abstraction (which constitutes the essence of thought, science and theory) to the concrete (which constitutes the essence of the real).

This is precisely Feuerbach's confusion; a confusion shared by Marx in his Feuerbachian period: not only does it provide ammunition for a mass-produced ideology popular today, but it also threatens to lead astray those taken in by the 'transparency' of its often considerable virtues as a protest, into hopeless theoretical blind-alleys. The critique which, in the last instance, counterposes the abstraction it attributes to theory and to science and the concrete it regards as the real itself, remains an ideological critique, since it denies the reality of scientific practice, the validity of its abstractions and ultimately the reality of that theoretical 'concrete' which is a knowledge. Hoping to be 'concrete' and hoping for the 'concrete', this conception hopes to be 'true' *qua* conception, so it hopes to be knowledge, but it starts by denying the reality of precisely the practice that produces knowledge! It remains in the very ideology that it claims to 'invert', that is, not in abstraction in general, but in a determinate ideological abstraction.[23]

It was absolutely necessary to come this far if we were to recognize that even within the process of knowledge, the 'abstract' generality with which the process starts and the 'concrete' generality it finishes with, Generality I and Generality III respectively, are not in essence the same generality, and, in consequence, the 'appearance' of the Hegelian conception of the auto-genesis of the concept, of the 'dialectical' movement whereby the abstract universal produces itself as concrete, depends on a confusion of the kinds of 'abstraction' or 'generality' in action in theoretical practice. Thus, when Hegel, as Marx puts it,[24] conceives 'the real as the result of self-synthesizing, self-deepening and self-moving thought' he is the victim of a *double* confusion:

(1) First, he takes the labour of production of scientific knowledge for 'the genetic process of the concrete (the real) itself'. But Hegel could not fall into this 'illusion' without opening himself to a second confusion.

(2) He takes the universal concept that figures at the beginning of

---

23   Feuerbach himself is an example. That is why his 'declarations of materialism' should be handled with great care. I have already drawn attention to this point (cf. *La Pensée*, March–April 1961, p. 8), in an article on the Young Marx in which I even used *certain notions that remained ideological*, notions that would fall under the ban of this present criticism. For example, the concept of a 'retreat' which acted as a reply to Hegel's 'supersession' and was intended to illustrate Marx's effort to get out of ideology, to free himself from myth and make contact with the *original* which Hegel had deformed – even used polemically, this concept of a 'retreat', by suggesting a return to the 'real', to the 'concrete' *anterior* to ideology, came within a handsbreadth of 'positivism'. Or again, the polemical refutation of even the *possibility* of a history of philosophy. The authority for this thesis came from a quotation from *The German Ideology* which does declare that philosophy (like religion, art, etc.) has no history. There also I was on the edge of positivism, only a step from reducing all ideology (and therefore philosophy) to a simple (temporary) phenomenon of a social formation (as *The German Ideology* is constantly tempted to do).

24   Marx, *Introduction* (*Werke*, Vol. XIII, p. 632).

the process of knowledge (for example, the concept of universality itself, the concept of 'Being' in the *Logic*) for the essence and motor of the process, for 'the self-engendering concept';[25] he takes the Generality I which theoretical practice is to transform into a knowledge (Generality III) for the essence and motor of the transformation process itself! Legitimately borrowing an analogy from another practice,[26] we might just as well claim that it is the fuel that by its dialectical auto-development produces the steam-engine, the factories and all the extraordinary technical, mechanical, physical, chemical and electrical apparatus which makes its extraction and its innumerable transformations possible today! So Hegel only falls victim to this 'illusion' because he imposes on the reality of theoretical practice an ideological conception of the universal, of its function and meaning. But in the dialectic of practice, the abstract generality at the beginning (Generality I), that is, the generality worked on, is not the same as the generality that does the work (Generality II) and even less is it the specific generality (Generality III) produced by this labour: a knowledge (the 'concrete-theoretical'). Generality II (which works) is not at all the simple development of Generality I, its passage (however complex) from the in-itself to the for-itself; for Generality II is the 'theory' of the science under consideration, and as such it is the result of a whole process (the history of the science from its foundation), which is a process of real transformations in the strongest sense of the word, that is, a process whose form is not the form of a simple development (according to the Hegelian model – the development of the in-itself into the for-itself), but of mutations and reconstructions that induce real qualitative discontinuities. So when Generality II works on Generality I it is never working on itself, neither at the moment of the science's foundation nor later in its history. That is why Generality I always emerges from this labour really transformed. It may retain the general 'form' of generality, but this form tells us nothing about it, for it has become a quite different generality – it is no longer an ideological generality, nor

---

25   *Ibid.*

26   This comparison is well founded: these two distinct practices have in common the general essence of practice.

one belonging to an earlier phase of the science, but in every case a qualitatively new specified scientific generality.

Hegel denies this reality of theoretical practice, this concrete dialectic of theoretical practice, that is, the qualitative discontinuity that intervenes or appears between the different generalities (I, II and III) even in the continuity of the production process of knowledges, or rather, he does not think of it, and if he should happen to think of it, he makes it the phenomenon of another reality, the reality he regards as essential, but which is really ideological through and through: the movement of the Idea. He projects this movement on to the reality of scientific labour, ultimately conceiving the unity of the process from the abstract to the concrete as the auto-genesis of the concept, that is, as a simple development via the very forms of alienation of the original in-itself in the emergence of its end-result, an end-result which is no more than its beginning. That is why Hegel fails to see the real, qualitative differences and transformations, the essential discontinuities which constitute the very process of theoretical practice. He imposes an ideological model on them, the model of the development of a simple interiority. That is to say, Hegel decrees that the ideological generality he imposes on them shall be the sole constitutive essence of the three types of generality – I, II and III – in action in theoretical practice.

Only now does the profound meaning of the Marxist critique of Hegel begin to appear in all its implications. Hegel's basic flaw is not just a matter of the 'speculative' illusion. This speculative illusion had already been denounced by Feuerbach and it consists of the identification of thought and being, of the process of thought and the process of being, of the concrete 'in thought' and the 'real' concrete. This is the speculative sin *par excellence*: the sin of abstraction which inverts the order of things and puts the process of the auto-genesis of the concept (the abstract) in the place of the process of the auto-genesis of the concrete (the real). Marx explains this to us quite clearly in *The Holy Family* [27] where we see, in Hegelian speculative philosophy,

---

27   *The Holy Family* was written in 1844. The same theme recurs in *The German Ideology* (1845) and *The Poverty of Philosophy* (1847).

the abstraction 'Fruit' produce the apple, the pear and the almond by its own movement of auto-determinant auto-genesis. . . . Feuerbach gave what was if possible an even better exposition and criticism of it in his admirable 1839 analysis of the Hegelian 'concrete universal'. Thus, there is a *bad* use of abstraction (the speculative and idealist use) which reveals to us the contrasting *good* use of abstraction (the materialist use). We understand, it is all quite clear and straightforward! And we prepare to put things straight, that is, to put abstraction in its right place by a liberating 'inversion' – for, of course, it is not the (general) concept of fruit which produces (concrete) fruits by auto-development, but, on the contrary, (concrete) fruits which produce the (abstract) concept of fruit. Is that all right?

No, strictly speaking, it is not all right. We cannot accept the ideological confusions which are implicit in this 'inversion' and which allow us to talk about it in the first place. There is no rigour in the inversion in question, unless we presuppose a basic ideological confusion, the confusion Marx had to reject when he really renounced Feuerbach and stopped invoking his vocabulary, when he had consciously abandoned the empiricist ideology which had allowed him to maintain that a scientific concept is produced exactly as the general concept of fruit 'should be' produced, by an abstraction acting on concrete fruits. When Marx says in the *Introduction* that any process of scientific knowledge begins from the abstract, from a generality, and not from the real concrete, he demonstrates the fact that he has actually broken with ideology and with the mere denunciation of speculative abstraction, that is, with its presuppositions. When Marx declares that the raw material of a science always exists in the form of a given generality (Generality I), in this thesis with the simplicity of a fact he is putting before us a new model which no longer has any relation to the empiricist model of the production of a concept by good abstraction, starting from real fruits and disengaging their essence by 'abstracting from their individuality'. This is now clear as far as the scientific labour is concerned; its starting-point is not 'concrete subjects' but Generalities I. But is this also true of this *Generality I*? Surely the latter is a preliminary stage of knowledge produced precisely by the *good abstraction* that Hegelian speculation merely uses in a bad way?

Unfortunately, this thesis cannot be an organic part of dialectical materialism, but only of an empiricist and sensualist ideology. This is the thesis Marx rejects when he condemns Feuerbach for conceiving 'sensuousness . . . only in the form of the object', that is, only in the form of an intuition without practice. Generality I, for example, the concept of 'fruit', is not the product of an 'operation of abstraction' performed by a 'subject' (consciousness, or even that mythological subject 'practice') – but the result of a complex process of elaboration which involves several distinct concrete practices on different levels, empirical, technical and ideological. (To return to our rudimentary example, the concept of fruit is itself the product of distinct practices, dietary, agricultural or even magical, religious and ideological practices – in its origins.) So as long as knowledge has not broken with ideology, every Generality I will be deeply impregnated by ideology, which is one of the basic practices essential to the existence of the social whole. The act of *abstraction* whereby the pure essence is extracted from concrete individuals *is an ideological myth*. In essence, Generality I is inadequate to the essence of the objects from which abstraction should extract it. It is this inadequacy that theoretical practice reveals and removes by the transformation of Generality I into Generality III. So Generality I itself is a rejection of the model from empiricist ideology presupposed by the 'inversion'.

To sum up: if we recognize that scientific practice starts with the abstract and produces a (concrete) knowledge, we must also recognize that Generality I, the raw material of theoretical practice, is qualitatively different from Generality II, which transforms it into 'concrete-in-thought', that is, into knowledge (Generality III). Denial of the difference distinguishing these two types of Generality and ignorance of the priority of Generality II (which works) over Generality I (which is worked on), are *the very bases of the Hegelian idealism* that Marx rejected: behind the still ideological semblance of the 'inversion' of abstract speculation to give concrete reality or science, this is the decisive point in which the fate of Hegelian ideology and Marxist theory is decided. The fate of Marxist theory, because we all know that the deep reasons for a rupture – not the reasons we admit, but those that act – will decide for ever whether the deliverance we expect from it will be only the expectation of freedom, that is, the absence of freedom, or freedom itself.

So that is why to maintain that the concept of 'inversion' is a *knowledge* is to endorse the ideology that underlies it, that is, to endorse a conception that denies even the reality of theoretical practice. The 'settlement' pointed out to us by the concept of 'inversion' cannot then consist merely of an inversion of the theory which conceives the auto-genesis of the concept as 'the genesis of the (real) concrete' itself, to give the opposite theory, the theory which conceives the auto-genesis of the real as the genesis of the concept (it is this opposition that, if it really had any basis, would authorize the term 'inversion'): this settlement consists (and this is the decisive point) of the rejection of an ideological theory foreign to the reality of scientific practice, to substitute for it a qualitatively different theory which, for its part, recognizes the essence of scientific practice, distinguishes it from the ideology that some have wanted to impose on it, takes seriously its particular characteristics, thinks them, expresses them, and thinks and expresses the practical conditions even of this recognition.[28] On reaching this point, we can see that in the last resort there can be no question of an 'inversion'. For a science is not obtained by inverting an ideology. A science is obtained on condition that the domain in which ideology believes that it is dealing with the real is abandoned,

---

28   This work of rupture was the result of one man's theoretical practice; that man was Karl Marx. This is not the place to return to a question I merely outlined in my article *On the Young Marx*. I should have to show why it is that Marx's theoretical practice, itself also a labour of transformation, should necessarily have taken on in theory the preponderant form of a rupture, of an epistemological break.

Might I suggest that the moment that Marx's relation to Hegel is no longer, in the last analysis, a relation of inversion, but a quite different relation, we may perhaps be better able to understand what seemed so prodigious and paradoxical to Lenin himself (in his immediate reactions of surprise in the *Notebooks*): that there are in Hegel utilizable analyses and even a number of – naturally – isolated demonstrations of a materialist character? Might I suggest that, if the relation between Marx and Hegel is not one of inversion, the 'rationality' of the Hegelian dialectic becomes infinitely more intelligible?

that is, by abandoning its ideological *problematic* (the organic presupposition of its basic concepts, and with this system, the majority of these concepts as well) and going on to establish the activity of the new theory 'in another element',[29] in the field of a new, scientific, problematic. I use these terms quite seriously, and, as a simple test, I defy anyone ever to produce an example of a true science which was constituted by inverting the problematic of an ideology, that is, on the basis of the very problematic of the ideology.[30] I only set one condition on this challenge: all words must be used in their strict sense, not metaphorically.

A 'Pre-given' Complex Structured Whole

'The simplest economic category . . . can only ever exist as the unilateral and abstract relation of a pre-given, living concrete whole . . .'

Karl Marx, *Introduction to the Critique of Political Economy*

We seem to have come a long way from the specificity of every contradiction – but, in fact, we have not moved one inch from it. We now know that this specificity is not the specification of any generality whatsoever, that is, in the limit case, the specification of an ideological generality. It is the specificity of a Generality III, of a knowledge.

What, then, is this 'specificity' of contradiction?

The dialectic is 'the study of contradiction in the very essence of

---

29   This 'theoretical image', borrowed from a paragraph by the Young Marx, was put forward on the occasion of my article in *La Nouvelle Critique*, December 1960, p. 36.

30   This sort of challenge will, I think, raise some echoes in all Marxists' political experience. For to defy anyone to make a real change in the effects without changing the cause, the basic determining structure, surely resembles the critique of reformism, the challenge that Communists throw down every day to all the world's reformists, to all those who believe that it is possible to invert the order of things on its own basis, for example, to invert social inequality into social equality, the exploitation of man by man into the mutual co-operation of men, on the very basis of existing social relations. The workers' song says: '*le monde va changer de base*'; it is theoretically irreproachable.

objects', or what comes to the same thing, 'the doctrine of the unity of opposites'. According to Lenin, 'this grasps the kernel of dialectics, but it requires explanations and development'. Mao refers to these texts and moves on to the 'explanations and development', that is, to the content of the 'kernel', in short, to the definition of the specificity of contradictions.

And then we suddenly come upon three very remarkable concepts. Two are concepts of distinction: (1) the distinction between the *principal contradiction* and the secondary contradictions; (2) the distinction between the *principal aspect* and the secondary *aspect* of each contradiction. The third and last concept: (3) the *uneven development* of contradiction. These concepts are presented to us as if 'that's how it is'. We are told that they are essential to the Marxist dialectic, since they are what is specific about it. It is up to us to seek out the deeper theoretical reasons behind these claims.

Mere consideration of the first distinction is enough to show that it presupposes immediately the existence of several contradictions (if not it would be impossible to oppose the principal ones to the secondary ones) in the same process. So it implies the existence of a complex process. In fact, according to Mao, 'A simple process contains only a single pair of opposites, while a complex process contains more'; for 'there are many contradictions in the course of development of any major thing'; but then, 'there are many contradictions in the process of development of a complex thing, and one of them is necessarily the principal contradiction'.[31] As the second distinction (the distinction between the principal and secondary aspects of each contradiction) merely reflects within each contradiction the complexity of the process, that is, the existence in it of a plurality of contradictions, one of which is dominant, it is this complexity that we must consider.

We have found the complexity of the process at the heart of these basic distinctions. Here again we are touching on one of the essential points of Marxism: the same essential point, but approached from another angle. When Mao sets aside the 'simple process with two

---

31 Mao Tse-tung, 'On Contradiction', *Selected Works* (English trans. of the second Chinese edition, Peking, 1965), Vol. 1, pp. 322, 331 and 337.

opposites', he seems to do so for factual reasons; it is irrelevant to his object, society, which does have a plurality of contradictions. But at the same time, surely, he provides for the pure possibility of this 'simple process with two opposites'? If so, it could be argued that this 'simple process with two opposites' is the essential, original process, and the others, the complex processes, are no more than complications of it, that is, the phenomenon developed. Is not Lenin leaning towards this view when he declares that 'The splitting of a single whole and the knowledge of its contradictory parts', already known to Philo . . . (Lenin's parenthesis), 'is the *essence* (one of the "essentials", one of the principal, if not the principal, characteristics or features) of the dialectic.'[32] In the single whole split into two contradictory parts, Lenin is surely not just describing a 'model' of contradiction, but the very 'womb' of all contradiction, the original essence manifest in all contradiction, even in its most complex forms? And this would surely make the complex merely the development and phenomenon of the simple? This is the decisive question. For this 'simple process with two opposites' in which the Whole is split into two contradictory parts is precisely the very *womb* of Hegelian contradiction.

Once again, we can and must put our interpretation to the test.

Of course, Mao only refers to the 'simple process' as a reminder, and gives no example of it. But throughout his analysis we never deal with anything but complex processes in which a structure with multiple and uneven determinations intervenes primitively, not secondarily; no complex process is presented as the development of a simple one, so the complex never appears as the phenomenon of the simple – on the contrary, it appears as the result of a process which is itself complex. So complex processes are never anything but given complexities, their reduction to simple origins is never envisaged, in fact or in principle. If we return to Marx's 1857 *Introduction*, we find the same requirement expressed with extraordinary rigour: in his reflections on the concepts of Political Economy, Marx does not only show that it is impossible to delve down to the birth or origin of the simple universal, 'production', since 'when we talk of production we always mean production

---

32   Lenin, *Philosophical Notebooks, op. cit.*, p. 359.

at a determinate stage in social development of the production of individuals living in *society*,[33] that is, in a structured social whole. Marx does not only deny us the ability to delve down beneath this complex whole (and this denial is a denial on principle: it is not ignorance which prevents us, but the very essence of production itself, its concept); Marx does not only show that every 'simple category' presupposes the existence of the structured whole of society,[34] but also, what is almost certainly more important, he demonstrates that far from being original, in determinate conditions, simplicity is merely the product of the complex process. This is simplicity's sole claim to existence (again, existence in a complex whole!): in the form of the existence of such and such a 'simple' category. Thus, labour: 'Labour seems a wholly simple category. Even the conception of labour in this generality – as Labour in general – is age-old. . . . However, economically conceived in this simplicity, "labour" is as modern a category as the relations which engender this simple abstraction.'[35] In the same way, the individual producer, or the individual as the elementary subject of production, which eighteenth-century mythology imagined to be at the origin of society's economic development, this economic 'cogito' only appeared, even as an 'appearance', in developed capitalist society, that is, in the society which had developed the social character of production to the highest degree. Similarly, exchange, the simple universal *par excellence*, 'did not appear historically in all its intensity until the most developed states of society. (This category) absolutely does not stride through every economic relation.'[36] So simplicity is not original; on the contrary, it is the structured whole which gives its meaning to the simple category, or which may produce the economic existence of certain simple categories as the result of a long process and under exceptional conditions.

Whatever the case, we are in a world foreign to Hegel: 'Hegel

---

33   Marx, *Introduction*, *op. cit.*, p. 616.
34   'The simplest economic category . . . can only ever exist as the unilateral and abstract relation of a pre-given, living, concrete whole . . .' (Karl Marx, *Introduction*, *op. cit.*, p. 632).
35   *Ibid.*, p. 634.
36   *Ibid.*, p. 634.

is right to begin his *Philosophy of Right* with possession as it is the subject's simplest legal relation. But no possession exists before the family or before master-slave relations, and these are much more concrete relations.'[37] The *Introduction* is no more than a long demonstration of the following thesis: the simple only ever exists within a complex structure; the universal existence of a simple category is never original, it only appears as the end-result of a long historical process, as the product of a highly differentiated social structure; so, where reality is concerned, we are never dealing with the pure existence of simplicity, be it essence or category, but with the existence of 'concretes' of complex and structured beings and processes. This is the basic principle that eternally rejects the Hegelian womb of contradiction.

Indeed, if we take the rigorous essence rather than the metaphorical sense of the Hegelian model, we can see that the latter does require this 'simple process with two opposites', this simple original unity, splitting into two opposites, that is still evoked in Lenin's reference. This is the original unity that constitutes the fragmented unity of the two opposites in which it is alienated, changing even as it stays the same; these two opposites are the same unity, but in duality, the same interiority, but in exteriority – and that is why each is for its own part the contradictory and abstraction of the other, since each is merely the abstraction of the other without knowing it, as in-itself – before restoring their original unity, but enriched by its fragmentation, by its alienation, in the negation of the abstraction which negated their previous unity; then they will be a single whole once again, they will have reconstituted a new simple 'unity', enriched by the past labour of their negation, the new simple unity of a totality produced by the negation of the negation. It is clear that the implacable logic of this Hegelian model rigorously interlinks the following concepts: simplicity, essence, identity, unity, negation, fission, alienation, opposites, abstraction, negation of the negation, supersession (*Aufhebung*), totality, simplicity, etc. The whole of the Hegelian dialectic is here, that is, it is completely dependent on the radical presupposition of a simple

---

37   *Ibid.*, p. 633.

original unity which develops within itself by virtue of its negativity, and throughout its development only ever restores the original simplicity and unity in an ever more 'concrete' totality.

Marxists may well invoke this model or use it as a short-cut or symbol, either inadvertently or intentionally,[38] but strictly conceived, Marxist theoretical practice rejects it, just as Marxist political practice does. Marxism rejects it precisely because it rejects the theoretical presupposition of the Hegelian model: the presupposition of an original simple unity. What Marxism refuses is the (ideological) philosophical pretension to coincide exhaustively with a 'root origin', whatever its form (the *tabula rasa*; the zero point in a process; the state of nature; the concept of the beginning that, for example, Hegel sees as being immediately identical with nothingness; the simplicity that, for Hegel once again, is the starting-point – and restarting-point, indefinitely – for every process, what restores it to its origin, etc.); it rejects, therefore, the Hegelian philosophical pretension which accepts this original simple unity (reproduced at each moment of the process) which will produce the whole complexity of the process later in its auto-development, but without ever getting lost in this complexity itself,[39] without ever losing in it either its simplicity or its unity – since the plurality and the complexity will never be more than its own 'phenomenon', entrusted with the manifestation of its own essence.[40]

Once again, I am afraid that we cannot reduce the rejection of this presupposition to its 'inversion'. This presupposition has not been 'inverted', it has been eliminated; totally eliminated (absolutely! and

---

38   Intentionally: for example, when Marx wanted to teach his contemporaries' *philosophical stupidity* a lesson, by 'coquetting' with Hegel's terminology in the First Volume of *Capital* ('*kokettieren*'). Do we still need this lesson?

39   Even its death is no more than the imminence of its Resurrection, as Good Friday is the imminence of Easter Sunday. These symbols are Hegel's own.

40   To forestall any misunderstanding, I should point out that it is this 'Hegelian dialectic' that reigns in glory over Marx's *1844 Manuscripts*, and what is more, in an extraordinarily pure and uncompromising state. To round off the demonstration I should add that the Hegelian dialectic in the *Manuscripts* has been rigorously 'inverted'. That is why the rigour of this rigorous text is not Marxist.

not in the sense of the *Aufhebung* that 'preserves' what it eliminates
. . .) and replaced by a *quite different* theoretical presupposition which
has nothing to do with the old one. Instead of the ideological myth of
a philosophy of origins and its organic concepts, Marxism establishes
in principle the recognition of the givenness of the complex structure
of any concrete 'object', a structure which governs both the development of the object and the development of the theoretical practice
which produces the knowledge of it. There is no longer any original
essence, only an ever-pre-givenness, however far knowledge delves
into its past. There is no longer any simple unity, only a structured,
complex unity. There is no longer any original simple unity (in any
form whatsoever), but instead, *the ever-pre-givenness of a structured
complex unity*. If this is the case, it is clear that the 'womb' of the
Hegelian dialectic has been proscribed and that its organic categories, in so far as they are specific and positively determined, cannot
survive it with theoretical status, particularly those categories that
'cash' the theme of the original simple unity, that is, the 'fission' of the
single whole, alienation, the abstraction (in the Hegelian sense) that
unites the opposites, the negation of the negation, the *Aufhebung*, etc.
Given this, it is not surprising that there is no trace of these organically Hegelian categories either in Marx's 1857 *Introduction* or in Mao
Tse-tung's text of 1937.

Of course, some of these categories might well be invoked in an
ideological context (for example, the struggle with Dühring), or in a
general exposition intended to illustrate the meaning of given results;
as long as it is on this level of ideological struggle, or of opposition and
illustration, these categories can be used with very real results in ideological practice (struggle) and in the general exposition of a conception.
But this last 'exposition' (the illustration of the laws of the dialectic by
such and such an example) must remain within the zone sanctioned by
theoretical practice – for in itself it does not constitute a true theoretical practice, producing new knowledges. On the other hand, where a
true practice is concerned, one which really transforms its object and
produces true results (knowledges, a revolution . . .), such as Marx's and
Lenin's theoretical and political practice, etc., then the margin of theoretical tolerance in respect to these categories disappears; the categories

themselves disappear. Where a true practice, organically constituted and developed over the years, is concerned, and not a simple application without organic effects, an application which makes no changes in its object (for example, to the practice of physics), to its real development; where the practice of a man truly committed to a true practice is concerned, a man of science who applies himself to the constitution and development of a science, or a political man who applies himself to the development of the class struggle – then there is no longer any question, there can no longer be any question, of imposing on the object even categories which are approximately correct. Then those categories which have nothing further to say are silent, or reduced to silence. Thus, in the only Marxist practices which have really been constituted, Hegelian categories have been dead a long time. They are 'absent' categories. No doubt that is why some people have collected together and displayed to every gaze, with the infinite care that is the due of the unique remains of some former age, the *two sole sentences*[41] to be found in the whole of *Capital*, that is, in some 2,300 octavo pages in the English edition; no doubt that is why they add force to these two sentences by adding to them another sentence, or rather a phrase, an exclamation, made by Lenin, which assures us very enigmatically that because Hegel went unread, Marx was not understood at all for half a century. But let us return to this simple fact: in the only Marxist practices that have really been constituted, the categories in use or in action are not Hegelian: in action in Marxist practice there are different categories, the categories of the Marxist dialectic.

---

41   One very metaphorical reference to the negation of the negation. Another, which I shall discuss, on the transformation of quantity into quality. Engels refers to these two texts and comments on them in the first part of *Anti-Dühring*, Chapters 12 and 13. One further word on the negation of the negation. Today it is official convention to reproach Stalin with having suppressed the 'laws of the dialectic', and more generally with having turned away from Hegel, the better to establish his dogmatism. At the same time, it is willingly proposed that a certain return to Hegel would be salutary. One day perhaps these declarations will become the object of some proof. In the meanwhile, it seems to me that it would be simpler to recognize that the expulsion of the 'negation of the negation' from the domain of the Marxist dialectic might be evidence of the real theoretical perspicacity of its author.

Structure in Dominance: Contradiction and Overdetermination

'The uneven relation of the development of material production with that, for example, of artistic production. . . . The only point difficult to grasp, here, is how production relations stand in uneven development to legal relations . . .'

Karl Marx, Introduction to the Critique of Political Economy

We still have to learn the essential feature of this practice: the law of uneven development. For, as Mao puts it in a phrase as clear as the dawn, 'Nothing in this world develops absolutely evenly.'

To understand the meaning of this law and its scope – and, contrary to what is sometimes thought, it does not concern Imperialism alone, but absolutely 'everything in this world' – we must return to the essential differences of Marxist contradiction which distinguish a principal contradiction in any complex process, and a principal aspect in any contradiction. So far I have only insisted on this 'difference' as an index of the complexity of the whole, arguing that it is absolutely necessary that the whole be complex if one contradiction in it is to dominate the others. Now we must consider this domination, no longer as an index, but in itself, and draw out its implications.

That one contradiction dominates the others presupposes that the complexity in which it features is a structured unity, and that this structure implies the indicated domination–subordination relations between the contradictions. For the domination of one contradiction over the others cannot, in Marxism, be the result of a contingent distribution of different contradictions in a collection that is regarded as an object. In this complex whole 'containing many contradictions' we cannot 'find' one contradiction that dominates the others as we might 'find' the spectator a head taller than the others in the grandstand at the stadium. Domination is not just an indifferent *fact*, it is a fact *essential* to the complexity itself. That is why complexity implies domination as one of its essentials: it is inscribed in its structure. So to claim that this unity is not and cannot be the unity of a simple, original and universal essence is not, as those who dream of that ideological concept foreign to Marxism, 'monism',[42] think, to sacrifice unity on the altar of 'pluralism' – it is to claim something quite different: that the unity discussed by Marxism is *the unity of the complexity itself*, that the mode of organization and articulation of the complexity is precisely what constitutes its unity. It is to claim that *the complex whole has the unity of a structure articulated in dominance*. In the last resort this specific structure is the basis for the relations of domination between contradictions and between their aspects that Mao described as essential.

This principle must be grasped and intransigently defended if Marxism is not to slip back into the confusions from which it had

---

42 *Monism*. This is the key concept in the personal conception of Haeckel, the great German biologist and valiant mechanical materialist combatant in the anti-religious and anti-clerical struggle between 1880 and 1910; active propagandist, author of 'popular' works which had a very wide diffusion; creator of the 'League of German Monists'. He held religion to be 'dualist' and counterposed to it 'monism'. As a 'monist' he held that there were not two substances (God and the world, Mind or soul and matter) but one only. Haeckel himself thought that this Unique Substance had two attributes (rather like the Spinozist substance with its two essential attributes): matter and energy. He held that all determinations, whether material or spiritual, were modes of this Substance, for which he claimed 'Omnipotence'. Plekhanov was to take up this theme of 'monism', and no doubt it had affinities with the mechanistic tendencies Lenin was later to reproach him with. Plekhanov was more 'consistent' than Haeckel; he recognized that modern idealism was also a 'monism', as it explained everything by a single substance, Spirit. He maintained that Marxism was a materialist monism (cf. Plekhanov: *The Development of the Monist View of History*). Perhaps it is to Plekhanov that I owe the simultaneous presence of the term 'monism' in the articles of G. Besse, R. Garaudy and G. Mury, and of expressions declaring that Marxism is essentially 'monist'. Engels and Lenin totally condemned this ideological concept because of its imprecision. Sometimes my critics use it in a strong sense (e.g. Mury), sometimes in a more or less weak sense; they do not oppose it to dualism, as Haeckel and Plekhanov did, but to 'pluralism'; so in their hands the term may be said to have taken on a methodological nuance, but still an ideological one. The concept has no positive use in Marxism, it is even theoretically dangerous. At the most, it might have a negative practical value: beware of 'pluralism'! It has no value as knowledge. To accord it such a value and draw out the theoretical consequences (Mury) is ultimately to deform Marx's thought.

delivered us, that is, into a type of thought for which only one model of unity exists: the unity of a substance, of an essence or of an act; into the twin confusions of 'mechanistic' materialism and the idealism of consciousness. If we were so precipitate as to assimilate the structured unity of a complex whole to the simple unity of a totality; if the complex whole were taken as purely and simply the development of one *single* essence or original and simple substance, then at best we would slide back from Marx to Hegel, at worst, from Marx to Haeckel! But to do so would be precisely to sacrifice the specific difference which distinguishes Marx from Hegel: the distance which radically separates the *Marxist type of unity* from the Hegelian type of unity, or the Marxist totality from the Hegelian totality. The concept of the 'totality' is a very popular concept today; no passport is required to cross from Hegel to Marx, from the *Gestalt* to Sartre, etc., beyond the invocation of one word: 'totality'. The word stays the same, but the concept changes, sometimes radically, from one author to another. Once the concept has been defined this tolerance must cease. In fact, the Hegelian 'totality' is not such a malleable concept as has been imagined, it is a concept that is perfectly defined and individualized by its theoretical role. Similarly, the Marxist totality is also definite and rigorous. All these two 'totalities' have in common is: (1) a word; (2) a certain vague conception of the unity of things; (3) some theoretical enemies. On the other hand, in their essence they are almost unrelated. The *Hegelian totality* is the alienated development of a simple unity, of a simple principle, itself a moment of the development of the Idea: so, strictly speaking, it is the phenomenon, the self-manifestation of this simple principle which persists in all its manifestations, and therefore even in the alienation which prepares its restoration. Once again, we are not dealing with concepts without consequences. For the unity of a simple essence manifesting itself in its alienation produces this result: that every concrete difference featured in the Hegelian totality, including the 'spheres' visible in this totality (civil society, the State, religion, philosophy, etc.), all these differences are negated as soon as they are affirmed: for they are no more than 'moments' of the simple internal principle of the totality, which fulfils itself by negating the alienated difference that it posed;

further, as alienations – phenomena – of the simple internal principle, these differences are all equally '*indifferent*', that is, practically equal beside it, and therefore equal to one another, and that is why one determinate contradiction *can never be dominant* in Hegel.[43] That is to say, the Hegelian whole has a 'spiritual' type of unity in which all the differences are only posed to be negated, that is, they are indifferent,

---

43 Hegel's theory should not be confused with Marx's judgement of Hegel. Surprising as it may seem to those who know Hegel only in Marx's judgement, in his theory of society Hegel is not the inverse of Marx. The 'spiritual' principle that constitutes the internal unity of the Hegelian historical totality cannot be assimilated at all to the one that features in Marx in the form of the 'determination in the last instance by the Economy'. The inverse principle – determination in the last instance by the State, or by Philosophy – is not to be found in Hegel. It was Marx who said that the Hegelian conception of society *amounts in reality* to making Ideology the motor of History, because it is an ideological conception. But Hegel says nothing of the kind. For him, there is no determination in the last instance *in society*, in the existing totality. Hegelian society is not unified by a basic instance that exists inside it, it is neither unified nor determined by any of its 'spheres', be it the political sphere, the philosophical sphere or the religious sphere. For Hegel, the principle unifying and determining the social totality is not such and such a 'sphere' of society but a principle which has no privileged place or body in society, for the simple reason that it resides in all places and all bodies. It is in every determination of society, in the economic, the political, the legal, etc., down to the most spiritual. For example, Rome: it is not its *ideology* that unifies and determines it for Hegel, but a 'spiritual' principle (itself a moment of the development of the Idea) manifest in every Roman determination, in its economy, its politics, its religion, its law, etc. This principle is *the abstract legal personality*. It is a 'spiritual' principle of which Roman Law is only one determination among others. In the modern world it is *subjectivity*, just as universal a principle: the economy is subjectivity, as is politics, religion, philosophy, music, etc. The totality of Hegelian society is such that its principle is simultaneously immanent to it and transcendent of it, but it never coincides in itself with any determinate reality of society itself. That is why the Hegelian totality may be said to be endowed with a unity of a 'spiritual' type in which each element is *pars totalis*, and in which the visible spheres are merely the alienated and restored unfolding of the said internal principle. In other words, there is nothing to justify the identification (even as an inversion) of the Hegelian totality's type of unity and the Marxist totality's type of unity.

in which they never exist for themselves, in which they only have a semblance of an independent existence, and in which, since they never manifest anything but the unity of the simple internal principle alienated in them, they are practically equal among themselves as the alienated phenomena of this principle. My claim is that the Hegelian totality: (1) is not really, but only apparently, articulated in 'spheres'; (2) that its unity is not its complexity itself, that is, the structure of this complexity; (3) that it is therefore deprived of the structure in dominance (*structure à dominante*) which is the absolute precondition for a real complexity to be a unity and really the object of a *practice* that proposes to transform this structure: political practice. It is no accident that the Hegelian theory of the social totality has never provided the basis for a *policy*, that there is not and cannot be a Hegelian politics.

This is not all. If every contradiction is a contradiction in a complex whole structured in dominance, this complex whole cannot be envisaged without its contradictions, without their basically uneven relations. In other words, each contradiction, each essential articulation of the structure, and the general relation of the articulations in the structure in dominance, constitute so many conditions of the existence of the complex whole itself. This proposition is of the first importance. For it means that the structure of the whole and therefore the 'difference' of the essential contradictions and their structure in dominance, is the very existence of the whole; that the 'difference' of the contradictions (that there is a principal contradiction, etc.; and that every contradiction has a principal aspect) is identical to the conditions of the existence of the complex whole. In plain terms this position implies that the 'secondary' contradictions are not the pure phenomena of the 'principal' contradiction, that the principal is not the essence and the secondaries so many of its phenomena, so much so that the principal contradiction might practically exist *without* the secondary contradictions, or without some of them, or might exist *before* or *after* them.[44] On the contrary, it implies that the secondary

---

44   This myth of origin is well illustrated by the theory of the 'bourgeois' social contract, which, for example, in Locke, and what a theoretical gem, defines an economic activity in the state of nature before (in principle or in fact, it matters little) any of its legal and political conditions of existence!

contradictions are essential even to the existence of the principal contradiction, that they really constitute its condition of existence, just as the principal contradiction constitutes their condition of existence. As an example, take the complex structured whole that is society. In it, the 'relations of production' are not the pure phenomena of the forces of production; they are also their condition of existence. The superstructure is not the pure phenomenon of the structure, it is also its condition of existence. This follows from Marx's principle, referred to above, that production without society, that is, without social relations, exists nowhere; that we can go no deeper than the unity that is the unity of a whole in which, if the relations of production do have production itself as their condition of existence, production has as its condition of existence its form: the relations of production. Please do not misunderstand me: this mutual conditioning of the existence of the 'contradictions' does not nullify the structure in dominance that reigns over the contradictions and in them (in this case, determination in the last instance by the economy). Despite its apparent circularity, this conditioning does not result in the destruction of the structure of domination that constitutes the complexity of the whole, and its unity. Quite the contrary, even within the reality of the conditions of existence of each contradiction, it is the manifestation of the structure in dominance that unifies the whole.[45] *This reflection of the conditions of existence of the contradiction within itself, this reflection of the structure articulated in dominance that constitutes the unity of the complex whole*

---

45   In the *Introduction* Marx gives us the best possible proof of the invariance of the structure in dominance within the apparent circularity of conditioning, when he analyses the identity of production, consumption and distribution through exchange. This might give the reader Hegelian vertigo – 'nothing simpler, then, for a Hegelian than to pose production and consumption as identical' (*op. cit.*, p. 625) – but this would be a complete misunderstanding. 'The result we have obtained is not that production, distribution, exchange and consumption are identical, but that they are all elements of one totality, differentiations within one unity' in which it is production in its specific difference that is determinant. 'So a determinate production determines a determinate consumption, distribution and exchange, and the determinate mutual relations of these different moments. For its part, production in its unilateral form is really determined by the other moments' (pp. 630–31).

within each contradiction, this is the most profound characteristic of the Marxist dialectic, the one I have tried recently to encapsulate in the concept of '*overdetermination*'.[46]

This becomes easier to understand if we make a detour via a familiar concept. When Lenin said that '*the soul of Marxism is the concrete analysis of a concrete situation*': when Marx, Engels, Lenin, Stalin and Mao explain that '*everything depends on the conditions*'; when Lenin describes the peculiar '*circumstances*' of Russia in 1917; when Marx (and the whole Marxist tradition) explains, with the aid of a thousand examples, that such and such a contradiction will dominate according to the case, etc., they are appealing to a concept that might appear to be *empirical*: the 'conditions', which are simultaneously the existing conditions and the conditions of existence of the phenomenon under consideration. Now this concept is essential to Marxism precisely because it is not an empirical concept: a statement about what exists. ... On the contrary, it is a *theoretical* concept, with its basis in the very essence of the object: the ever-pre-given complex whole. In fact, these conditions are no more than the very existence of the whole in a determinate 'situation', the 'current situation' of the politician, that is, the complex relation of reciprocal conditions of existence between the articulations of the structure of the whole. That is why it is theoretically possible and legitimate to speak of the 'conditions' as of something that enables us to understand that the Revolution, 'the task of the day', could only break out here, in Russia, in China, in Cuba, in 1917, in 1949, in 1958, and not elsewhere; and not in another 'situation'; that the revolution, governed by capitalism's basic contradiction, did not succeed until Imperialism, and succeeded in the 'favourable' conditions that were

---

46   I did not invent this concept. As I pointed out, it is borrowed from two existing disciplines: specifically, from linguistics and psychoanalysis. In these disciplines it has an objective dialectical 'connotation', and – particularly in psychoanalysis – one sufficiently related formally to the content it designates here for the loan not to be an arbitrary one. A new word is necessarily required to designate a new acquisition. A neologism might have been invented. Or it was possible to 'import' (in Kant's words) a concept sufficiently related to make its domestication (Kant) easy. And in return, this 'relatedness' might open up a path to psychoanalytic reality.

precisely points of historical rupture, the 'weakest links': not England, France or Germany, but 'backward' Russia (Lenin), China and Cuba (ex-colonies, lands exploited by Imperialism). If it is theoretically acceptable to talk of the conditions without sliding into the empiricism or the irrationality of 'that's how it is' and of 'chance', it is because Marxism conceives the 'conditions' as the (real, concrete, current) existence of the contradictions that constitute the whole of a historical process. That is why Lenin's invocation of the 'existing conditions' in Russia was not a lapse into empiricism; he was analysing the very existence of the complex whole of the process of Imperialism in Russia in that 'current situation'.

But if the conditions are no more than the current existence of the complex whole, they are its very contradictions, each reflecting in itself the organic relation it has with the others in the structure in dominance of the complex whole. Because each contradiction reflects in itself (in its specific relations of unevenness with the other contradictions, and in the relation of specific unevenness between its two aspects) the structure in dominance of the complex whole in which it exists, and therefore because of the current existence of this whole and therefore of its current 'conditions', the contradiction is identical with these conditions: so when we speak of the 'existing conditions' of the whole, we are speaking of its 'conditions of existence'.

Is it necessary to return to Hegel once again to show that, for him, the 'circumstances' or 'conditions' are ultimately no more than phenomena and therefore evanescent, since in that form of 'contingency' christened the 'existence of Necessity', they can never express more than a manifestation of the movement of the Idea; that is why 'conditions' do not really exist for Hegel since, under cover of simplicity developing into complexity, he always deals with a pure interiority whose exteriority is no more than its phenomenon. That in Marxism the '*relation to nature*', for example, is organically part of the 'conditions of existence'; that it is one of the terms, the principal one, of the principal contradiction (forces of production/relations of production); that, as their condition of existence, it is reflected in the 'secondary' contradictions of the whole and their relations; that the conditions of existence are therefore a real absolute, the given-ever-pre-givenness of the existence of the complex whole which reflects them inside its own structure – all this is quite foreign to Hegel, who, in one movement, rejects both the structured complex whole and its conditions of existence by his prior assumption of a pure, simple interiority. That is why, for example, the relation to nature, the conditions of existence of any human society, merely has the role of a contingent given for Hegel, the role of the 'inorganic', of climate, of geography (America, that 'syllogism whose middle term – the Isthmus of Panama – is very narrow'!), the role of the famous 'that's how it is!' (Hegel's comment at the sight of the mountains), designating the material nature which must be 'superseded' (*aufgehoben*!) by the Spirit which is its 'truth'. Yes, thus reduced to geographical nature, the conditions of existence really are the very contingency that will be resorbed, negated–superseded by the Spirit which is its free necessity and which already exists in Nature even in the form of contingency (the contingency that makes a small island produce a great man!). This is because natural or historical conditions of existence are never more than *contingency* for Hegel, because in no respect do they determine the spiritual totality of society; for Hegel, the absence of conditions (in the non-empirical, non-contingent sense) is a necessary counterpart to the absence of any real structure in the whole, and to the absence of a structure in dominance, the absence of any basic determination and the absence of that reflection of the conditions in the contradiction which its '*overdetermination*' represents.

I am insisting on this 'reflection' that I propose to call '*overdetermination*' at this point because it is absolutely essential to isolate it, identify it and give it a name, so that we can explain its reality theoretically, the reality which is forced on us by the political practice of Marxism as well as by its theoretical practice. Let us try to delimit this concept more accurately. Overdetermination designates the following essential quality of contradiction: the reflection in contradiction itself of its conditions of existence, that is, of its situation in the structure in dominance of the complex whole. This is not a univocal 'situation'. It is not just its situation '*in principle*' (the one it occupies in the hierarchy of instances in relation to the determinant instance: in society, the economy) nor just its situation '*in fact*' (whether, in the phase under consideration, it is dominant or subordinate) but *the relation of this situation in fact to this situation in principle*, that is, the very relation which makes of this situation in fact *a 'variation' of the – 'invariant' – structure, in dominance, of the totality*.

If this is correct, we must admit that contradiction can no longer be univocal (categories can no longer have a role and meaning fixed once and for all) since it reflects in itself, in its very essence, its relation to the unevenness of the complex whole. But we must add that, while no longer univocal, it has not for all that become 'equivocal', the product of the first-comer among empirical pluralities, at the mercy of circumstances and 'chance', their pure reflection, as the soul of some poet is merely that passing cloud. Quite the contrary, once it has ceased to be univocal and hence determined once and for all, standing to attention in its role and essence, it reveals itself as determined by the structured complexity that assigns it to its role, as – if you will forgive me the astonishing expression – complexly-structurally-unevenly-determined. I must admit, I preferred a shorter term: overdetermined.

It is this very peculiar type of determination (this overdetermination) which gives Marxist contradiction its specificity, and enables us to explain Marxist *practice* theoretically, whether it is theoretical or political. Only overdetermination enables us to understand the concrete variations and mutations of a structured complexity such as a social formation (the only one that has really been dealt with by Marxist practice up to now), not as the accidental variations and mutations produced by external 'conditions' in a fixed structured whole, in its categories and their fixed order (this is precisely mechanism) – but as so many concrete restructurations inscribed in the essence, the 'play' of each category, in the essence, the 'play' of each contradiction, in the essence, the 'play' of the articulations of the complex structure in dominance which is reflected in them. Do we now need to repeat that unless we assume, think this very peculiar type of determination once we have identified it, we will never be able to think the possibility of political action, or even the possibility of theoretical practice itself, that is, very precisely, the essence of the object (the raw material) of *political* and *theoretical* practice, that is, the structure of the 'current situation' (in theory or politics) to which these practices apply; do we need to add that unless we conceive this overdetermination we will be unable to explain theoretically the following simple reality: the prodigious 'labour' of a theoretician, be it Galileo, Spinoza or Marx, and of a revolutionary, Lenin and all his companions, devoting their suffering, if not their lives, to the resolution of these small 'problems': the elaboration of an *'obvious'* theory, the making of an *'inevitable'* revolution, the realization in their own personal 'contingency'(!) of the Necessity of History, theoretical or political, in which the future will soon quite naturally be living its 'present'?

To make this point clear, let us take up the very terms of Mao Tse-tung. If all contradictions are under the sway of the great law of unevenness, and to be a Marxist and to be able to act politically (and, I should add, to be able to produce theoretically), it is necessary at all costs to distinguish the principal from the secondary among contradictions and their aspects, and if this distinction is essential to Marxist theory and practice – this is, Mao comments, because we must face up to concrete reality, to the reality of the history that men are living, if we are to explain a reality in which the *identity of opposites* is supreme, that is (1) the passage in indeterminate conditions, of one opposite into the place of another,[47] the exchange of roles between contradictions and their aspects (I shall call this phenomenon of substitution *displacement*); (2) the 'identity' of opposites in a real unity (I shall call this phenomenon of 'fusion' *condensation*). Indeed, the great lesson of practice is that if the structure in dominance remains constant, the disposition of the roles within it changes; the principal contradiction becomes a secondary one, a secondary contradiction takes its place, the principal aspect becomes a secondary one, the secondary aspect becomes the principal one. There is always one principal contradiction and secondary ones, but they exchange their roles in the structure articulated in dominance while this latter remains stable. *'There is no doubt at all that at every stage in the development of a process, there is only one principal contradiction which plays the leading role,'* says Mao Tse-tung. But this principal contradiction produced by *displacement* only becomes 'decisive', explosive, by *condensation* (by 'fusion'). It is the latter that constitutes the 'weakest link' that, as Lenin said, must

---

47   *On Contradiction, op. cit.*, pp. 338, 339.

be grasped and pulled in political practice (or in theoretical practice . . .) so that the whole chain will follow, or, to use a less linear image, it is the latter which occupies the strategic nodal position that must be attacked in order to produce '*the dissolution of (the existing) unity*'.[48] Here again, we must not be taken in by the appearance of an arbitrary succession of dominations; for each one constitutes one stage in a complex process (the basis for the 'periodization' of history) and the fact that we are concerned with the dialectics of a complex process is the reason why we are concerned with those overdetermined, specific 'situations', the 'stages', 'phases' and 'periods', and with the mutations of specific domination that characterize each stage. The nodality of the development (the specific phases) and the specific nodality of the structure at each phase are the very existence and reality of the complex process. This is the basis of the reality, decisive in and for political practice (and obviously also for theoretical practice), of the displacements of domination and the condensations of the contradictions, which Lenin gave us such a clear and profound example of in his analysis of the 1917 Revolution (the 'fusion' point of the contradictions; in both senses of the word, the point where several contradictions *condense* – 'fuse' – so that this point becomes the *fusion* point – the critical point – and the point of revolutionary *mutation*, of '*recrystallization*').

Perhaps these gestures will help us to understand why the great law of unevenness suffers no exceptions.[49] This unevenness suffers no exceptions because it is not itself an exception: not a derivatory law, produced by peculiar conditions (Imperialism, for example) or intervening in the interference between the developments of distinct social formations (the unevenness of economic development, for example, between 'advanced' and 'backward' countries, between colonizers and colonized, etc.). Quite the contrary, it is a primitive law, with priority over these peculiar cases and able to account for them precisely in so far as it does not derive from their existence. Only because every social formation is affected by unevenness, are the

---

48   *Ibid.*, p. 342.
49   *Ibid.*, pp. 335–6.

relations of such a social formation with other formations of different economic, political and ideological maturity affected by it, and it
enables us to understand how these relations are possible. So it is not
external unevenness whose intervention is the basis for an internal
unevenness (for example, the so-called meeting of civilizations), but,
on the contrary, the internal unevenness has priority and is the basis
for the role of the external unevenness, up to and including the effects
this second unevenness has within social formations in confrontation.
Every interpretation that reduces the phenomena of internal unevenness (for example, explaining the 'exceptional' conjuncture in Russia
in 1917 solely by its relation of external unevenness: international
relations, the uneven economic development of Russia as compared
with the West, etc.) slides into mechanism, or into what is frequently
an alibi for it: a theory of the reciprocal interaction of the inside and
the outside. So it is essential to get down to the primitive internal
unevenness to grasp the essence of the external unevenness.

The whole history of Marxist theory and practice confirms this point.
Marxist theory and practice do not only approach unevenness as the
external effect of the interaction of different existing social formations,
but also within each social formation. And within each social formation, Marxist theory and practice do not only approach unevenness in
the form of simple exteriority (the *reciprocal action* of infrastructure and
superstructure), but in a form organically *internal* to each instance of
the social totality, to each contradiction. It is '*economism*' (mechanism)
and not the true Marxist tradition that sets up the hierarchy of instances
once and for all, assigns each its essence and role and defines the universal meaning of their relations; it is economism that identifies roles and
actors eternally, not realizing that the necessity of the process lies in an
exchange of roles 'according to circumstances'. It is economism that
identifies eternally in advance the determinant-contradiction-in-the-
last-instance with the *role* of the dominant contradiction, which for
ever assimilates such and such an 'aspect' (forces of production, economy, practice) to the principal *role*, and such and such another 'aspect'
(relations of production, politics, ideology, theory) to the secondary
role – whereas in real history determination in the last instance by the
economy is exercised precisely in the permutations of the principal role

between the economy, politics, theory, etc. Engels saw this quite clearly and pointed it out in his struggle with the opportunists in the Second International, who were awaiting the arrival of socialism through the action of the economy alone. The whole of Lenin's political work witnesses to the profundity of this principle: that determination in the last instance by the economy is exercised, according to the phases of the process, not accidentally, not for external or contingent reasons, but essentially, for internal and necessary reasons, by permutations, displacements and condensations.

So unevenness is internal to a social formation because the structuration in dominance of the complex whole, this structural invariant, *is itself the precondition for the concrete variation of the contradictions* that constitute it, and therefore for their displacements, condensations and mutations, etc., and inversely because *this variation is the existence of that invariant*. So uneven development (that is, these same phenomena of displacement and condensation observable in the development process of a complex whole) is not external to contradiction, but constitutes its most intimate essence. So the unevenness that exists in the 'development' of contradictions, that is, in the process itself, exists in the essence of contradiction itself. If it were not that the concept of *unevenness* has been associated with an external comparison of a quantitative character, I should gladly describe Marxist contradiction as '*unevenly determined*' granted recognition of the internal essence designated by this unevenness: *overdetermination*.

We still have one last point to examine: the *motor* role of contradiction in the development of a process. An understanding of contradiction is meaningless unless it allows us to understand this motor.

What has been said of Hegel enables us to understand in what sense the Hegelian dialectic is a motive force, and in what sense the concept is 'auto-development'. In a text as beautiful as the night, the *Phenomenology* celebrates '*the labour of the negative*' in beings and works, the Spirit's sojourn even in death, the universal trouble of negativity dismembering the corpse of Being to give birth to the glorious body of that infinity of nothingness become Being, the Spirit – and every philosopher trembles in his soul as if he was in the presence of the Mysteries. But negativity can only contain the motor principle

of the dialectic, the negation of the negation, as a strict reflection of
the Hegelian theoretical presuppositions of simplicity and origin. The
dialectic is negativity as an abstraction of the negation of the negation, itself an abstraction of the phenomenon of the restoration of
the alienation of the original unity. That is why the End is in action
in every Hegelian beginning; that is why the origin does no more
than grow by itself and produce in itself its own end, in its alienation.
So the Hegelian concept of '*what maintains itself in being-other-than-
itself*' is the existence of negativity. So contradiction is a motive force
for Hegel as negativity, that is, as a pure reflection of 'the being-in-
itself even in being-other-than-itself', therefore as a pure reflection of
the principle of alienation itself: the simplicity of the Idea.

This cannot be true for Marx. If the only processes we are dealing
with are processes of the complex structure in dominance, the concept
of negativity (and the concepts it reflects: the negation of the negation, alienation, etc.) cannot help towards a scientific understanding
of their development. Just as the development's type of necessity
cannot be reduced to the ideological necessity of the reflection of
the end on its beginning, so the motor principle of this development
cannot be reduced to the development of the idea in its own alienation. So, in Marxism, *negativity* and *alienation* are *ideological* concepts
that can *only* designate their own *ideological* content. Nevertheless,
the fact that the Hegelian type of necessity and the Hegelian essence
of development should be rejected does not mean at all that we are in
the theoretical void of subjectivity, of 'pluralism' or of contingency.
Quite the contrary, only on condition that we free ourselves from
these Hegelian presuppositions can we be really sure of escaping
this void. Indeed, it is because the process is complex and possesses
a structure in dominance that its development, and all the typical
aspects of this development, can really be explained.

I shall only give one example of this here. How is it possible, theoretically, to sustain the validity of this basic Marxist proposition: '*the
class struggle is the motor of history*'; that is, sustain theoretically the
thesis that it is by *political* struggle that it is possible to '*dissolve the
existing unity*', when we know very well that it is not politics but the
economy that is determinant in the last instance? How, other than with

the reality of the complex process with structure in dominance, could we explain theoretically the real difference between the economic and the political in the class struggle itself, that is, to be exact, the real difference between the economic struggle and the political struggle, a difference that will always distinguish Marxism from any spontaneous or organized form of opportunism? How could we explain our necessity to go through the distinct and specific level of *political* struggle if the latter, although distinct, and because it is distinct, were the simple phenomenon and not the real *condensation*, the nodal strategic point, in which *is reflected the complex whole* (economic, political and ideological)? How, finally, could we explain the fact that the Necessity of History itself thus goes in decisive fashion through *political practice*, if the structure of contradiction did not make this practice possible in its concrete reality? How could we explain the fact that even Marx's theory which made this necessity comprehensible to us could have been *produced* if the structure of contradiction did not make the concrete reality of this production possible?

So, in Marxist theory, to say that contradiction is a motive force is to say that it implies *a real struggle, real confrontations, precisely located within the structure of the complex whole*; it is to say that the locus of confrontation may vary according to the relation of the contradictions in the structure in dominance in any given situation; it is to say that the *condensation* of the struggle in a strategic locus is inseparable from the *displacement* of the dominant among these contradictions; that the organic phenomena of *condensation* and *displacement* are the very existence of the 'identity of opposites' until they produce the globally visible form of the *mutation* or qualitative leap that sanctions the revolutionary situation when the whole is recrystallized. Given this, we can explain the crucial distinction for political practice between the distinct moments of a process: '*non-antagonism*', '*antagonism*' and '*explosion*'. Contradiction, says Lenin, is always at work, in every moment. So these three moments are merely three forms of its existence. I shall characterize the first as the moment when the overdetermination of a contradiction exists *in the dominant form of displacement* (the 'metonymic' form of what has been enshrined in the phrase: '*quantitative changes*' in history or theory); the second, as the moment when overdetermination exists *in the dominant form of condensation* (acute class conflict in the case of society, theoretical crisis in a science, etc.); and the last, the revolutionary explosion (in society, in theory, etc.), as the moment of unstable global condensation inducing the dissolution and resolution of the whole, that is, a global restructuring of the whole on a qualitatively new basis. So the purely 'accumulative' form, in so far as this 'accumulation' can be purely quantitative (addition is only *exceptionally* dialectical), seems to be only a subordinate form, and Marx only ever gave one pure example of it, an unmetaphorical example this time, but an 'exceptional' one (an exception with a basis in its own conditions), in the unique passage from *Capital* which became the object of a famous commentary by Engels in *Anti-Dühring* (Part 1, Chapter 12).

*

If I may close by summing up the argument of this analysis, imperfect and didactic as it obviously is, I hope I shall be allowed to remind the reader that I merely undertook to give a theoretical expression of the specific difference of the Marxist dialectic active in the theoretical and political practices of Marxism, and that this was the object of the problem I had posed: the problem of the nature of Marx's 'inversion' of the Hegelian dialectic. If this analysis is not too unfaithful to the elementary demands of theoretical investigation I defined at the outset, then its theoretical solution should provide us with *more theoretical information*, that is, some knowledges.

If this is indeed the case, we should have acquired a theoretical result that might be expressed schematically in the following form:

The specific difference of Marxist contradiction is its 'unevenness', or 'overdetermination', which reflects in it its conditions of existence, that is, the specific structure of unevenness (in dominance) of the ever-pre-given complex whole which is its existence. Thus understood, contradiction is the motor of all development. Displacement and condensation, with their basis in its overdetermination, explain by their dominance the phases (non-antagonistic, antagonistic and explosive) which constitute the existence of the complex process, that is, 'of the development of things'.

If, as Lenin said, the dialectic is the conception of the contradiction in the very essence of things, the principle of their development and disappearance, then with this definition of the specificity of Marxist contradiction we should have reached *the Marxist dialectic* itself.[50]

Like every theoretical expression, this definition only exists in the concrete contents it enables us to think.

Like every theoretical expression, this definition should first of all enable us to think these concrete contents.

It cannot claim to be Theory in the general sense of the term, unless it enables us to think the whole set of concrete contents, those it did not arise from as well as those it did.

We have expressed this definition of the dialectic *vis-à-vis* two concrete contents: the theoretical practice and the political practice of Marxism.

To justify its general scope, to verify that this definition of the dialectic really does go beyond the domain *vis-à-vis* which it was expressed and can therefore claim a theoretically tempered and tested universality, it remains to put it to the test of other concrete contents, *other practices*; for example, the test of the theoretical practice of the

---

50 Those put off by this abstract definition might consider the fact that it explains no more than the essence of the dialectic at work in the concrete of Marxist thought and action. Those surprised by this unusual definition might consider the fact that it concerns very exactly the understanding of the 'development', of the 'birth and death' of phenomena, which a long tradition has associated with the word 'dialectic'. Those disconcerted by this definition (which does not regard any Hegelian concept as essential, neither negativity, negation, fission, the negation of the negation, alienation, 'supersession') might consider the fact that it is always a gain to lose an inadequate concept if the concept gained in exchange is more adequate to real practice. Those yearning after the simplicity of the Hegelian 'womb' might consider the fact that in 'certain determinate conditions' (really, exceptional conditions) the materialist dialectic can represent in a very limited sector, a 'Hegelian' form, but, precisely because it is an exception, it is not this form itself, that is, the exception, but its conditions that must be generalized. To think these conditions is to think the possibility of its own 'exceptions'. The Marxist dialectic thus enables us to think what constituted the 'crux' of the Hegelian dialectic: for example, the *non-development*, the stagnation of the 'societies without history' be they primitive or otherwise; for example, the phenomenon of real 'survivals', etc.

natural sciences, the test of the theoretical practices which are still problematic in the sciences (epistemology, the history of science, of ideology, philosophy, etc.) to check on their scope and eventually, as must be, to correct their formulation, in short, to see whether in the '*particular*' that has been examined, the universal has really been grasped that made of it this '*particularity*'.

This could and should be the occasion for new investigations.

April–May 1963

Part Seven

Marxism and Humanism

'My analytical method does not start from man but from the economically given social period.'

Karl Marx, *Randglossen zur Wagners Lehrbuch . . ., 1879–80.*

I

Today, Socialist 'Humanism' is on the agenda.

As it enters the period which will lead it from socialism (to each according to his labour) to communism (to each according to his needs), the Soviet Union has proclaimed the slogan: All for Man, and introduced new themes: the freedom of the individual, respect for legality, the dignity of the person. In workers' parties the achievements of socialist humanism are celebrated and justification for its theoretical claims is sought in *Capital*, and more and more frequently, in Marx's Early Works.

This is a historical event. I wonder even whether socialist humanism is not such a reassuring and attractive theme that it will allow a dialogue between Communists and Social-Democrats, or even a wider exchange with those 'men of good will' who are opposed to war and poverty. Today, even the high-road of Humanism seems to lead to socialism.

In fact, the objective of the revolutionary struggle has always been the end of exploitation and hence the liberation of man, but, as Marx foresaw, in its first historical phase, this struggle had to take the form of the struggle between *classes*. So revolutionary humanism could only be a 'class humanism', 'proletarian humanism'. The end of the exploitation of man meant the end of *class* exploitation. The liberation of man meant the liberation of the working *class* and above all liberation by the dictatorship of the proletariat. For more than forty years, in the U.S.S.R., amid gigantic struggles, 'socialist humanism' was expressed in the terms of class dictatorship rather than in those of personal freedom.[1]

The end of the dictatorship of the proletariat in the U.S.S.R. opens up a second historical phase. The Soviets say, in our country antagonistic classes have disappeared, the dictatorship of the proletariat has fulfilled its function, the State is no longer a class State but the State of the whole people (of everyone). In the U.S.S.R. men are indeed now treated without any class distinction, that is, as *persons*. So, *in ideology*, we see the themes of class humanism give way before the themes of a socialist humanism of the person.

Ten years ago socialist humanism only existed in one form: that of class humanism. Today it exists in two forms: class humanism, where the dictatorship of the proletariat is still in force (China, etc.), and (socialist) personal humanism where it has been superseded (the U.S.S.R.). Two forms corresponding to two necessary historical phases. In 'personal' humanism, 'class' humanism contemplates its own future, realized.

This transformation in history casts light on certain transformations in the mind. The dictatorship of the proletariat, rejected by Social-Democrats in the name of (bourgeois) personal 'humanism', and which bitterly opposes them to Communists, has been superseded in the U.S.S.R. Even better, it is foreseeable that it might take peaceful and short-lived forms in the West. From here we can see in outline a sort of meeting between two personal 'humanisms', socialist humanism and Christian or bourgeois liberal humanism. The 'liberalization' of the U.S.S.R. reassures the latter. As for socialist humanism,

---

1   Here I am using 'class humanism' in the sense of Lenin's statement that the October socialist revolution had given power to the working classes, the workers and the poor peasants, and that, *on their behalf*, it had secured conditions of life, action and development that they had never known before: democracy *for* the working classes, dictatorship *over* the oppressors. I am not using 'class humanism' in the sense adopted in Marx's early works, where the proletariat in its 'alienation' represents the human essence itself, whose 'realization' is to be assured by the revolution; this 'religious' conception of the proletariat (the 'universal class', since it is the 'loss of man' in 'revolt against its own loss') was re-adopted by the young Lukács in his *Geschichte und Klassenbewusstsein*.

it can see itself not only as a critique of the contradictions of bourgeois humanism, but also and above all as the consummation of its 'noblest' aspirations. Humanity's millenarian dreams, prefigured in the drafts of past humanisms, Christian and bourgeois, will at last find realization in it: in man and between men, the reign of Man will at last begin.

Hence the fulfilment of the prophetic promise Marx made in the *1844 Manuscripts*: '*Communism . . . as the real appropriation of the human essence through and for men . . . this communism as a fully developed naturalism – Humanism*'.

II

To see beyond this event, to understand it, to know the meaning of socialist humanism, it is not enough just to register the event, nor to record the concepts (humanism, socialism) in which the event itself thinks itself. The theoretical claims of the concepts must be tested to ensure that they really do provide us with a truly scientific knowledge of the event.

But precisely in the couple 'humanism–socialism' there is a striking theoretical unevenness: in the framework of the Marxist conception, the concept 'socialism' is indeed a scientific concept, but the concept 'humanism' is no more than an *ideological* one.

Note that my purpose is not to dispute the reality that the concept of socialist humanism is supposed to designate, but to define the *theoretical* value of the concept. When I say that the concept of humanism is an ideological concept (not a scientific one), I mean that while it really does designate a set of existing relations, unlike a scientific concept, it does not provide us with a means of knowing them. In a particular (ideological) mode, it designates some existents, but it does not give us their essences. If we were to confuse these two orders we should cut ourselves off from all knowledge, uphold a confusion and risk falling into error.

To show this clearly, I shall briefly invoke Marx's own experience, for he only arrived at a scientific theory of history at the price of a radical critique of the philosophy of man that had served as his theoretical basis during the years of his youth (1840–45). I use the words 'theoretical basis' in their strict sense. For the young Marx, 'Man' was not just a cry denouncing poverty and slavery. It was the theoretical principle of his world outlook and of his practical attitude. The 'Essence of Man' (whether freedom–reason or community) was the basis both for a rigorous theory of history and for a consistent political practice.

This can be seen in the two stages of Marx's humanist period.

The First Stage was dominated by a liberal–rationalist humanism closer to Kant and Fichte than to Hegel. In his conflict with censorship, Rhenish feudal laws, Prussian despotism, Marx's political struggle and the theory of history sustaining it were based theoretically on a philosophy of man. Only the essence of man makes history, and this essence is freedom and reason. *Freedom*: it is the essence of man just as weight is the essence of bodies. Man is destined to freedom, it is his very being. Whether he rejects it or negates it, he remains in it for ever: '*So much is freedom the essence of Man that even its adversaries are realizing it when they fight against its reality. . . . So freedom has always existed, in one way or another, sometimes only as a particular privilege, sometimes as a general right.*'[2] This distinction illuminates the whole of history: thus, feudalism is freedom, but in the 'non-rational' form of privilege; the modern State is freedom, but in the rational form of a universal right. *Reason*: man is only freedom as reason. Human freedom is neither caprice, nor the determinism of interest, but, as Kant and Fichte meant it, autonomy, obedience to the inner law of reason. This reason, which has '*always existed though not always in a rational form*'[3] (e.g. feudalism), in modern times does at least exist in the form of reason in the State, the State of law and right. '*Philosophy regards the State as the great organism in which legal, moral and political freedom should find their realization and in which the individual citizen, when he obeys the State's laws, is only obeying the natural laws of his own reason, of human reason.*'[4]

---

2   *Die Rheinische Zeitung*, 'The Freedom of the Press', 12 May 1842.
3   Letter to Ruge, September 1843 – an admirable formulation, the key to Marx's early philosophy.
4   *Die Rheinische Zeitung*, 'On the leading article in no. 179 of the *Kölnische Zeitung*', 14 July 1842.

Hence the task of philosophy: '*Philosophy demands that the State be the State of human nature.*'[5] This injunction is addressed to the State itself: if it would recognize its essence it would become reason, the true freedom of man, through its own reform of itself. Therefore, politico-philosophical criticism (which reminds the State of its duty to itself) sums up the whole of politics: the free Press, the free reason of humanity, becomes politics itself. This political practice – summed up in *public theoretical criticism*, that is, in public criticism by way of the Press – which demands as its absolute precondition the *freedom of the Press* is the one Marx adopted in the *Rheinische Zeitung*. Marx's development of his theory of history was the basis and justification for his own *practice*: the journalist's public criticism that he saw as political action *par excellence*. This Enlightenment Philosophy was completely rigorous.

The Second Stage (1842–5) was dominated by a new form of humanism: Feuerbach's 'communalist' humanism. The Reason-State had remained deaf to reason: there was no reform of the Prussian State. History itself delivered this judgement on the illusions of the humanism of reason: the young German radicals had been expecting that when he was King the heir to the throne would keep the liberal promises he had made before his corona-tion. But the throne soon changed the liberal into a despot – the State, which should at last have become reason, since it was in itself reason, gave birth merely to unreason once again. From this enormous disappointment, lived by the young radicals as a true historical and theoretical crisis, Marx drew the conclusion: '*The political State . . . encapsulates the demands of reason precisely in its modern forms. But it does not stop there. Everywhere it presupposes realized reason. But everywhere it also slides into the contradiction between its theoretical definition and its real hypotheses.*' A decisive step had been taken: the State's abuses were no longer conceived as misappropriations of the State *vis-à-vis* its essence, but as a real contradiction between its essence (reason) and its existence (unreason). Feuerbach's humanism made it possible to think just

---

5   *Ibid.*

this contradiction by showing in unreason the alienation of reason, and in this alienation the history of man, that is, his realization.[6]

Marx still professes a philosophy of man: 'To be radical is to grasp things by the root; but for man the root is man himself' (1843). But then man is only freedom–reason because he is first of all '*Gemeinwesen*', 'communal being', a being that is only consummated theoretically (science) and practically (politics) in universal human relations, with men and with his objects (external nature 'humanized' by labour). Here also the essence of man is the basis for history and politics.

History is the alienation and production of reason in unreason, of the true man in the alienated man. Without knowing it, man realizes the essence of man in the alienated products of his labour (commodities, State, religion). The loss of man that produces history and man must presuppose a definite pre-existing essence. At the end of history, this man, having become inhuman objectivity, has merely to re-grasp as subject his own essence alienated in property, religion and the State to become total man, true man.

This new theory of man is the basis for a new type of political action: the politics of *practical* reappropriation. The appeal to the simple reason of the State disappears. Politics is no longer simply theoretical criticism, the enlightenment of reason through the free

---

6   This confluence of Feuerbach and the theoretical crisis in which history had thrown the young German radicals explains their enthusiasm for the author of the *Provisional Theses*, of the *Essence of Christianity* and of the *Principles of the Philosophy of the Future*. Indeed, Feuerbach represented the *theoretical* solution to the young intellectuals' theoretical crisis. In his humanism of alienation, he gave them the theoretical concepts that enabled them to think the alienation of the human essence as an indispensable moment in the realization of the human essence, unreason (the irrational *reality* of the State) as a necessary moment in the realization of reason (the idea of the State). It thus enabled them to *think* what they would otherwise have suffered as irrationality itself: the necessary *connexion* between reason and unreason. Of course, this relation remained trapped in a philosophical anthropology, its basis, with this theoretical proviso: the remanipulation of the concept of man, indispensable to think the historical relation between historical reason and unreason. Man ceases to be defined by reason and freedom: he becomes, in his very principle, 'communalist', concrete intersubjectivity, love, fraternity, 'species being'.

Press, but man's practical reappropriation of his essence. For the State, like religion, may well be man, but man dispossessed: man is split into citizen (State) and civil man, two abstractions. In the heaven of the State, in 'the citizen's rights', man lives in imagination the human community he is deprived of on the earth of the 'rights of man'. So the revolution must no longer be merely *political* (rational liberal reform of the State), but '*human*' ('communist'), if man is to be restored his nature, alienated in the fantastic forms of money, power and gods. From this point on, this practical revolution must be the common work of philosophy and of the proletariat, for, in philosophy, man is theoretically affirmed; in the proletariat he is practically negated. The penetration of philosophy into the proletariat will be the conscious revolt of the affirmation against its own negation, the revolt of man against his inhuman conditions. Then the proletariat will negate its own negation and take possession of itself in communism. The revolution is the very *practice* of the logic immanent in alienation: it is the moment in which criticism, hitherto unarmed, recognizes its arms in the proletariat. It gives the proletariat the theory of what it is; in return, the proletariat gives it its armed force, a single unique force in which no one is allied except to himself. So the revolutionary alliance of the proletariat and of philosophy is once again sealed in the essence of man.

III

In 1845, Marx broke radically with every theory that based history and politics on an essence of man. This unique rupture contained three indissociable elements.

(1) The formation of a theory of history and politics based on radically new concepts: the concepts of social formation, productive forces, relations of production, superstructure, ideologies, determination in the last instance by the economy, specific determination of the other levels, etc.

(2) A radical critique of the *theoretical* pretensions of every philosophical humanism.

(3) The definition of humanism as an *ideology*.

This new conception is completely rigorous as well, but it is a new rigour: the essence criticized (2) is defined as an ideology (3), a category belonging to the new theory of society and history (1).

This rupture with every *philosophical* anthropology or humanism is no secondary detail; it is Marx's scientific discovery.

It means that Marx rejected the problematic of the earlier philosophy and adopted a new problematic in one and the same act. The earlier idealist ('bourgeois') philosophy depended in all its domains and arguments (its 'theory of knowledge', its conception of history, its political economy, its ethics, its aesthetics, etc.) on a problematic of *human nature* (or the essence of man). For centuries, this problematic had been transparency itself, and no one had thought of questioning it even in its internal modifications.

This problematic was neither vague nor loose; on the contrary, it was constituted by a coherent system of precise concepts tightly articulated together. When Marx confronted it, it implied the two complementary postulates he defined in the Sixth Thesis on Feuerbach:

(1) that there is a universal essence of man;

(2) that this essence is the attribute of '*each single individual*' who is its real subject.

These two postulates are complementary and indissociable. But their existence and their unity presuppose a whole empiricist–idealist world outlook. If the essence of man is to be a universal attribute, it is essential that *concrete subjects* exist as absolute givens; this implies an *empiricism of the subject*. If these empirical individuals are to be men, it is essential that each carries in himself the whole human essence, if not in fact, at least in principle; this implies an *idealism of the essence*. So empiricism of the subject implies idealism of the essence and vice versa. This relation can be inverted into its 'opposite' – empiricism of the concept/idealism of the subject. But the inversion respects the basic structure of the problematic, which remains fixed.

In this type-structure it is possible to recognize not only the principle of theories of society (from Hobbes to Rousseau), of political economy (from Petty to Ricardo), of ethics (from Descartes to Kant), but also the very principle of the (pre-Marxist) idealist and materialist 'theory of knowledge' (from Locke to Feuerbach, via Kant). The content of the human essence or of the empirical subjects may vary (as can be seen from Descartes to Feuerbach); the subject may change from empiricism to idealism (as can be seen from Locke to Kant): the terms presented and their relations only vary within the invariant type-structure which constitutes this very problematic: *an empiricism of the subject always corresponds to an idealism of the essence (or an empiricism of the essence to an idealism of the subject).*

By rejecting the essence of man as his theoretical basis, Marx rejected the whole of this organic system of postulates. He drove the philosophical categories of the *subject*, of *empiricism*, of the *ideal essence*, etc., from all the domains in which they had been supreme. Not only from political economy (rejection of the myth of *homo œconomicus*, that is, of the individual with definite faculties and needs as the *subject* of the classical economy); not just from history (rejection of social atomism and ethico-political idealism); not just from ethics (rejection of the Kantian ethical idea); but also from philosophy itself: for Marx's materialism excludes the empiricism of the subject (and its inverse: the transcendental subject) and the idealism of the concept (and its inverse: the empiricism of the concept).

This total theoretical revolution was only empowered to reject the old concepts because it replaced them by new concepts. In fact, Marx established a new problematic, a new systematic way of asking questions of the world, new principles and a new method. This discovery is immediately contained in the theory of historical materialism, in which Marx did not only propose a new theory of the history of societies, but at the same time implicitly, but necessarily, a new 'philosophy', infinite in its implications. Thus, when Marx replaced the old couple individuals/human essence in the theory of history by new concepts (forces of production, relations of production, etc.), he was, in fact, simultaneously proposing a new conception of 'philosophy'. He replaced the old postulates (empiricism/idealism of the subject, empiricism/idealism of the essence) which were the basis not only for idealism but also for pre-Marxist materialism, by a

historico-dialectical materialism of *praxis*: that is, by a theory of the
different specific *levels* of *human practice* (economic practice, political
practice, ideological practice, scientific practice) in their characteristic
articulations, based on the specific articulations of the unity of human
society. In a word, Marx substituted for the 'ideological' and universal concept of Feuerbachian 'practice' a concrete conception of the
specific differences that enables us to situate each particular practice
in the specific differences of the social structure.

So, to understand what was radically new in Marx's contribution,
we must become aware not only of the novelty of the concepts of
historical materialism, but also of the depth of the theoretical revolution they imply and inaugurate. On this condition it is possible to
define humanism's status, and reject its *theoretical* pretensions while
recognizing its practical function as an ideology.

Strictly in respect to theory, therefore, one can and must speak
openly of *Marx's theoretical anti-humanism*, and see in this *theoretical anti-humanism* the absolute (negative) precondition of the
(positive) knowledge of the human world itself, and of its practical transformation. It is impossible to *know* anything about
men except on the absolute precondition that the philosophical
(theoretical) myth of man is reduced to ashes. So any thought
that appeals to Marx for any kind of restoration of a theoretical
anthropology or humanism is no more than ashes, *theoretically*.
But in practice it could pile up a monument of pre-Marxist ideology that would weigh down on real history and threaten to lead it
into blind alleys.

For the corollary of theoretical Marxist anti-humanism is the
recognition and knowledge of humanism itself: as an *ideology*. Marx
never fell into the idealist illusion of believing that the knowledge of
an object might ultimately replace the object or dissipate its existence.
Cartesians, knowing that the sun was two thousand leagues away,
were astonished that this distance only looked like two hundred
paces: they could not even find enough of God to fill in this gap. Marx
never believed that a knowledge of the nature of *money* (a social relation) could destroy its *appearance*, its form of existence – a thing, for
this appearance was its very being, as necessary as the existing mode

of production.[7] Marx never believed that an ideology might be dissi-pated by a knowledge of it: for the knowledge of this ideology, as the knowledge of its conditions of possibility, of its structure, of its specific logic and of its practical role, within a given society, is simul-taneously knowledge of the conditions of its necessity. So Marx's theoretical *anti-humanism* does not suppress anything in the histori-cal *existence* of humanism. In the real world philosophies of man are found after Marx as often as before, and today even some Marxists are tempted to develop the themes of a new theoretical humanism. Furthermore, Marx's theoretical anti-humanism, by relating it to its conditions of existence, recognizes a necessity for humanism as an *ideology*, a conditional necessity. The recognition of this neces-sity is not purely speculative. On it alone can Marxism base a policy in relation to the existing ideological forms, of every kind: religion, ethics, art, philosophy, law – and in the very front rank, humanism. When (eventually) a Marxist policy of humanist ideology, that is, a

---

7   The whole, fashionable, theory of 'reification' depends on a projec-tion of the theory of alienation found in the early texts, particularly the *1844 Manuscripts*, onto the theory of 'fetishism' in *Capital*. In the *1844 Manuscripts*, the objectification of the human essence is claimed as the indis-pensable preliminary to the reappropriation of the human essence by man. Throughout the process of objectification, man only exists in the form of an objectivity in which he meets his own essence in the appearance of a foreign, non-human, essence. This 'objectification' is not called 'reification' even though it is called *inhuman*. Inhumanity is not represented *par excellence* by the model of a 'thing': but sometimes by the model of animality (or even of pre-animality – the man who no longer even has simple animal relations with nature), sometimes by the model of the omnipotence and fascination of transcendence (God, the State) and of money, which is, of course, a 'thing'. In *Capital* the only social relation that is presented in the form of a *thing* (this piece of metal) is *money*. But the conception of money as a *thing* (that is, the confusion of value with use-value in money) does not correspond to the reality of this 'thing': it is not the brutality of a simple 'thing' that man is faced with when he is in direct relation with money; it is a *power* (or a *lack* of it) over things and men. An ideology of reification that sees 'things' everywhere in human relations confuses in this category 'thing' (a category more foreign to Marx cannot be imagined) every social relation, conceived according to the model of a money-thing ideology.

political attitude to humanism, is achieved – a policy which may be either a rejection or a critique, or a use, or a support, or a development, or a humanist renewal of contemporary forms of ideology in the *ethico-political* domain – this policy will only have been possible on the absolute condition that it is based on Marxist philosophy, and a precondition for this is theoretical *anti-humanism*.

IV

So everything depends on the knowledge of the nature of humanism as an ideology.

There can be no question of attempting a profound definition of ideology here. It will suffice to know very schematically that an ideology is a system (with its own logic and rigour) of representations (images, myths, ideas or concepts, depending on the case) endowed with a historical existence and role within a given society. Without embarking on the problem of the relations between a science and its (ideological) past, we can say that ideology, as a system of representations, is distinguished from science in that in it the practico-social function is more important than the theoretical function (function as knowledge).

What is the nature of this social function? To understand it we must refer to the Marxist theory of history. The 'subjects' of history are given human societies. They present themselves as totalities whose unity is constituted by a certain specific type of *complexity*, which introduces instances, that, following Engels, we can, very schematically, reduce to three: the economy, politics and ideology. So in every society we can posit, in forms which are sometimes very paradoxical, the existence of an economic activity as the base, a political organization and 'ideological' forms (religion, ethics, philosophy, etc.). *So ideology is as such an organic part of every social totality*. It is as if human societies could not survive without these *specific formations*, these systems of representations (at various levels), their ideologies. Human societies secrete ideology as the very element and atmosphere indispensable to their historical respiration and life. Only an ideological world outlook could have imagined societies *without ideology* and accepted the utopian idea of a world in which ideology (not just one of its historical forms) would disappear without trace, to be replaced by *science*. For example, this utopia is the principle behind the idea that ethics, which is in its essence ideology, could be replaced by science or become scientific through and through; or that religion could be destroyed by science which would in some way take its place; that *art* could merge with knowledge or become 'everyday life', etc.

And I am not going to steer clear of the crucial question: *historical materialism cannot conceive that even a communist society could ever do without ideology*, be it ethics, art or 'world outlook'. Obviously it is possible to foresee important modifications in its ideological forms and their relations and even the disappearance of certain existing forms or a shift of their functions to neighbouring forms; it is also possible (on the premise of already acquired experience) to foresee the development of new ideological forms (e.g. the ideologies of 'the scientific world outlook' and 'communist humanism') but in the present state of Marxist theory strictly conceived, it is not conceivable that communism, a new mode of production implying determinate forces of production and relations of production, could do without a social organization of production, and corresponding ideological forms.

So ideology is not an aberration or a contingent excrescence of History: it is a structure essential to the historical life of societies. Further, only the existence and the recognition of its necessity enable us to act on ideology and transform ideology into an instrument of deliberate action on history.

It is customary to suggest that ideology belongs to the region of 'consciousness'. We must not be misled by this appellation which is still contaminated by the idealist problematic that preceded Marx. In truth, ideology has very little to do with 'consciousness', even supposing this term to have an unambiguous meaning. It is profoundly *unconscious*, even when it presents itself in a reflected form (as in pre-Marxist 'philosophy'). Ideology is indeed a system of representations, but in the majority of cases these representations have nothing to do with 'consciousness': they are usually images and occasionally concepts, but it is above all as *structures* that they impose on the vast majority of men, not via their 'consciousness'. They are perceived–accepted–suffered cultural objects and they act functionally on men via a process that escapes them. Men 'live' their ideologies as the Cartesian 'saw' or did not see – if he was not looking at it – the moon two hundred paces away: *not at all as a form of consciousness, but as an object of their 'world'* – as their *'world'* itself. But what do we mean, then, when we say that ideology is a matter of men's 'consciousness'? First, that ideology is distinct from other social instances, but also that men *live* their actions, usually referred to freedom and 'consciousness' by the classical tradition, in ideology, *by and through ideology*; in short, that the 'lived' relation between men and the world, including History (in political action or inaction), passes through ideology, or better, *is ideology itself*. This is the sense in which Marx said that it is in ideology (as the locus of political struggle) that men *become conscious* of their place in the world and in history, it is within this ideological unconsciousness that men succeed in altering the 'lived' relation between them and the world and acquiring that new form of specific unconsciousness called 'consciousness'.

So ideology is a matter of the *lived* relation between men and their world. This relation, that only appears as '*conscious*' on condition that it is *unconscious*, in the same way only seems to be simple on condition that it is complex, that it is not a simple relation but a relation between relations, a second degree relation. In ideology men do indeed express, not the relation between them and their conditions of existence, but *the way* they live the relation between them and their conditions of existence: this presupposes both a real relation and an '*imaginary*', '*lived*' relation. Ideology, then, is the expression of the relation between men and their 'world', that is, the (overdetermined) unity of the real relation and the imaginary relation between them and their real conditions of existence. In ideology the real relation is inevitably invested in the imaginary relation, a relation that *expresses* a *will* (conservative, conformist, reformist or revolutionary), a hope or a nostalgia, rather than describing a reality.

It is in this overdetermination of the real by the imaginary and of the imaginary by the real that ideology is *active* in principle, that it reinforces or modifies the relation between men and their conditions of existence, in the imaginary relation itself. It follows that this action can never be purely *instrumental*; the men who would use an ideology purely as a means of action, as a tool, find that they have been caught by it, implicated by it, just when they are using it and believe themselves to be absolute masters of it.

This is perfectly clear in the case of a *class society*. The ruling ideology is then the ideology of the ruling *class*. But the ruling class does not maintain with the ruling ideology, which is its own ideology, an external and lucid relation of pure utility and cunning. When, during the eighteenth century, the 'rising class', the bourgeoisie, developed a humanist ideology of equality, freedom and reason, it gave its own demands the form of universality, since it hoped thereby to enroll at its side, by their education to this end, the very men it would liberate only for their exploitation. This is the Rousseauan myth of the origins of inequality: the rich holding forth to the poor in 'the most deliberate discourse' ever conceived, so as to persuade them to live their slavery as their freedom. In reality, the bourgeoisie has to believe in its own myth before it can convince others, and not only so as to convince others, since what it lives in its ideology is *the very relation* between it and its real conditions of existence which allows it simultaneously to act on itself (provide itself with a legal and ethical consciousness, and the legal and ethical conditions of economic liberalism) and on others (those it exploits and is going to exploit in the future: the 'free labourers') so as to take up, occupy and maintain its historical role as a ruling class. Thus, in a very exact sense, the bourgeoisie *lives* in the ideology of *freedom* the relation between it and its conditions of existence: that is, *its* real relation (the law of a liberal capitalist economy) *but invested in an imaginary relation* (all men are free, including the free labourers). Its ideology consists of this play on the word *freedom*, which betrays the bourgeois wish to mystify those ('free men'!) it exploits, blackmailing them with freedom so as to keep them in harness, as much as the bourgeoisie's need to *live* its own class rule as the freedom of those it is exploiting. Just as a people that exploits another cannot be free, so a class that *uses* an ideology is its captive too. So when we speak of the class function of an ideology it must be understood that the ruling ideology is indeed the ideology of the ruling class and that the former serves the latter not only in its rule over the exploited class, *but in its own constitution of itself as the ruling class*, by making it accept the lived relation between itself and the world as real and justified.

But, we must go further and ask what becomes of *ideology* in a society in which classes have disappeared. What we have just said allows us to answer this question. If the whole social function of ideology could be summed up cynically as a myth (such as Plato's 'beautiful lies' or the techniques of modern advertising) fabricated and manipulated from the outside by the ruling class to fool those it is exploiting, then ideology would disappear with classes. But as we have seen that even in the case of a class society ideology is active on the ruling class itself and contributes to its moulding, to the modification of its attitudes to adapt it to its real conditions of existence (for example, legal freedom) – it is clear that *ideology (as a system of mass representations) is indispensable in any society if men are to be formed, transformed and equipped to respond to the demands of their conditions of existence*. If, as Marx said, history is a perpetual transformation of men's conditions of existence, and if this is equally true of a socialist society, then men must be ceaselessly transformed so as to adapt them to these conditions; if this 'adaptation' cannot be left to spontaneity but must be constantly assumed, dominated and controlled, it is in ideology that this demand is expressed, that this distance is measured, that this contradiction is lived and that its resolution is 'activated'. It is in ideology that the classless society *lives* the inadequacy/adequacy of the relation between it and the world, it is in it and by it that it transforms men's 'consciousness', that is, their attitudes and behaviour so as to raise them to the level of their tasks and the conditions of their existence.

In a class society ideology is the relay whereby, and the element in which, the relation between men and their conditions of existence is settled to the profit of the ruling class. In a classless society ideology is the relay whereby, and the element in which, the relation between men and their conditions of existence is lived to the profit of all men.

V

We are now in a position to return to the theme of socialist humanism and to account for the theoretical disparity we observed between a scientific term (socialism) and an ideological one (humanism).

In its relations with the existing forms of bourgeois or Christian *personal* humanism, socialist personal humanism presents itself as an ideology precisely in the *play on words* that authorizes this meeting. I am far from thinking that this might be the meeting of a cynicism and a naïvety. In the case in point, the play on words is still the index of a *historical reality*, and simultaneously of a lived ambiguity, and an expression of the desire to overcome it. When, in the relations between Marxists and everyone else, the former lay stress on a socialist personal humanism, they are simply demonstrating their *will* to bridge the gap that separates them from possible allies, and they are simply anticipating the movement, trusting to future history the task of providing the old words with a new content.

It is this content that matters. For, once again, the themes of Marxist humanism are not, first of all, themes for the use of *others*. The Marxists who develop them necessarily do so *for themselves* before doing so for others. Now we know what these developments are based on: on the new conditions existing in the Soviet Union, on the end of the dictatorship of the proletariat and on the transition to communism.

And this is where everything is at stake. This is how I should pose the question. *To what* in the Soviet Union does the manifest development of the themes of (socialist) personal humanism correspond? Speaking of the idea of man and of humanism in *The German Ideology*, Marx commented that the idea of human nature, or of the essence of man, concealed a *coupled value judgement*, to be precise, the couple human/inhuman; and he wrote: 'the "inhuman" as much as the "human" is a product of present conditions; it is their negative side'. The couple human/inhuman is the hidden principle of all humanism which is, then, no more than a way of living–sustaining–resolving this contradiction. Bourgeois humanism made man the principle of all theory. This luminous essence of man was the visible counterpart to a shadowy inhumanity. By this part of shade, the content of the human essence, that apparently absolute essence, announced its rebellious birth. The man of freedom–reason denounced the egoistic and divided man of capitalist society. In the two forms of this couple inhuman/human, the bourgeoisie of the eighteenth century lived in 'rational-liberal' form, the German left radical intellectuals in 'communalist' or 'communist' form, the relations between them and their conditions of existence, as a rejection, a demand and a programme.

What about contemporary socialist humanism? It is also a *rejection* and a denunciation: a rejection of all human discrimination, be it racial, political, religious or whatever. It is a rejection of all economic exploitation or political slavery. It is a rejection of war. This rejection is not just a proud proclamation of victory, an exhortation and example addressed to outsiders, to all men oppressed by Imperialism, by its exploitation, its poverty, its slavery, its discriminations and its wars: it is also and primarily turned *inwards*: to the Soviet Union itself. In personal socialist humanism, the Soviet Union accepts on its own account the supersession of the period of the dictatorship of the proletariat, but it also rejects and condemns the 'abuses' of the latter, the aberrant and 'criminal' forms it took during the period of the 'cult of personality'. Socialist humanism, in its internal use, deals with the historical reality of the supersession of the dictatorship of the proletariat and of the 'abusive' forms it took in the U.S.S.R. It deals with a 'dual' reality: not only a reality superseded by the rational *necessity* of the development of the forces of production of socialist relations of production (the dictatorship of the proletariat) – but also a reality which *ought not to have had to be superseded*, that new form of '*non-rational existence of reason*', that part of historical '*unreason*' and of the 'inhuman' that the past of the U.S.S.R. bears within it: terror, repression and dogmatism – precisely what has not yet been completely superseded, in its effects or its misdeeds.

But with this wish we move from the shade to the light, from the inhuman to the human. The communism to which the Soviet Union is committed is a world without economic exploitation, without violence, without discrimination – a world opening up before the Soviets the infinite vistas of progress, of science, of culture, of bread and freedom, of free development – a world that can do without shadows or tragedies. Why then all this stress so deliberately laid on *man*? What need do the Soviets have for an *idea of man*, that is, an idea of themselves, *to help them live their history*? It is difficult here to avoid relating together the necessity to prepare and realize an important historical mutation (the transition to communism, the end of the dictatorship of the proletariat, the withering-away of the State apparatus, presupposing the creation of new forms of political, economic and cultural organization, corresponding to this transition) on the one hand – and, on the other, the *historical conditions* in which this transition must be put into effect. Now it is obvious that *these conditions*, too, bear the characteristic mark of the U.S.S.R.'s past and of its difficulties – not only the mark of the difficulties due to the period of the '*cult of personality*', *but also* the mark of the more distant difficulties characteristic of the '*construction of socialism in one country*', and in addition in a country economically and culturally 'backward' to start with. Among these 'conditions', first place must be given to the 'theoretical' conditions inherited from the past.

The present disproportion of the historical tasks to their conditions explains the recourse to this ideology. In fact, the themes of socialist humanism designate the existence of real problems: *new* historical, economic, political and ideological problems that the Stalinist period kept in the shade, but still produced while producing socialism – problems of the forms of economic, political and cultural *organization* that correspond to the level of development attained by socialism's productive forces; problems of the new form of *individual development* for a new period of history in which the State will no longer take charge, *coercively*, of the leadership or control of the destiny of each individual, in which from now on each man will *objectively* have *the choice*, that is, *the difficult task* of becoming by himself what he is. The themes of socialist humanism (free development of the individual, respect for socialist legality, dignity of the person, etc.) are the way the Soviets and other socialists are *living* the relation between themselves and these problems, that is, the *conditions* in which they are posed. It is striking to observe that, in conformity with the necessity of their development, in the majority of socialist democracies as in the Soviet Union, problems of politics and ethics have come to the fore and that for their part, Western parties, too, are obsessed with these problems. Now, it is not less striking to see that these problems are occasionally, if not frequently, dealt with *theoretically* by recourse to concepts derived from Marx's early period, from his philosophy of man: the concepts of alienation, fission, fetishism, the total man, etc. However, considered in themselves, these problems are basically problems that, far from calling for a 'philosophy of man', involve the preparation of new forms of *organization* for economic, political and ideological life (including new forms of individual development) in the socialist countries during the phase of the withering-away or supersession of the dictatorship of the proletariat. Why is it that these problems are posed by certain ideologues as a function of the concepts of a *philosophy of man* – instead of being openly, fully and rigorously posed in the economic, political and ideological terms of Marxist theory? Why do so many Marxist philosophers seem to feel the need to appeal to the pre-Marxist ideological concept of *alienation* in order supposedly to think and 'resolve' these concrete historical problems?

We would not observe the temptation of this ideological recourse if it were not in its own way the index of a necessity which cannot nevertheless take shelter in the protection of other, better established, forms of necessity. There can be no doubt that Communists are correct in opposing the economic, social, political and cultural *reality* of socialism to the 'inhumanity' of Imperialism in general; that this contrast is a part of the confrontation and struggle between socialism and imperialism. But it might be equally dangerous to use an ideological concept like humanism, with neither discrimination nor reserve, as if it were a theoretical concept, when it is inevitably charged with associations from the ideological unconsciousness and only too easily blends into themes of petty-bourgeois inspiration (we know that the petty bourgeoisie and its ideology, for which Lenin predicted a fine future, have not yet been buried by History).

Here we are touching on a deeper reason, and one doubtless difficult to express. Within certain limits this recourse to ideology might indeed be envisaged as the substitute for a recourse to theory. Here again we would find the *theoretical conditions* currently inherited by Marxist theory from its past – not just the dogmatism of the Stalinist period, but also, from further back, the heritage of the disastrously opportunist interpretations of the Second International which Lenin fought against throughout his life, but which have neither as yet been buried by History. These conditions have hindered the development which was indispensable if Marxist theory was to acquire precisely those concepts demanded by the new problems: concepts that would have allowed it to pose these problems today in scientific, not ideological terms; that would have allowed it to call things by their names, that is, by the appropriate Marxist concepts, rather than, as only too often happens, by ideological concepts (alienation) or by concepts without any definite status.

For example, it is regrettable to observe that the concept by which Communists designate an important historical phenomenon in the history of the U.S.S.R. and of the workers' movement: the concept of the 'cult of personality' would be an 'absent', unclassifiable concept in Marxist theory if it were taken as a theoretical concept; it may well describe and condemn a mode of behaviour, and on these grounds, possess a doubly practical value, but, to my knowledge, Marx never regarded a mode of political behaviour as directly assimilable to a historical *category*, that is, to a *concept* from the theory of historical materialism: for if it does designate a reality, it is not its concept. However, everything that has been said of the 'cult of personality' refers exactly to the domain of the *superstructure* and therefore of State organization and ideologies; further it refers largely to *this domain alone*, which we know from Marxist theory possesses a 'relative autonomy' (which explains very simply, in theory, how the socialist *infrastructure* has been able to develop without essential damage during this period of errors affecting the superstructure). Why are existing, known and recognized Marxist concepts not invoked to think and situate this phenomenon, which is in fact described as a mode of behaviour and related to one man's 'psychology', that is, merely *described* but not thought? If one man's 'psychology' could take on this *historical* role, why not pose in Marxist terms the question of the historical conditions of the possibility of this apparent promotion of 'psychology' to the dignity and dimensions of a historical fact? Marxism contains in its principles the wherewithal to pose this problem in terms of theory, and hence the wherewithal to clarify it and help to resolve it.

It is no accident that the two examples I have invoked are the concept of alienation and the concept of the 'cult of personality'. For the concepts of socialist humanism, too (in particular the problems of law and the person), have as their object problems arising in the domain of the superstructure: State organization, political life, ethics, ideologies, etc. And it is impossible to hold back the thought that the recourse to ideology is the shortest cut there, too, a substitute for an insufficient theory. Insufficient, but latent and potential. Such is the role of this temptation of the recourse to ideology; to fill in this absence, this delay, this gap, without recognizing it openly, by making one's need and impatience a theoretical argument, as Engels put it, and by taking the need for a theory for the theory itself. The philosophical humanism which might easily become a threat to us and which shelters behind the unprecedented achievements of socialism itself, is this complement which, in default of theory, is destined to give certain Marxist ideologues the *feeling* of the theory that they lack; a feeling that cannot lay claim to that most precious of all the things Marx gave us – the possibility of scientific knowledge.

That is why, if today socialist humanism is on the agenda, the good reasons for this ideology can in no case serve as a caution against the bad ones, without dragging us into a confusion of ideology and scientific theory.

Marx's philosophical anti-humanism does provide an understanding of the necessity of existing ideologies, including humanism. But at the same time, because it is a critical and revolutionary theory, it also provides an understanding of the tactics to be adopted towards them; whether they should be supported, transformed or combated. And Marxists know that there can be no tactics that do not depend on a strategy – and no strategy that does not depend on theory.

October 1963

A Complementary Note on 'Real Humanism'

Just a word or two on the phrase 'real humanism'.[1]

The specific difference lies in the adjective: *real*. Real-humanism is scientifically defined by its opposition to unreal humanism, ideal(ist), abstract, speculative humanism, and so on. This *reference* humanism is simultaneously invoked as a reference and rejected for its abstraction, unreality, etc., by the new real-humanism. So the old humanism is judged by the new as an abstract and illusory humanism. Its illusion is to aim at an unreal object, to have as its content an object which is not the real object.

Real humanism presents itself as the humanism that has as its content not an abstract speculative object, but a real object.

But this definition remains a negative one: it is sufficient to express the rejection of a certain content, but it does not provide the new content as such. The content aimed at by real-humanism is not in the concepts of humanism or 'real' as such, but outside these concepts. The adjective real is *gestural*; it points out that to find the content of this new humanism you must look in *reality* – in society, the State, etc. So the concept of real-humanism is linked to the concept of humanism as its theoretical reference, but it is opposed to it through its rejection of the latter's abstract object – and by providing a concrete, real, object. The word *real* plays a dual role. It shows up the idealism and abstraction in the old humanism (negative function of the concept of reality); and at the same time it designates the *external reality* (external to the old humanism) in which the new humanism will find its content (positive function of the concept of reality). However, this positive function of the word 'real' is not a positive function of *knowledge*, it is a positive function of *practical gesture*.

What, indeed, is this 'reality' which is to transform the old

---

1 The concept of 'real-humanism' sustains the argument of an article by Jorge Semprun published in *Clarté*, no. 58 (see *Nouvelle Critique*, no. 164, March 1965). It is a concept borrowed from Marx's Early Works.

humanism into real-humanism? It is society. The Sixth Thesis on Feuerbach goes so far as to say that the non-abstract 'man' is 'the ensemble of the social relations'. Now if we take this phrase literally as an adequate definition *it means nothing at all*. Try and give it a literal explication and you will see that there is no way out without recourse to a periphrasis of the following kind: 'If anyone wants to know what reality is, not the reality corresponding adequately to the concept of man, or of humanism, but the reality which is directly at issue in these concepts, it is not an abstract essence but the ensemble of the social relations.' This periphrasis immediately highlights the *inadequacy* of the concept of man to its definition: the ensemble of the social relations. Between these two terms (man/ensemble of the social relations) there is, doubtless, some relation, but it is not legible in the definition, *it is not a relation of definition, not a relation of knowledge*.

But this inadequacy has a meaning, this relation has a meaning: a *practical* meaning. This inadequacy manifestly designates an *action to be achieved*, a *displacement* to be put into effect. It means that to find the reality alluded to by seeking abstract man no longer but real man instead, it is necessary *to turn to society*, and to undertake an analysis of the ensemble of the social relations. In the phrase real-humanism, in my opinion, the concept 'real' is a practical concept, the equivalent of a *signal*, of a notice-board that 'points out' what movement is to be put into effect and in what direction, to what place, must there be *displacement* to reach the real earth rather than the heaven of abstraction. 'The real this way!' We follow this *guide* and we come out into society, the social relations, and the conditions of their real possibility.

But it is then that the shocking paradox appears: once this *displacement* has really been put into effect, once the scientific analysis of this real object has been undertaken, we discover that a knowledge of concrete (real) men, that is, a knowledge of the ensemble of the social relations is only possible on condition that we do completely without the *theoretical services* of the concept of man (in the sense in which it existed in its theoretical claims even before the displacement). In fact, this concept seems to me to be useless from a scientific viewpoint, not because it is abstract! – but because it is not scientific. To think the reality of society, of the ensemble of social relations, we must put into effect a radical *displacement*, not only a spatial displacement (from the abstract to the concrete) but also a conceptual displacement (we change our basic concepts). The concepts whereby Marx thought reality, which real-humanism pointed out, never ever again introduce as *theoretical* concepts, the concepts of man or humanism; but other, quite new concepts, the concepts of mode of production, forces of production, relations of production, superstructure, ideology, etc. This is the paradox: the practical concept that pointed out for us the destination of the displacement has been consumed in the displacement itself, the concept that pointed out for us the site for investigation is from now on absent from the investigation itself.

This is a characteristic phenomenon of the *transitions-breaks* that constitute the advent of a new problematic. At certain moments in the history of ideas we see these *practical concepts* emerge, and typically they are *internally unbalanced* concepts. In one aspect they belong to the old ideological universe which serves as their 'theoretical' reference (humanism); but in the other they concern a new domain, pointing out the *displacement* to be put into effect to get to it. In the first aspect they retain a 'theoretical' meaning (the meaning in their universe of reference); in the second their only meaning is as a *practical* signal, pointing out a direction and a destination, but without giving an adequate concept of it. We still remain in the domain of the earlier ideology; we are approaching its frontier and a signpost points out to us a beyond, a direction and a destination. 'Cross the frontier and go on in the direction of society and you will find the real.' The signpost is still standing in the ideological domain, *the message is written in its language*, even if it does use 'new' words, even the rejection of ideology is written in ideological language, as we see so strikingly in Feuerbach; the 'concrete', the 'real', these are the names that the opposition to ideology bears in ideology.

You can stay indefinitely at the frontier line, ceaselessly repeating concrete! concrete! real! real! This is what Feuerbach did, and Feuerbach, too, spoke of society and State, and never stopped talking about real man, man with needs, concrete man, who is merely the ensemble of his developed human needs, of politics and industry.

He stayed with the words which in their concreteness itself referred him to the image of man whose *realization* he called for (Feuerbach, too, said that real man is society, in a definition *then adequate* to its concept, since society was for him in each of its historical moments never more than the progressive manifestation of the *human essence*).

Or, on the contrary, you can cross the frontier for good and penetrate into the domain of reality and embark 'seriously on its study', as Marx puts it in *The German Ideology*. Then the signal will have played its practical part. It remains in the old domain, in the domain *abandoned* by the very fact of *displacement*. There you are face to face with your real object, obliged to forge the requisite and adequate concepts, to think it, obliged to accept the fact that the old concepts and in particular the concept of real-man or real-humanism will not allow you to *think the reality of man*, that to reach this immediacy, which is precisely not an immediacy, it is necessary, as always where knowledge is concerned, to make a long detour. You have abandoned the old domain, the old concepts. Here you are in a new domain, for which new concepts will give you the knowledge. The sign that a real change in locus and problematic has occurred, and that a new adventure is beginning, the adventure of science in development.

So are we condemned to repeat the same experience? Real-humanism may today be the *slogan* of a rejection and a programme and thus in the best of cases a *practical* signal, the rejection of an abstract 'humanism' which only existed in the discourse and not in the reality of institutions – and the gesture towards a beyond, a reality which is still *beyond*, which is not yet truly *realized*, but only hoped for, the programme of an aspiration to be brought to life. It is only too clear that profound rejections and authentic wishes, as well as an impatient desire to overcome still unconquered obstacles, are, in their own way, translated in this concept of real-humanism. It is also certain that in every epoch of history men must make their own experiments on their own account, and it is no accident that some of them retrace the 'paths' taken by their elders and ancestors. It is certainly indispensable that Communists should take seriously the real meaning concealed in this wish, the realities for which this practical concept is an index. It is certainly indispensable that Communists should pass to and fro between the still uncertain, confused and ideological forms in which this wish or some new experiment are expressed – and their own theoretical concepts; that they should, when the need has been absolutely proved, forge new theoretical concepts adequate to the upheavals of practice in our own time.

But we should not forget that the frontier separating ideology from scientific theory was crossed about one hundred and twenty years ago by Marx; that this great undertaking and this great discovery have been recorded in the works and inscribed in the conceptual system of a knowledge whose effects have little by little transformed the face of the earth and its history. We cannot and must not for one instant renounce the benefits of this irreplaceable gain, the benefits of these theoretical resources which far transcend in wealth and potential the use that has so far been made of them. We must not forget that an understanding of what is going on in the world today and the political and ideological interchange indispensable to the broadening and reinforcement of the bases of socialism are only possible if, for our part, we do not fall *behind* what Marx gained for us, as far behind as that still uncertain frontier between ideology and science. We can give help to all those who are near to crossing that frontier, but only on condition that we have crossed it ourselves, and have inscribed in our concepts the irreversible result of this change of scene.

For us, the 'real' is not a *theoretical slogan*; the real is the real object that exists independently of its knowledge – but which can only be defined by its knowledge. In this second, theoretical, relation, the real is identical to the means of knowing it, the real is its known or to-be-known structure, it is the very object of Marxist theory, the object marked out by the great theoretical discoveries of Marx and Lenin, the immense, living, constantly developing field, in which the events of human history can from now on be mastered by men's practice, because they will be within their conceptual grasp, their knowledge.

This is what I meant when I demonstrated that real-humanism or socialist humanism may be the object of a recognition or of a misunderstanding, according to the status assigned it in respect to theory; that it can serve as a *practical, ideological* slogan in so far as it is exactly adequate to its function and not confused with a quite different function; that there is no way in which it can abrogate the attributes of a *theoretical* concept. I also meant that this slogan is not itself its own light, but can at most point out the *place*, *beyond it*, where light reigns. I meant that a certain *inflation* of this practical, ideological concept might induce Marxist theory to fall behind its own frontiers; and what is more, might even hinder, if not bar, the way to truly *posing*, and hence truly solving, the problems whose existence and urgency it is intended to designate, in its own way. Simply put, the recourse to ethics so deeply inscribed in every humanist ideology may play the part of an imaginary treatment of real problems. Once *known*, these problems are posed in precise terms; they are organizational problems of the forms of economic life, political life and individual life. To pose these problems correctly and to resolve them in reality, they must be called by their names, *their scientific names*. The slogan of humanism has no theoretical value, but it does have value as a practical index: we must get down to the concrete problems themselves, that is, to their knowledge, if we are to produce the historical transformation whose necessity was thought by Marx. We must be careful that in this process no *word*, justified by its practical function, usurps a theoretical function; but that in performing its practical function, it simultaneously disappears from the field of theory.

January 1965

Glossary

ABSTRACT (*abstrait*). For Althusser, the theoretical opposition between the abstract and the concrete lies wholly in the realm of *theory*. The abstract is the starting-point for theoretical practice, its Generality I (q.v.), while the concrete is its end-point (Generality III). The common theoretical view that regards theory as abstract and reality as concrete is characteristic of the works of Feuerbach and of Marx's own youth.

ALIENATION (*aliénation*, *Entäusserung*). An ideological concept used by Marx in his Early Works (q.v.) and regarded by the partisans of these works as the key concept of Marxism. Marx derived the term from Feuerbach's anthropology where it denoted the state of man and society where the essence of man is only present to him in the distorted form of a god, which, although man created it in the image of his essence (the species-being), appears to him as an external, pre-existing creator. Marx used the concept to criticize the State and the economy as confiscating the real self-determining labour of men in the same way. In his later works, however, the term appears very rarely, and where it does it is either used ironically, or with a different conceptual content (in *Capital*, for instance).

BREAK, EPISTEMOLOGICAL (*coupure epistémologique*). A concept introduced by Gaston Bachelard in his *La Formation de l'esprit scientifique*, and related to uses of the term in studies in the history of ideas by Canguilhem and Foucault (see Althusser's *Letter to the Translator*, p. 224). It describes the leap from the pre-scientific world of ideas to the scientific world; this leap involves a radical break with the whole pattern and frame of reference of the pre-scientific (ideological) notions, and the construction of a new pattern (problematic q.v.). Althusser applies it to Marx's rejection of the Hegelian and Feuerbachian ideology of his youth and the construction of the basic concepts of dialectical and historical materialism (q.v.) in his later works.

CONCRETE-IN-THOUGHT/REAL-CONCRETE (*concret-de-pensée/concret-réel*). In Feuerbach's ideology, the speculative abstract (q.v.), theory, is opposed to the concrete, reality. For the mature Marx, however, the theoretical abstract and concrete both exist in thought as Generalities I and III (q.v.). The concrete-in-thought is produced wholly in thought, whereas the real-concrete 'survives independently outside thought before and after' (Marx).

CONJUNCTURE (*conjoncture*). The central concept of the Marxist science of politics (cf. Lenin's 'current moment'); it denotes the exact balance of forces, state of overdetermination (q.v.) of the contradictions at any given moment to which political tactics must be applied.

CONSCIOUSNESS (*conscience*). A term designating the region where ideology is located ('false consciousness') and superseded ('true consciousness'), contaminated by the pre-Marxist ideology of the Young Marx. In fact, Althusser argues, ideology is profoundly *unconscious* – it is a structure imposed involuntarily on the majority of men.

CONTRADICTION (*contradiction*). A term for the articulation of a practice (q.v.) into the complex whole of the social formation (q.v.). Contradictions may be antagonistic or non-antagonistic according to whether their state of overdetermination (q.v.) is one of fusion or condensation, or one of displacement (q.v.).

CONTRADICTIONS, CONDENSATION, DISPLACEMENT AND FUSION OF (*condensation, déplacement et fusion des contradictions*). Condensation and displacement were used by Freud to indicate the two ways dream-thoughts are represented in the dream-work – by the compression of a number of dream-thoughts into one image, or by transferring psychical intensity from one image to another. Althusser uses the analogy of these processes of psychical overdetermination to denote the different forms of the overdetermination (q.v.) of contradictions in the Marxist theory of history. In periods of stability the essential contradictions of the social formation are neutralized by displacement; in a revolutionary situation, however, they may condense or fuse into a revolutionary rupture.

DEVELOPMENT, UNEVEN (*développement inégal*). A concept of Lenin and Mao Tse-tung: the overdetermination (q.v.) of all the contradictions in a social formation (q.v.) means that none can develop simply; the different overdeterminations in different times and places result in quite different patterns of social development.

DIALECTIC OF CONSCIOUSNESS (*dialectique de la conscience*). The Hegelian dialectic, or any dialectic where the various elements or moments are externalizations of a single, simple, internal principle, as Rome in Hegel's *Philosophy of History* is an expression of the abstract legal personality, etc.

EFFECTIVITY, SPECIFIC (*efficacité spécifique*). The characteristic of Marx's later theory: the different aspects of the social formation are not related as in Hegel's dialectic of consciousness (q.v.) as phenomena and essence, each has its precise influence on the complex totality, the structure in dominance (q.v.). Thus base and superstructure (q.v.) must not be conceived as vulgar Marxism conceives them, as essence and phenomenon, the State and ideology are not mere expressions of the economy, they are autonomous within a structured whole where one aspect is dominant, this dominance being determined in the last instance by the economy.

EMPIRICISM (*empirisme*). Althusser uses the concept of empiricism in a very wise sense to include all 'epistemologies' that oppose a given subject to a given object and call knowledge the abstraction by the subject of the essence of the object. Hence the knowledge of the object is part of the object itself. This remains true whatever the nature of the subject (psychological, historical, etc.) or of the object (continuous, discontinuous, mobile, immobile, etc.) in question. So as well as covering those epistemologies traditionally called 'empiricist', this definition includes classical idealism, and the epistemology of Feuerbach and the Young Marx.

FORMATION, SOCIAL (*formation sociale*). [A concept denoting 'society' so-called. L.A.]* The concrete complex whole comprising economic practice, political practice and ideological practice (q.v.) at a certain place and stage of development. Historical materialism is the science of social formations.

GENERALITIES I, II AND III (*Généralités I, II et III*). In theoretical practice (q.v.), the process of the production of knowledge, Generalities I are the abstract, part-ideological, part-scientific generalities that are the raw material of the science, Generalities III are the concrete, scientific generalities that are produced, while Generalities II are the theory of the science at a given moment, the means of production of knowledge (q.v.).

HUMANISM (*humanisme*). Humanism is the characteristic feature of the ideological problematic (q.v.) from which Marx emerged and, more generally, of most modern ideology; a particularly conscious form of humanism is Feuerbach's anthropology, which dominates Marx's Early Works (q.v.). As a science, however, historical materialism, as exposed in Marx's later works, implies a theoretical anti-humanism. 'Real-humanism' characterizes the works of the break (q.v.): the humanist form is retained, but usages such as 'the ensemble of the social relations' point forward to the concepts of historical materialism. However, the *ideology* (q.v.) of a socialist society may be a humanism, a proletarian 'class humanism' [an expression I obviously use in a provisional, half-critical sense. L.A.].

IDEOLOGY (*idéologie*). Ideology is the 'lived' relation between men and their world, or a reflected form of this unconscious relation, for instance a 'philosophy' (q.v.), etc. It is distinguished from a science not by its falsity, for it can be coherent and logical (for instance, theology), but by the fact that the practico-social predominates in it over the theoretical, over knowledge. Historically, it precedes the science that is produced by making an epistemological break (q.v.) with it, but it survives alongside science as an essential element of every social formation (q.v.), including a socialist and even a communist society.

---

* The author's interpolations are indicated by square brackets.

KNOWLEDGE (*connaissance*). Knowledge is the product of theoretical practice (q.v.); it is Generalities III (q.v.). As such it is clearly distinct from the practical recognition (*reconnaissance*) of a theoretical problem.

MATERIALISM, DIALECTICAL AND HISTORICAL (*matérialisme dialectique et historique*). Historicists, even those who claim to be Marxists, reject the classical Marxist distinction between historical and dialectical materialism since they see philosophy as the self-knowledge of the historical process, and hence identify philosophy and the science of history; at best, dialectical materialism is reduced to the historical method, while the science of history is its content. Althusser, rejecting historicism, rejects this identification. For him, historical materialism is the science of history, while dialectical materialism, Marxist philosophy, is the theory of scientific practice (see THEORY).

NEGATION OF THE NEGATION (*négation de la négation*). A Hegelian conception that Marx 'flirts' with even in his mature works. It denotes the process of destruction and resumption (supersession/ *Aufhebung* q.v.) whereby the Spirit moves from one stage of its development to another. For Marx, it describes the fact that capitalism, having come into being by the destruction of feudalism, is itself destined to be destroyed by the rise of socialism and communism [this description makes a *metaphorical* use of the notion. L.A.].

OVERDETERMINATION (*surdétermination*, *Überdeterminierung*). Freud used this term to describe (among other things) the representation of the dream-thoughts in images privileged by their condensation of a number of thoughts in a single image (condensation/ *Verdichtung*), or by the transference of psychic energy from a particularly potent thought to apparently trivial images (displacement/ *Verschiebung- Verstellung*). Althusser uses the same term to describe the effects of the contradictions in each practice (q.v.) constituting the social formation (q.v.) on the social formation as a whole, and hence back on each practice and each contradiction, defining the pattern of dominance and subordination, antagonism and non-antagonism of the contradictions in the structure in dominance (q.v.) at any given historical moment. More precisely, the overdetermination of a contradiction is the reflection in it of its conditions of existence within the complex whole, that is, of the other contradictions in the complex whole, in other words its uneven development (q.v.).

'PHILOSOPHY'/PHILOSOPHY (*'philosophie'/philosophie*). 'Philosophy' (in inverted commas) is used to denote the reflected forms of ideology (q.v.) as opposed to Theory (q.v.). See Althusser's own 'Remarks on the Terminology Adopted', p. 126. Philosophy (without inverted commas) is used in the later written essays to denote Marxist philosophy, i.e. dialectical materialism.

PRACTICE, ECONOMIC, POLITICAL, IDEOLOGICAL AND THEORETICAL (*pratique économique, politique, idéologique et théorique*). Althusser takes up the theory introduced by Engels and much elaborated by Mao Tse-tung that economic, political and ideological practice are the three practices (processes of production or transformation) that constitute the social formation (q.v.). Economic practice is the transformation of nature by human labour into social products, political practice the transformation of social relations by revolution, ideological practice the transformation of one relation to the lived world into a new relation by ideological struggle. In his concern to stress the distinction between science and ideology (q.v.), Althusser insists that theory constitutes a fourth practice, theoretical practice, that transforms ideology into knowledge with theory. The determinant moment in each practice is the work of production which brings together raw materials, men and means of production – *not* the men who perform the work, who cannot therefore claim to be the subjects of the historical process. Subsidiary practices are also discussed by Althusser, e.g. technical practice (*pratique technique*).

PROBLEMATIC (*problématique*). A word or concept cannot be considered in isolation; it only exists in the theoretical or ideological framework in which it is used: its problematic. A related concept can clearly be seen at work in Foucault's *Madness and Civilization* (but see Althusser's *Letter to the Translator*). It should be stressed that the problematic is *not* a world-view. It is not the essence of the thought of an individual or epoch which can be deduced from a body of texts by an empirical, generalizing reading; it is centred on the *absence* of problems and concepts within the problematic as much as their presence; it can therefore only be reached by a symptomatic reading (*lecture symptomale* q.v.) on the model of the Freudian analyst's reading of his patient's utterances.

READING (*lecture*). The problems of Marxist theory (or of any other theory) can only be solved by learning to read the texts correctly (hence the title of Althusser's later book, *Lire le Capital*, 'Reading *Capital'*); neither a superficial reading, collating literal references, nor a Hegelian reading, deducing the essence of a corpus by extracting the 'true kernel from the mystified shell', will do. Only a symptomatic reading (*lecture symptomale* – see PROBLEMATIC), constructing the problematic, the unconsciousness of the text, is a reading of Marx's work that will allow us to establish the epistemological break that makes possible historical materialism as a science (q.v.).

SCIENCE (*science*). See IDEOLOGY and PRACTICE.

SPONTANEITY (*spontanéité*) A term employed by Lenin to criticize an ideological and political tendency in the Russian Social-Democratic movement that held that the revolutionary movement should base itself on the 'spontaneous' action of the working class rather than trying to lead it by imposing on this action, by means of a party, policies produced by the party's theoretical work. [For Lenin, the *real* spontaneity, capacity for action, inventiveness, and so on, of the 'masses', was to be respected as *the most precious* aspect of the workers' movement: but at the same time Lenin condemned the 'ideology of spontaneity' (a dangerous ideology) shared by his opponents (populists and 'Socialist Revolutionaries'), and recognized that the *real* spontaneity of the masses was to be sustained and criticized in the mean time in order to 'liberate' it from the influence of bourgeois ideology. L.A.] In this sense, Lenin argued that to make *concessions* to 'spontaneity' was to hand the revolutionary movement over to the power of bourgeois ideology, and hence to the counter-revolution. Althusser generalizes this by arguing that each practice (q.v.) and its corresponding science must not be left to develop on their own, however successful they may temporarily be, since to do so leaves the field open for an ideology (characteristically pragmatism) to seize hold of the science, and for the counter-revolution to seize the practice. The 'unity of theory and practice' cannot be the simple unity of a reflection, it is the complex one of an epistemological break (q.v.) [in theory. In *political* practice this unity takes another form (not examined in this book). L.A.].

STRUCTURE, DECENTRED (*structure décentrée*). The Hegelian totality (q.v.) presupposes an original, primary essence that lies behind the complex appearance that it has produced by externalization in history; hence it is a structure with a centre. The Marxist totality, however, is never separable in this way from the elements that constitute it, as each is the condition of existence of all the others (see OVERDETERMINATION); hence it has no centre, only a dominant element, and a determination in the last instance (see STRUCTURE IN DOMINANCE): it is a decentred structure.

STRUCTURE IN DOMINANCE (*structure à dominante*). The Marxist totality (q.v.) is neither a whole each of whose elements is equivalent as the phenomenon of an essence (Hegelianism), nor are some of its elements epiphenomena of any one of them (economism or mechanism); the elements are asymmetrically related but autonomous (contradictory); one of them is *dominant*. [The economic base '*determines*' ('in the last instance') *which* element is to be *dominant* in a social formation (see *Lire le Capital*). L.A.] Hence it is a structure in dominance. But the dominant element is not fixed for all time, it varies according to the overdetermination (q.v.) of the contradictions and their uneven development (q.v.). In the social formation this overdetermination is, in the last instance, determined by the economy (*determiné en dernière instance de l'économie*). This is Althusser's clarification of the classical Marxist assertion that the superstructure (q.v.) is relatively autonomous but the economy is determinant in the last instance. The phrase 'in the last instance' does not indicate that there will be some ultimate time or ever was some starting-point when the economy will be or was solely determinant, the other instances preceding it or following it: 'the last instance never comes', the structure is always the co-presence of all its elements and their relations of dominance and subordination – it is an 'ever-pre-given structure' (*structure toujours-déjà-donnée*).

STRUCTURE, EVER-PRE-GIVEN (*structure toujours-déjà-donnée*). See STRUCTURE IN DOMINANCE

SUPERSESSION (*depassement, Aufhebung*). A Hegelian concept popular among Marxist-humanists, it denotes the process of historical development by the destruction and retention at a higher level of an old historically determined situation in a new historically determined situation – e.g. socialism is the supersession of capitalism, Marxism a supersession of Hegelianism. Althusser asserts that it is an ideological concept, and he substitutes for it that of the historical transition, or, in the development of a science, by the epistemological break (q.v.).

SUPERSTRUCTURE/STRUCTURE (*superstructure/structure*). In classical Marxism the social formation (q.v.) is analysed into the components economic structure – determinant in the last instance – and relatively autonomous superstructures: (1) the State and law; (2) ideology. Althusser clarifies this by dividing it into the structure (the economic practice) and the superstructure (political and ideological practice). The relation between these three is that of a structure in dominance (q.v.), determined in the last instance by the structure.

THEORY, 'THEORY', THEORY (*théorie, 'théorie', Théorie*). For Althusser theory is a specific, scientific theoretical practice (q.v.). In Chapter 6, 'On the Materialist Dialectic', a distinction is also made between 'theory' (in inverted commas), the determinate theoretical system of a given science, and Theory (with a capital T), the theory of practice in general, i.e. dialectical materialism (q.v.). [In a few words in the preface to the Italian translation of *Lire le Capital*, reproduced in the new French edition of the book, and to be published in the English translation (New Left Books), I have pointed out that I *now* regard my definition of philosophy (Theory as 'the Theory of theoretical practice') as a unilateral and, in consequence, *false* conception of dialectical materialism. Positive indications of the new definition I propose can be found: (1) in an interview published in *L'Unità* in February 1968 and reproduced in the Italian translation of *Lire le*

Capital (Feltrinelli) and in *La Pensée* (April 1968); (2) in *Lénine et la philosophie*, the text of a lecture I gave to the Société Française de Philosophie in February 1968, and published under the same title by François Maspero in January 1969. The new definition of philosophy can be resumed in three points: (1) philosophy 'represents' the class struggle in the realm of *theory*, hence philosophy is neither a science, nor a pure theory (Theory), but a *political practice of intervention* in the realm of theory; (2) philosophy 'represents' scientificity in the realm of political practice, hence philosophy is not *the* political practice, but a theoretical practice of intervention in the realm of politics; (3) philosophy is an original 'instance' (differing from the instances of *science* and *politics*) that represents the one instance alongside (*auprès de*) the other, in the form of a specific *intervention* (political-theoretical). L.A.]

TOTALITY (*totalité*, *Totalität*). An originally Hegelian concept that has become confused by its use by all theorists who wish to stress the whole rather than the various parts in any system. However, the Hegelian and the Marxist totalities are quite different. The Hegelian totality is the essence behind the multitude of its phenomena, but the Marxist totality is a decentred structure in dominance (q.v.).

WORKS OF MARX, EARLY, TRANSITIONAL AND MATURE (*Œuvres de jeunesse, de maturation et de la maturité de Marx*). Althusser rejects the view the Marx's works form a theoretical unity. He divides them as follows: Early Works (1840–45); Works of the Break (*Œuvres de la Coupure* – 1845); Transitional Works (1845–7); Mature Works (1857–83). It should be remembered, however, that the epistemological break (q.v.) can neither be *punctual*, nor made once and for all: it is to be thought as a 'continuous break', and its criticism applies even to the latest of Marx's works, which 'flirt' with Hegelian expressions and contain pre-Marxist 'survivals'.

A Letter to the Translator

Thank you for your glossary; what you have done in it is *extremely* important from a political, educational and theoretical point of view. I offer you my warmest thanks.

I return your text with a whole series of corrections and interpolations (some of which are fairly long and important, you will see why).

A minor point: you refer twice to Foucault and once to Canguilhem *vis-à-vis* my use of 'break' and, I think, of 'problematic'. I should like to point out that Canguilhem has lived and thought in close contact with the work of Bachelard for many years, so it is not surprising if he refers somewhere to the term 'epistemological break', although this term is rarely to be found as such in Bachelard's texts (on the other hand, if the term is uncommon, the *thing* is there all the time from a certain point on in Bachelard's work). But Canguilhem has not used this concept *systematically*, as I have tried to do. As for Foucault, the uses he explicitly or implicitly makes of the concepts 'break' and 'problematic' are echoes either of Bachelard, or of my own systematic 'use' of Bachelard (as far as 'break' is concerned) and of what I owe to my unfortunate friend Martin (for 'problematic'). I am not telling you this out of 'author's pride' (it means nothing to me), but out of respect both for the authors referred to and for the readers.

As for these authors: *Canguilhem*'s use of the concept 'break' differs from mine, although his interpretation does tend in the same direction. In fact, this should be put the other way round: *my debt to Canguilhem is incalculable*, and it is my interpretation that tends in the direction of his, as it is a *continuation* of his, going beyond the point where his has (for the time being) stopped. *Foucault*: his case is quite different. He was a pupil of mine, and 'something' from my writings has passed into his, including certain of my formulations. But (and it must be said, concerning as it does his own philosophical personality) under his pen and in his thought even the meanings he gives to formulations he has borrowed from me are transformed into another, quite different meaning than my own. Please take these corrections into account; I entrust them to you in so far as they may enlighten the English reader (who has access in particular to that *great* work, *Madness and Civilization*), and guide him in his references.

Much more important are the corrections I have suggested for some of your rubrics. In most cases they are merely *corrections* (*precisions*) which do not affect the state of the theoretical concepts that figure in the book (*For Marx*). They cast a little more light on what you yourself have very judiciously clarified. But in other cases they are corrections of a different kind: bearing on a certain point in Lenin's thought, for example (my interpolation on the question of spontaneity). And finally, in other cases (see my last interpolation), I have tried to give some hints to guide the English reader in the road I have travelled since the (now quite distant) publication of the articles that make up *For Marx*. You will understand why I am so *insistent* on all these corrections and interpolations. I urge you to give them a place in your glossary, and add that (1) I have myself gone over the text of the glossary line by line, and (2) I have made changes in matters of detail (which need not be indicated) and a few *important interpolations*.

As a result, everything should be perfectly clear. And we shall have removed the otherwise inevitable snare into which readers of 1969 would certainly have 'fallen', if they were allowed to believe that the author of texts that appeared one by one between 1960 and 1965 has *remained in the position* of these old articles whereas time has not ceased to pass. . . . You can easily imagine the theoretical, ideological and political misunderstandings that could not but have arisen from this 'fiction', and how much time and effort would have had to be deployed to 'remove' these misunderstandings. The procedure I suggest has the advantage that it removes any misunderstanding of this kind *in advance*, since, *on the one hand*, I leave the system of concepts of 1960 to 1965 as it was, while *on the other*, *I* indicate the *essential point* in which I have developed in the intervening years – since, *finally*, I give *references* to the new writings that contain the new definition of philosophy that I now hold, and I summarize the *new conception* which I have arrived at (provisionally – but what is not provisional?).

LOUIS ALTHUSSER

Index

Index

233